THE

FINAL

EXODUS

CHRISTINE PAXSON
AND ROSE SPILLER

THE

FINAL

EXODUS

DECIPHERING THE
BOOK OF REVELATION

AMBASSADOR INTERNATIONAL
GREENVILLE, SOUTH CAROLINA & BELFAST, NORTHERN IRELAND
www.ambassador-international.com

THE FINAL EXODUS

Deciphering the Book of Revelation
©2022 by Christine Paxson and Rose Spiller
All rights reserved

Paperback ISBN: 978-1-64960-305-0
eISBN: 978-1-64960-327-2

Cover Design by Hannah Linder Designs
Interior Design by Dentelle Design
Edited by Katie Cruice Smith

Scripture taken from The Holy Bible, English Standard Version. ESV® Text Edition: 2016. Copyright © 2001 by Crossway Bibles, a publishing ministry of Good News Publishers.

No part of this publication may be reproduced, distributed, or transmitted in any form or by any means, including photocopying, recording, or other electronic or mechanical methods, without the prior written permission of the publisher, except in the case of brief quotations embodied in critical reviews and certain other noncommercial uses permitted by copyright law. For permission requests, contact the publisher using the information below.

AMBASSADOR INTERNATIONAL
Emerald House
411 University Ridge, Suite B14
Greenville, SC 29601
United States
www.ambassador-international.com

AMBASSADOR BOOKS
The Mount
2 Woodstock Link
Belfast, BT6 8DD
Northern Ireland, United Kingdom
www.ambassadormedia.co.uk

The colophon is a trademark of Ambassador, a Christian publishing company.

As always, we dedicate this book to ours husbands, John and Ed, and our families, who are the joy of our life and who often blow us away with their unconditional love and support. They patiently share us and encourage us as we spend many, many hours studying, researching, reading, writing, podcasting, teaching, editing, posting, and the myriad of other tasks it takes for us to keep Proverbs 9:10 Ministries going. This book is as much your accomplishment as it is ours!

—Chris and Rose

TABLE OF CONTENTS

ACKNOWLEDGMENTS 9

INTRODUCTION 11

CHAPTER 1
THERE'S NO "S" IN REVELATION 15

STUDY GUIDE 29

CHAPTER 2
THERE'S A PROBLEM WITH YOUR CHURCH 33

STUDY GUIDE 62

CHAPTER 3
PULLING BACK THE CURTAIN 65

STUDY GUIDE 81

CHAPTER 4
ALL HELL'S GONNA BREAK LOOSE 85

STUDY GUIDE 99

CHAPTER 5
SOUND THE TRUMPETS! 103

STUDY GUIDE 117

CHAPTER 6
"EAT YOUR SCRIPTURE!" 121

STUDY GUIDE 134

CHAPTER 7
RELEASE THE KRACKEN 137
STUDY GUIDE 157

CHAPTER 8
THE LORD'S DAY OF VENGEANCE 161
STUDY GUIDE 175

CHAPTER 9
TIME'S UP! THE BATTLE OF ARMAGEDDON 177
STUDY GUIDE 194

CHAPTER 10
THE MOTHER OF ALL PROSTITUTES
AND OBSCENITIES 197
STUDY GUIDE 212

CHAPTER 11
HOW IT'S ALL GONNA GO DOWN 215
STUDY GUIDE 233

CHAPTER 12
WHAT WILL ETERNITY BE LIKE? 237
STUDY GUIDE 250

CONCLUSION 253
BIBLIOGRAPHY 255
DISCOGRAPHY 261

ACKNOWLEDGMENTS

As always, we thank our sovereign, gracious, triune God. Thank You, Lord, for choosing two undeserving and sinful women to be saved and to serve You. Thank You for instilling in us a passion and hunger to not only know You and Your Truth, but also to teach it to others. Thank You for the countless hours You continually give us to pursue that endeavor. Even when life overwhelms us and we are flying by the seat of our pants, You are faithful, and You give us just what we need at the exact time we need it! Thank You for giving us each other to partner with as we strive to honor and glorify You. There is no one we would rather grow with, learn with, laugh with, disagree at times with, cry with, and serve You with than each other! Most of all, Lord, thank You that we have been chosen *"according to the foreknowledge of God the Father, in the sanctification of the Spirit, for obedience to Jesus Christ and for sprinkling with his blood"* **(1 Peter 1:2)**. May every word in this book be to Your praise and Your glory!

INTRODUCTION

Have you ever marveled at a hungry infant? They can be screaming and crying, but once they get a feel of the nipple in their mouths, they chow down on their bottle like that milk is the most delicious and satisfying food in the whole world. And to them, it is! Their little digestive systems couldn't handle anything harsher; and since they have never tasted anything else, for them, there is nothing better! Once they start getting older, however, all that changes. Who can forget their baby's face the first time they had pears or applesauce? They love the sweet, fruity taste! When you introduce peas and carrots, the reaction may not be the same; but we keep feeding it to them because it's what they need to grow into healthy, strong children. And once they try pizza and ice cream, any desire for satisfying their hunger with bottles of milk are long gone! Most children would be happy to live on pizza and ice cream, but as parents, we know that is not what's best for them. We need to insert chicken and broccoli between the junk food. We want our children happy, but we also want them healthy! Part of our job as their parent is to give them what they need when they need it.

Our spiritual walk is much the same. As baby Christians, the nurturing milk is the Gospel message. We chow down on the beautiful message that even though we were dead in our sins and under the wrath of the Almighty God, He has made us alive and reconciled us to Himself through the saving blood and resurrection of our Lord Jesus. As we mature, we feed on the sanctifying work of the Holy Spirit as He indwells in us, allowing us to see God's presence and love in our lives. But to truly mature as a Christian, we need to not *just* feed on the love of God. We need the chicken and broccoli of His Word. We need to learn and understand all of His Truth—His holiness, His sovereignty, His justice, His mercy, and even His righteous wrath. This book was written for all of us who want to grow and deepen our walk with Jesus. It is filled with the spiritual chicken and broccoli we need to mature in our sanctification, knowledge, and wisdom.

The Final Exodus: Deciphering the Book of Revelation originated as a twelve-part series we did on our podcast, *No Trash, Just Truth*, in the fall of 2020. Not surprisingly, the twelve 30-to 40-minute episodes took hundreds of hours of studying, research, writing, and re-writing. The series was so well-received and we had so much additional material that we weren't able to fit into the podcast series that we decided to write *The Final Exodus: Deciphering the Book of Revelation*. The title is fitting because, as we will see, the book of Revelation is the ultimate fulfillment of the book of Exodus and God's ultimate deliverance of His people from sin, Satan, and death. We were encouraged by so many, including one person who told us, "The market is flooded with sensationalized, misguided, and heretical books on Revelation. More that are grounded in Scripture and truth are definitely needed."

What is it about the book of Revelation?! Some treat it like a futuristic comic book. Some consider it is too complex to try and understand. Some worry about getting the interpretation wrong—or worse, right! Some read it trying to "break the code," as if God had John write the book in a secret code expecting Christians to try and crack it. And then there are those who are terrified of the book and the images, so they just avoid it altogether. For them, ignorance is bliss.

If you fall into any of those categories, we urge you to put your preconceived notions aside and try a different approach. Walk with us through the book of Revelation as we interpret it the same way every other book in the Bible is to be interpreted—with contextualization, exposition, and careful exegesis. Instead of pulling out one or two lines of a passage, we will look at whole passages so that they can be put into the proper context. Once context is established, we will compare what it says with other parts of Scripture to further establish the meaning, as rule number one of biblical exegesis is Scripture must interpret Scripture. We will ask questions like, *Where have we seen this before? Is this passage meant to be taken literally, symbolically, or metaphorically? Has this passage already been interpreted somewhere else in Scripture? Does our conclusion of the passage line up with everything else in the Bible? Is this passage telling us something new, or is it a picture of something already seen in the Old Testament or other parts of the New Testament?* This takes a lot of work, for sure, but it is the only way to get a solid, biblical interpretation of Revelation. As you read through this book, you will see lots of Scripture references. That is very intentional. As always, we do not want to give you our opinion or our thoughts. We only want to present God's Truth—something crucial, especially with the book of Revelation, where there are so many vastly different interpretations, it can make your head spin! As you will see in the following chapters, the key to *The Final Exodus: Deciphering the Book of Revelation* is not to find some outlandish new meaning, but instead, to look back at what the previous sixty-five books of the Bible tell us!

We pray that you are blessed and nourished as you read this book and answer the study questions at the end of each chapter. One thing we can promise is that after digging into Revelation with us, you will see the truths of this book throughout the entire Bible. So grab your Bible and let's dive in!

CHAPTER 1
THERE'S NO "S" IN REVELATION

Are we in the end times? This is a question we have heard over and over many times in the past couple of years. The simple answer is yes! We are! The not so simple answer is that we have been in the end times since Jesus ascended into Heaven and will continue to be until He comes back. Every day, we get closer to Jesus' second coming, but we have no way of knowing when that will be. We do have the book of Revelation, though. And that book is meant to teach us and encourage us in the wait.

Even before we dive into the text of the book to begin expositing it, there are things that will be helpful to know. First, for most of us, it is a foregone conclusion that John, the apostle, wrote the book of Revelation. However, this has been debated throughout history with some believing Revelation was written pseudonymously, with the author using John's name. Others believe it is indeed a John who wrote the book, just not John the Apostle. And then, of course, there are those who conclude that it was John the Apostle who wrote Revelation. The debate on all sides could fill a book. We strongly take the position that it was John the Apostle who penned Revelation. In summary, at the beginning of the book, John identifies himself as the author who wrote the book while he was exiled to the island of Patmos. John the Apostle was exiled to Patmos after an attempt to kill him by boiling in oil failed. (God miraculously saved John from death). If it was another author, he would have had to either been exiled to Patmos at the same time as John or would have had to lie about it.

16 THE FINAL EXODUS

Also, John died in 98 A.D. Up until 150 A.D., the book of Revelation was attributed to him by the Church and by people who had personally known him. John's authorship was not called into question until after 150 A.D. by some, but not by the Church fathers. They firmly held to a John the Apostle authorship. Additionally, the vast majority of credible biblical scholars throughout history have agreed that John the Apostle is the author. And, finally, in early historical writings, John the Apostle is given credit for writing Revelation.

So, that being a settled matter, the apostle John wrote Revelation in 95 A.D., during the reign of Domitian, emperor of Rome. Domitian, like so many of the Roman emperors, thought himself to be divine and required that all his subjects refer to him as lord and god. As you can imagine, many Christians of that time refused, which led to their widespread, horrific persecution. John wrote Revelation to encourage those persecuted Christians, as well as persecuted Christians for all time. The book is meant to fortify believers to persevere in their faith, understanding that perseverance could very well lead to martyrdom. God, through John, gave His people the book of Revelation so they could ultimately win their battle with the enemy, knowing that for some, that victory would come through their death.

The book of Revelation is part epistle, part apocalyptic. An epistle is a letter that is meant to be read publicly. Chapters two and three contain seven letters John wrote to seven churches. We will look at these letters in detail in the next chapter, but John wrote these letters with the expectation that they would be read out loud to God's people.

The remainder of the book of Revelation is apocalyptic. It is the prophecy John received from Jesus through oracles and visions. *Apocalyptic* can be defined as, "forecasting the ultimate destiny of the world," or "ultimately decisive."[1] The book of Revelation certainly shows us the destiny of the world; and as has been the case since before the creation of the earth, God's plan

---

1   *Merriam-Webster*, s.v. "Apocalyptic," accessed March 30, 2019, https://www.merriam-webster.com/dictionary/apocalyptic.

for it and for His people is ultimately decided. Revelation reveals to us the fulfillment of that plan.

THE CAMPS OF REVELATION

Like some of the other prophetical books of the Bible, how you approach the events in the book of Revelation will influence how you interpret the book. The book of Revelation has different "camps" of interpretation. Most have at least some biblical credibility. When you see the difference in the methods and expectations of each of the camps, you can see why there are so many differing views on Revelation out there.

Let's start with the view that has been called heresy by all credible Bible scholars—the *full preterist view*. This view believes everything in the book of Revelation (even Jesus' second coming) has already happened. This view is easily disputed. In regards to Jesus' second coming, Revelation 1:7 says, *"Behold, he is coming with the clouds, and **every** eye will see him, even those who pierced him, and all tribes of the earth will wail on account of him"* (emphasis added). If you are reading this and you haven't seen Jesus coming with the clouds, you know this view can't be correct. Also, full preterists do not believe in a future bodily resurrection, which is counter to Scripture. As **Acts 24:15** says, *"There will be a resurrection of both the just and the unjust."*

There are five other views that have some or full biblical credibility. While we go through the book, we will show contradictions and affirmations to some of them by using Scripture. They are considered biblically credible because *the essentials* they believe do line up with Scripture. More on that shortly.

Let's start with the *partial preterist view*. This is not to be confused with the full preterist view previously mentioned. Partial preterists believe that except for the second coming of Jesus and the events surrounding it, everything else in the book of Revelation has already occurred. This is a view held by many sound, biblical theologians. Their reasoning for believing that most of the events have already occurred is that they adhere to an earlier writing date of Revelation. Instead of believing the book was written in 95 A.D., they support a writing date prior to 70 A.D. They contend that much of what is described in the book is referring to the Roman Empire and their destruction of the temple and Jerusalem in 70 A.D.

Another view is the *historist view.* Historists believe that all of the events described in the book are in chronological order, beginning with the establishment of the Church in the first century all the way through Jesus' second coming, and that they are literal. Historists assign a specific, historical event to each happening described in Revelation; symbols and images in the book are assigned to a specific person or people group. You may have heard some wondering if the Covid-19 vaccine was the "mark of the beast." This belief is probably from either a historist or a futurist view.

You may have never heard the term *futurist,* but you are probably familiar with their viewpoint. The futurist approach is also known as dispensationalism. This approach to Revelation was made popular by C.I. Scofield in 1909 when he published his *Scofield Reference Bible. The Scofield Reference Bible* teaches the theology of dispensationalism that was devised in the nineteenth century by John Nelson Darby. The study notes in Scofield's Bible influenced many fundamental Christians in the U.S.[2] This view contradicts much of what is in Scripture, but it is the prevailing view amongst evangelicals today. It gained huge popularity when this approach was used for the fictional *Left Behind* series by Tim LaHaye and Jerry Jenkins. Like the historist view, the futurist approach sees the entire book of Revelation as literal. But unlike historists, people who adhere to the futurist view believe that the events won't happen until right before Jesus comes back. This approach looks forward to a time in history when chaos will come on suddenly, and all pandemonium breaks loose!

People who view this book literally—dispensationalists—have made predictions about exactly when things would occur. When those predicted events come and go without ever happening, they change their prediction. Does

---

2   *Theopedia,* s.v. "Cyrus I. Scofield," accessed February 21, 2021, https://www.theopedia.com/cyrus-i-scofield.

that sound like they are speaking God's Truth? The Old Testament prophets spoke the message God gave them. Everything they said in the Old Testament concerning judgment on Israel and Judah, the coming of the Messiah, and the punishment and destruction of enemy nations happened exactly as God said it would. Exactly! Would God now be erratic and inconsistent in giving "new prophets" messages that don't happen as He says? Of course not! These events and situations don't happen the way they have been prophesied because the person who spoke them is not a prophet and they do not speak for God; they speak out of their own mind. They aren't trying to glorify God; they are trying to glorify themselves by portraying themselves as the smartest person in the room. They figured out the "code." They know when the end of things will take place, even though Jesus clearly says in the gospel of Matthew that these things are not meant to be known **(Matt. 10:26)**. Think about that! We should be calling out these false teachers, not giving them a platform to speak their lies and encourage them by buying their books, DVDs, or whatever else they are selling.

Quite the opposite of the historist and futurist approach is the *idealist* approach. Rather than seeing the events in Revelation as chronological and literal, the idealist approaches the events in Revelation as repeating cycles of metaphors and symbols that all depict the same timeless, cosmic struggle between good and evil, specifically between the Church and Satan. For example, the previous three views see the whore Babylon in Revelation 17 as either a specific first-century, historical, or end-time figure, respectively; whereas, idealists argue that the whore Babylon *symbolizes* various political and religious powers who have opposed and persecuted the Church throughout history.

The last approach to the book of Revelation is the *eclectic* approach. This one is fairly new. Eclectics glean the strengths of the other four views that we just mentioned, while avoiding the pitfalls of each. It pulls the most credible parts of the other views together. Many leading evangelical scholars today have embraced the eclectic approach, arguing that it provides a balanced approach to Revelation. The eclectic approach does not have a consistent approach to the entire book. It interprets some events as literal, some as symbolic, and some as metaphorical, using contextualization and other Scripture throughout the Bible as its guide.

This book is written from an eclectic, idealist approach. We realize that's a bit of a curveball, but this view is held by many sound, biblical teachers and theologians. We believe this is the most scripturally grounded approach. While much of Scripture supports the idealist view that Revelation is a series of symbolic, repeating cycles depicting the struggle the Church has had with evil and Satan since Christ ascended and will have up until His second coming, it also contains specificities of actual events. Although the intensity differs, these events have simultaneously already occurred, are occurring now, and are still to occur. These events are the "already and not yet occurred" events. This will become much clearer as we go through the book.

We said that five of the six views to Revelation are considered somewhat biblically credible, with full preterism being the exception, because they agree on "the essentials." None of the five views are discrepant in how the "life and death" passages are interpreted. It is on the other passages that some of them have huge holes and contradictions in them. Now, of course, every word of Scripture is important; but some truths are life and death—like the Gospel message; salvation; Jesus' victory over Satan, sin, and death; and others. These are the passages on which our salvation depends! We absolutely cannot get these wrong, and shouldn't get them wrong, since God's Word, when properly studied and applied, leaves us with only one possible interpretation of them. There are other passages, though, that are not life and death. For example, whether you believe that there is one actual antichrist who will appear in the future or that the antichrist is a symbol of everyone throughout history who has opposed God and His people is not necessarily going to affect your salvation.

So, why then does the approach we take matter? Well, even though for your salvation it might not, it does matter for your sanctification and for how you live out your faith. Your approach to and interpretation of Revelation can make a huge difference in these areas. And as with anything you believe, you should want to make sure that it is scripturally grounded. And while all the views may agree on the essentials, there is much on which they disagree. Take the Tribulation, for instance. Depending on the approach you take, you could believe that the suffering in the Tribulation has already occurred, is occurring now, will occur sometime in the future, or that the Church will be raptured before it occurs and will not have to suffer through it. We may prefer one of these scenarios over another, but as followers of Jesus, it is not about our preference but about what God has revealed to us in His Word.

DATING THE BOOK OF REVELATION

As if we haven't muddied the waters enough, we mentioned earlier that there is a dating discrepancy for Revelation, with some believing it was written before 70 A.D. and some believing it was written in 95 A.D. Again, we will be using the later date of 95 A.D., but it's worth noting that whether the book was written before 70 A.D. or in 95 A.D., first-century Christians were in the exact same situation. They were being persecuted mercilessly by the emperors and government of Rome. The Roman Empire did not need much of an excuse to torture and kill the followers of Jesus in horrendous ways. So, whether John the Apostle wrote Revelation before 70 A.D. or in 95 A.D., keep in mind that this was the atmosphere into which he was speaking.

Early in the book, John tells us that the tribulation was happening at that time. In **Revelation 1:9**, he says to the churches to whom he is writing, *"I, John, your brother and partner in the tribulation."* John's exile on Patmos, as well as the torture and martyrdom of the other apostles and other followers, is evidence that the Tribulation was already occurring. To say that the events John was writing about in Revelation were all still far in the future to him, as dispensationalists or futurists believe, is to say that God told John to write about some terrible things God's people will face in the future, while John had seen every one of his fellow apostles and other disciples murdered in horrendous ways for their faith and while he himself had been boiled in oil and exiled to a remote island. It just doesn't make any sense.

But John's writing was not just for the first-century church. He also wrote this book for every church and every Christian throughout all of history. Just as tribulation was going on in John's time, it also has continued throughout history and will continue until Jesus returns. This makes the book of Revelation relevant to every Christian of every time. This book is meant to encourage Christians for all time. What will sustain a believer who is being persecuted, no matter when in history it occurs, is clinging to two important truths—the goodness of God and the sovereignty of God. Revelation clearly shows us both. It also reminds all of God's people Whom they serve and how and why they were redeemed. We are here because of one Man, Who willingly submitted to persecution, torture, and death on a cross but Who rose again and overcame that persecution and death. Even in our darkest hour, we can be encouraged that we serve the one, true God Who created, sustains, and is completely sovereign over the entire universe and every molecule in it. We belong to the God Who is in control of every single detail of every second, every minute, every day, and every year. And even more, our almighty, powerful God is completely good. Scripture shows us the mercy and grace of God over and over. And the ultimate sign of His goodness is that Jesus willingly gave up His own life to pay the penalty we deserve so that we could spend eternity with Him in Heaven.

THERE'S NO "S" IN REVELATION

Contrary to how many people pronounce the title of this book and contrary to what some may believe about this book, its title is singular. It is Revelation, not Revelations. (Although we confess to accidentally adding an "s" on it at times!) The entire book is one revelation, not a series of many revelations. It is one revelation *from* Jesus *about* Jesus. This is important because the whole book has one major theme—God is sovereign over all. And never will this be more evident than when Jesus returns and brings His already-won victory over Satan, sin, and death and the redemption of His people to completion.

Revelation 1:17-18 sums up this theme: "*Fear not, I am the first and the last, and the living one. I died, and behold I am alive forevermore, and I have the keys of Death and Hades.*" If we read the book of Revelation knowing that God has been completely in control over all of history and brings everything to consummation in Jesus, we will understand what we need to understand. Even if we don't fully grasp or agree on some of the details, we will understand the essential truths. The purpose of the book of Revelation is the same as the purpose of every other book of the Bible—to point us to Jesus as Lord and Savior and to show that He is the definitive representative and manifestation of God.

THE APOCALYPTIC LANGUAGE

There's one last point that's important to note about the book of Revelation. We mentioned that the book is part epistle and part apocalyptic. It's the apocalyptic language that trips people up and makes the book difficult to understand. While this language would have been familiar to John's initial audience, it isn't familiar to many of us; but it will become more familiar if we read and study the Old Testament, especially the prophetic books. Revelation has some five hundred allusions to the Old Testament.[3] John alludes to almost every book in the Old Testament, although he mostly uses Psalms, Isaiah, Ezekiel, and Daniel. If you have a grasp and understanding on these books and the whole Old Testament overall, Revelation will be much easier to understand. As we said in our book *The Bible Blueprint: A Guide to Better Understanding the Bible from Genesis to Revelation*, "Trying to tackle Revelation without any understanding of the Old Testament is like trying to comprehend Calculus without having a working knowledge of basic math!"[4]

For example, understanding Genesis is crucial to understanding Revelation. Genesis is the story of how man's rebellion derailed creation. Revelation is the story of God putting creation back to the way it was always

---

3 David Guzik, "Revelation 1 - Introduction; A Vision of Jesus," Enduring Word.com, Accessed November 1, 2021, https://enduringword.com/bible-commentary/revelation-1
4 Christine Paxson and Rose Spiller, *The Bible Blueprint: A Guide to Better Understanding the Bible from Genesis to Revelation* (Greenville: Ambassador International, 2020).

meant to be. In addition, much of what is in the book of Revelation is driven by the book of Exodus. The book of Exodus tells of how God delivered the nation of Israel from slavery in Egypt at that time. Revelation is the culmination of Exodus—God delivering all His people from the slavery of sin, Satan, and death forever!

Just as Jesus did not come the first time to teach anything radical or new, neither does Revelation. Jesus didn't come to change Old Testament teachings but to show us how they were originally meant to be understood. He didn't alter anything from the Old Testament; He fulfilled it! The same can be said for the book of Revelation. It is the final chapter on how Jesus fulfills the Old Testament. The contents are nothing new or radical; rather, it is the realization of the "Day of the Lord" that was often spoken about in the Old Testament.

Understanding the Old Testament and getting familiar with apocalyptic language isn't the only stumbling block to interpreting Revelation. It can also be made more difficult by the attitude some have toward the book. Some approach the book (or maybe won't approach the book) because of fear. They are either afraid of getting the interpretation wrong, or they are afraid of getting it right and finding out that it says something horrible is going to occur! Some will even marginalize the book, thinking it's not relevant. Incredibly, Martin Luther did not think the book of Revelation had relevancy or value. No disrespect, Dr. Luther, but every word, every comma, and every period in the Bible is important and relevant because it is God's Word to us!

Along those same lines, there has also been the problem of sensationalizing the book. Instead of seeing Revelation through the same lens as the other sixty-five books of the Bible which God has laid out for us to better understand Him, His commands, and His Truth, they see it as a futuristic comic book. They treat it as mysterious and as if the goal is to "crack the code" by figuring out precisely what everything means. There are several things throughout Scripture that we cannot figure out precisely. For example, exactly who were the Nephilim **(Gen. 6)**, or should women still be wearing head coverings **(1 Cor. 11)**?

One of our favorite seminary professors, Dr. Sean McDonough, has said that interpreting Revelation is fifty percent orientation and fifty percent perspiration.[5] We need to read the book of Revelation, putting the passages and imagery into context and putting them against other Scripture. It's a lot of work, but it's the only way to obtain the full blessing from the book and to avoid fearing, marginalizing, or sensationalizing the book.

NUMBERS

Something prevalent throughout the book is the use of numbers. Revelation is full of numbers. There are some people—historists and futurists mostly—who interpret these numbers literally. But like the other prophetic books in the Bible and other books in the apocalyptic genre, numbers in Revelation are used symbolically. We will go into detail when we get to the specific passages, but just as an overview, the number seven is used a lot in the book. The number seven is used throughout Scripture to symbolize perfect completeness. In Revelation, we will see the number seven signifying complete, perfect judgment, victory, and glory.

Another number used in the book is twelve. In the Bible, there are twelve tribes of Israel and twelve apostles. Along those lines, twelve is used in Revelation to represent the complete people of God. Revelation 14 talks about the 144,000 people who have Jesus' name on their foreheads. There are not literally 144,000 people saved. The number—twelve times twelve times one thousand—symbolizes the complete number of people God has chosen to save.

Another prominent number is three. The number three represents completeness, but in a different way than the number seven. It has a Trinitarian reference. More on that when we get to it.

And the last number we will touch on for now is the number four. The number four represents creation. **Revelation 7:1** says, *"I saw four angels standing at the four corners of the earth, holding back the four winds of the earth."*

---

5   Dr. Sean McDonough, "New Testament Survey II—The End of All Things," Lecture, Gordon Conwell Theological Seminary's Dimension of Faith Program, May 2017.

In other words, God has complete dominion over all creation, including angels, the earth, and nature.

Finally, the entire book of Revelation is designed to bring glory, honor, and laud to our sovereign Father and our Lord and Savior Jesus Christ through the power of the Holy Spirit. Keep that in mind as we go through it.

THE FIRST BEATITUDE

Let's finish up the chapter by looking at the beginning three verses of Revelation 1, or the prologue to the book. **Revelation 1:1-3** says,

> *The revelation of Jesus Christ, which God gave him to show to his servants the things that must soon take place. He made it known by sending his angel to his servant John, who bore witness to the word of God and to the testimony of Jesus Christ, even to all that he saw. Blessed is the one who reads aloud the words of this prophecy, and blessed are those who hear, and who keep what is written in it, for the time is near.*

There are seven beatitudes in the book of Revelation. Here we see the first one: *"Blessed is the one who reads aloud the words of this prophecy, and blessed are those who hear, and who keep what is written in it, for the time is near."* You are probably familiar with beatitudes from Matthew 5. Beatitudes are meant for believers. They are who believers are right now, although not perfected yet. They are also what believers will be like when God's Kingdom comes in its fullness in the new heavens and new earth when their sins are totally removed and they are able to live holy lives.[6] John is writing this epistle and this beatitude to seven churches. He was telling them that what he was writing (the book of Revelation) should be read aloud in church! In John's time, there were no written copies of the entire Bible. There were scrolls of the Old Testament and New Testament writings, but they were not widely available to people. When John wrote this letter, it would have been delivered to a specific place, and someone

---

6   Christine Paxson and Rose Spiller, "Episode 45: An Unobtainable Directive Part 1," *No Trash, Just Truth* Podcast, July 27, 2020, 20:26, https://www.buzzsprout.com/615385/4319417.

would have had the privilege of reading it out loud to the congregation to bring encouragement to the people and to bring them hope in their darkest hours.

We see this in the later part of this beatitude, where John says, *"Blessed are those who hear."* John is talking about persecution. He was being persecuted at the time of writing; he was aware that his fellow apostles had been killed; he had seen followers of Christ persecuted and murdered; and he knew that more persecution was to come. We love what Dr. Baucham says about this. He says, "John has no idea what the future holds—he is exiled on a remote island. Then Jesus comes and says, I want to show you something and I want you to write it down. John knows it's a blessing to hear this book because it was a blessing for him to hear it!"[7]

The last part of the beatitude says, *"Blessed are those who keep what is written"* **(Rev. 1:3)**. Regardless, if you were an original listener to this, or you are hearing it for the first time today, the message is the same. With the help of the Holy Spirit, we are to continue on the journey God has intended for us, regardless of how we are being persecuted by the world or by the government. We aren't to run and hide somewhere until Jesus comes back because the world is a scary place. We are to endure the persecution until either we die or Jesus comes back for us.

This is a direct reference back to the Old Testament. In Jeremiah 29, God had Jeremiah send a letter to those who had been conquered and exiled to Babylon. He told them that even though they were under oppression and persecution, they should build houses, plant gardens, marry, have children, etc. We see this theme of perseverance through oppression and persecution in Daniel and Ezekiel, also.

We will wrap up the chapter with this. When you study and go through the book of Revelation, you can't help but see how God shows us a stark contrast between those on the inside and those on the outside. It's not about

---

[7] Baucham, Voddie, Jr. "An Introduction to Revelation." Lecture, February 21, 2021. YouTube Sermon Series preached at Grace Family Baptist Church on May 27, 2012.

whether or not we understand everything John shows us, but whether or not we believe and obey what is said in the book. The book shows the decided difference between those who belong to Jesus and, having been sealed by the Holy Spirit, would rather die than deny their Lord and Savior and those who do not belong to Jesus and have been marked by the beast and whose biggest concern is saving their physical lives. That is why for many, there is an urgency to "crack the code" of Revelation. Those who do not belong to Jesus are trying to save themselves and, therefore, want as much "inside information" as they can get so they can get a jump on things. But for those of us who are believers, there is no such urgency. We know that God has everything well in hand and will work everything out for our spiritual good. For our part, we need just to have faith, obey, and trust. For those on the side of belonging to Jesus, the message of Revelation is hope and blessing.

In light of all of this, let's begin digging into Revelation as we would study any other book of the Bible. Let's study it in order to better know God, grow in our faith, and to be blessed and edified by His Word!

CHAPTER 1
STUDY GUIDE

GETTING YOUR TOES WET

How would you describe your experience with the book of Revelation?

Why do you think people view the book of Revelation differently than any other book in the Bible?

After reading the descriptions of the different "camps" there are in approaching Revelation, which camp best describes how you view Revelation at this time?

What is the main thing you hope to get out of studying the book of Revelation?

DIVING IN DEEP

Revelation 1:9 makes it clear that John was writing about a tribulation that was going on at the time of his writing—a tribulation that began right after Jesus ascended into Heaven (Acts 1:9). *How do these other New Testament verses support that followers of Jesus were, and are, in the midst of the tribulation?*

John 15:18-21

Romans 8:33-37

30 THE FINAL EXODUS

2 Timothy 3:10-14

1 Peter 4:12-19

Read the Beatitudes in **Matthew 5:2-12**. The Beatitudes are not a list of how believers are expected to live. They are a beautiful promise of how Kingdom people *can* live because we have been freed from the bondage of sin and have the Holy Spirit indwelling in us. It is who believers are right now, although not perfected yet, and also what believers will be like when God's Kingdom comes in its fullness in the new heavens and new earth. *How do the following verses support this definition of the Beatitudes?*

Romans 12:1-2

2 Corinthians 5:14-19

Colossians 3:1-4

In light of the above definition, how should we understand this beatitude we see in **Revelation 1:3**: *"Blessed is the one who reads aloud the words of this prophecy and blessed are those who hear, and who keep what is written in it, for the time is near"?*

BACK ON DRY LAND

The book of Revelation is one revelation. It is the revelation about Jesus given by Jesus. It is the culmination of the entire Bible and the fulfillment of all of the promises of the Old Testament. It is not new and radical teaching or prophecy. In fact, there are some five hundred allusions back to the Old Testament.

As part of the new social justice movement, there has been a call by some "Christian" pastors to unhitch the Old Testament from the Bible because it is offensive and insensitive to some. *How do these verses show the foolishness of this teaching?*

Psalm 119:9-16

Matthew 4:1-4

2 Timothy 3:16-17

Given what we know about Revelation, what disasters can you see coming from "unhitching" the Old Testament from the Bible?

What comfort is there in knowing that the book of Revelation is not new or radical teaching but, instead, the fulfillment of the other sixty-five books of the Bible?

CHAPTER 2
THERE'S A PROBLEM WITH YOUR CHURCH

Search the internet for information on the island of Patmos today and you'll want to cruise there. Bright blue water and sandy beaches, beautiful white stucco homes, and private yachts in the pristine harbor tell us it's a place most of us would like to be "exiled" to. But John was exiled to an island with other prisoners, and tradition claims that he lived in a cave. Despite not knowing many of the circumstances on the island at that time, John makes it clear that being there was no picnic. He considers himself a *"partner in the tribulation . . . and the patient endurance that are in Jesus"* **(Rev. 1:9)**.

As we said in chapter one, persecution of Christ's Church had been going on since the time of Jesus' ascension. The time of "great tribulation" had already started way back then. As we'll see going through Revelation's entire twenty-two chapters, trial and tribulation for God's people continues throughout the entire Church Age until Jesus comes again. The Church marches on through much of God's judgment on the wicked. The wicked hate her because they hate her Savior. But she is Christ's Church, and the gates of Hell will not prevail against her as she does what she's supposed to—stand firm for her Savior, despite persecution, until the end.

Revelation discloses unseen realities. This book is the revelation of Jesus Christ, revealing what God the Father, Who is seated on the throne, gave Him to reveal. It was Jesus Who gave this revelation in symbolic visions to John through an angel. John addressed the letter to seven churches and opened with a greeting from all three Persons of the Trinity: *"Grace to you and peace from him who is and who was and who is to come [God, the Father], and from the seven spirits who are before his throne [the Holy Spirit] and from Jesus Christ the faithful witness, the firstborn of the dead, and the ruler of kings on earth"* **(Rev. 1:4-5)**.

This letter to the seven churches in Asia was in the form of a pastor writing a letter to churches under his pastoral care. It addresses how they were faring spiritually and what was going on in each of them, good and bad. The admonitions and praises for these churches wasn't just for the congregants of those specific seven churches. The number seven is used symbolically to mean perfect completeness. Jesus' selection of these seven churches to have John address in this letter is symbolic of all of God's people throughout the Church Age. What was said to the seven churches in Revelation has been relevant for every church since and is still relevant for all churches today.

Jesus declares Himself *"the faithful witness, the firstborn of the dead, and the ruler of kings on earth"* **(Rev. 1:5)**. He came as the faithful suffering servant, who triumphed over death. He wants His suffering Church to be assured that He has not only triumphed over death, but also that He is sovereign over all earthly powers. No earthly king has ever been (nor ever will be) out of God's complete sovereign rule. That means that nothing happens without God ordaining it to. Even when we can't understand why we are suffering or going through trials, He has a plan for our good and for His glory. In those times, the Church can remember that we are part of Jesus' Kingdom, which has been inaugurated, but not yet fully culminated. We live within the theological tension of an already/not-yet framework. Jesus loves us and *"has freed us from our sins by his blood and made us a kingdom, priests to his God and Father"* **(Rev. 1:5-6)**, but the full realization of that freedom and that kingdom won't happen until Jesus returns.

Jesus is coming back. **Revelation 1:7** says, *"Behold, he is coming with the clouds."* We are to "behold" Jesus' second coming. In other words, this is something we should be watching for expectantly. He may not be coming right now or even in the near future; but we should be waiting joyfully, with anticipation, much like waiting for a loved one to step off the plane after a long deployment. When Jesus comes, every eye will see Him, *"even those who pierced him, and all tribes of the earth will wail on account of him"* **(Rev. 1:7)**. This is a reference to those who actually pierced Jesus at His crucifixion as well as all people who've "pierced" Him through their unbelief. Many will wail or mourn on that day, something that most scholars consider the reaction of the unsaved to the coming judgment and the wrath they realize they're going to suffer.

Twice in the first chapter of Revelation—here in verse eight and again in verse seventeen—Jesus declares His divine eternity. He is the *"'Alpha and the Omega . . . who is and who was and who is to come, the Almighty'"* **(Rev. 1:8)**. Jesus is *the* Almighty—the eternal Ruler of all, having unrestricted power and absolute dominion over everything, and He is living and reigning in Heaven right now.

Along with these statements proclaiming the majesty and authority of Jesus, John writes in **Revelation 1:10**, *"I was in the Spirit on the Lord's day, and I heard behind me a loud voice like a trumpet."* It is Jesus who is speaking, and the highly symbolic description John gives of His appearance in **Revelation 1:13-16** is similar to visions in **Daniel 7:9** and **Ezekiel 43:2**. It's the picture of our Great High Priest reigning and ruling from Heaven.

Jesus' voice and appearance weren't the only things that grabbed John's attention. Where Jesus was located in the vision is of utmost importance for the Church. John writes, *"I saw seven golden lampstands, and in the midst of the lampstands one like a son of man"* **(Rev. 1:12-13)**. As it says in verse twenty, the seven lampstands are the seven churches to whom Revelation is addressed. Where is Jesus? Present with His Church. Apocalyptic literature was used to comfort people in times of trouble and harsh persecution to give them hope for the future. If Jesus had given no further revelation than chapter one, it should be enough to comfort every believer for all time. What could be more comforting for God's people in the harsh grip of persecution than being reminded that Jesus is with them? And not only that, but He also controls death and the eternal destiny of every person who has ever lived!

The vision of Jesus standing among the lampstands was so overwhelming, it made John drop over like a dead man. But Jesus allays his fear, saying, *"'Fear not, I am the first and the last, and the living one. I died, and behold I am alive forevermore, and I have the keys of Death and Hades'"* **(Rev. 1:17-18)**. Jesus' resurrection from death to life is a foundational truth in which Christians place their hope. No one took Jesus' own life from Him. As He says in **John 10:18**, *"No one takes it from me, but I lay it down of my own accord. I have authority to lay it down, and I have authority to take it up again."* Because He is God, He has the power to take human life at any time, as He did with Ananias and Sapphira in Acts 5. Jesus also has the power to raise people to life as He did with Jairus' daughter **(Mark 5)** and Lazarus **(John 11)**. There can be no denying Jesus wants His persecuted Bride to have complete confidence that He is alive and that He holds the power over life and death.

Not only does Jesus hold the power of life and death, but Jesus also holds *"the keys of Death and Hades"* **(Rev. 1:18)**, defined in **Luke 16:23** as *"being in torment."* This is where Satan and his demons and all of the unsaved will be cast someday. Believers can take comfort in the fact that God is sovereign over everything, including Satan and his demons. Jesus' dominion and authority extend everywhere and over all things, including the eternal destiny of every single person.

Jesus commanded John to write about the things *"that are to take place after this"* **(Rev. 1:19)**. We'll get to those in the other chapters. But first, John writes about *"the things . . . that are"* **(Rev. 1:19)**—the spiritual state of seven churches in Asia Minor at that time, according to Jesus' evaluation of them. Let's see what King Jesus has to say to His Bride.

THE SEVEN CHURCHES

Starting in chapter two, John conveys what Jesus had to say to each of the seven churches about their strengths and weaknesses. Because these seven churches represent the "complete" Church, we can look for these strengths and weaknesses in our own churches today. Each of the letters is addressed to "the angel" of the specific church. Although this could be an actual angel sent as a messenger to each church, it is likely that it is a personification of the church Jesus is addressing. We can be absolutely be sure these are the words of Jesus, not only because He tells us so but because the beginning of each section uses some of the attributes that described Him in chapter one, all uniquely used to fit specifically with each church's issues.

THE EPHESUS CHURCH

The first church John mentions is the church in Ephesus, described in **Revelation 2:1-7**.

The city of Ephesus was situated on the coast of Asia in modern-day Turkey and was abundantly rich. It was the home of a grand theater dedicated to the worship of the false goddess, Artemis, where more than twenty thousand local citizens and visitors could gather to chant, "Great is Artemis of the Ephesians," while on their way to the temple named for her. Worship of Artemis was so substantial and wealth was so abundant amongst the pagan Ephesians that just three centuries later, the people used their own funds to rebuild the temple after it was destroyed in a fire, refusing funding offered by Alexander the Great. There were other pagan religions thriving in the city, as well as worship of the pagan rulers of the day, both before and after the time that John wrote the book of Revelation. This is the environment in which the Ephesian Christians found themselves living.

Despite the living conditions in the city, the Ephesus church was doing some things well. The believers there were commended by Jesus, *"who holds the seven stars in his right hand, who walks among the seven golden lampstands"* **(Rev. 2:1)** for several things. Her ministering servants—*the seven stars* in the grip of His right hand—are commended for their good deeds, their patient endurance, and their vigilant watch over their doctrine (they didn't put up with false teachers). One of the false teaching groups they dealt with was the Nicolaitans, a heretical Christian group who lived lives of unrestrained indulgence.[8] They practiced antinomianism, the idea that once you're saved, grace allows you to lead a sinful life as much as you want! Jesus commends the Ephesus church for standing against the teaching, saying, *"'You hate the works of the Nicolaitans, which I also hate'"* **(Rev. 2:6)**. Antinomianism is still taught and practiced by some who claim to be Christians today. If Jesus hates something, it's obvious Christians shouldn't be doing it.

Jesus also commended the Ephesian church for *"bearing up"* **(Rev. 2:3)** under persecution for the sake of His name. However, they are not perfect. Jesus admonished the Ephesians, saying, *"'But I have this against you, that you have abandoned the love you had at first'"* **(Rev. 2:4)**. To find out what this means, we need take a look back at what the apostle Paul had to say in his letter to them decades before.

The apostle Paul had written to his protégé, Timothy, about the church in Ephesus sometime in the mid-sixties. Paul had left Timothy there when he headed to Macedonia, telling him to *"charge certain persons not to teach any different doctrine, nor to devote themselves to myths and endless genealogies, which promote speculations"* **(1 Tim. 1:3-4)**. It's clear from the good things Jesus says about this church in Revelation that Paul's teaching and Timothy's leadership of this church laid a solid foundation for its members. Knowing what you believe and why is crucial in the life of a Christian. It becomes even more so in times of persecution. Churches need strong leaders with correct doctrine and theology who won't tolerate false teaching.

---

8 Study Notes for Revelation 2:6—Nicolaitans, *ESV Study Bible: English Standard Version* (Wheaton, IL: Crossway Bibles, 2016).

In the letter Paul had written to the church itself, he commended them for their *"faith in the Lord Jesus and your love toward all the saints"* **(Eph. 1:15)**. Later in that same letter, Paul gives the church advice to *"[speak] the truth in love"* **(Eph. 4:15)**. This advice was in the context of teaching biblical truth. In other words, they were to teach and correct others lovingly when correcting theology and doctrine. Fighting for correct theology and doctrine causes strife. Keeping the doctrine and theology biblically sound in a church causes issues! This happens because the sinful default of the human heart makes us want to believe and interpret the Bible in our own way. When correcting doctrine or theology, things often get ugly.

There's something for all Christians to learn from Jesus' words to the Ephesian church. We should hate false teaching and correct it when we hear it, including calling out false teachers by name to warn others about them, just as Paul did in **2 Timothy 2:16-17**: *"But avoid irreverent babble, for it will lead people into more and more ungodliness, and their talk will spread like gangrene. Among them are Hymenaeus and Philetus, who have swerved from the truth, saying that the resurrection has already happened."* Hating and correcting false teaching implies that all believers need to make every effort to learn the Bible through reading and studying. You can't correct false teaching if you don't recognize it. God never intended for His people to remain infants in the faith, always needing milk or shallow theology. **Ephesians 4:14** tells us why we need to grow up into maturity in our knowledge: *"So that we may no longer be children, tossed to and fro by the waves and carried about by every wind of doctrine, by human cunning, by craftiness in deceitful schemes."*

But teaching and correcting false doctrine and theology isn't the only thing that matters—*how* we do that is also important. We need to remember *"the love [we] had"* **(Rev. 2:4)** for our brothers and sisters in the faith. If we are teaching or correcting a fellow believer in their doctrine or theology, we should do it lovingly. We are all members of the body of Christ. If we use our gifts in a harsh and unloving manner, regardless of how correct we may be, we are nothing more than *"a noisy gong or a clanging cymbal"* **(1 Cor. 13:1)**.

And in addition to that, we all know that it's very hard to admit you are wrong, even to yourself. If you're the one being corrected, be thankful that you're in a church where people desire correct theology and doctrine! Be thankful for the correction you receive, even when a brother or sister fails to do it lovingly. In that case, follow Paul's advice also found in his letter to the Ephesians: *"Let all bitterness and wrath and anger and clamor and slander be put away from you, along with all malice. Be kind to one another, tenderhearted, forgiving one another, as God in Christ forgave you"* **(Eph. 4:31)**.

Jesus gave the Ephesus church a remedy to having lost their first love: *"Remember therefore from where you have fallen; repent, and do the works you did at first"* **(Rev. 2:5)**. What does loving each other have to do with being a church? **First John 4:7-8** says, *"Beloved, let us love one another, for love is from God, and whoever loves has been born of God and knows God. Anyone who does not love does not know God, because God is love."* If we've been born again by God, we will love our brothers and sisters in the faith. Yes, we are to show love to unbelievers, but a church that's doing good deeds for the "world" yet hating and fighting each other needs to examine itself. Jesus gave the Ephesians a warning for not obeying Him: *"If not, I will come to you and remove your lampstand from its place"* **(Rev. 2:5)**. The warning to the Ephesus church is that they could cease to be a light to a dark world.

Jesus finished the letter to His worshipers in Ephesus by saying, *"To the one who conquers I will grant to eat of the tree of life"* **(Rev. 2:7)** in the new heavens and earth—something that was banned after the fall of Adam and Eve. That's quite a promise! Who can be a conqueror? **Romans 8:37** tells us that it is believers who *"are more than conquerors through [Christ]."* Jesus started this letter to His faithful servants proclaiming the Gospel in Ephesus reminding them that He had them in His hand. That's the safest place anyone can be because Jesus tells us, *"For I have come down from heaven, not to do my own will,* *but to do the will of him who sent me. And this is the will of him who sent me, that I shall lose nothing of all that he has given me but raise it up at the last day"* **(John 6:39)**. *"He who has an ear, let him hear"* **(Rev. 2:7)**.

THE SMYRNA CHURCH

The next church Jesus addressed was the one located in the city of Smyrna. It's the first of only two churches for which Jesus had no admonishment. The church in Smyrna was located in what is now Izmir, the third largest city in Turkey. The name *Smyrna* means "myrrh," a substance taken from a tree that produces a fragrance when crushed. It was a fitting name for the church located here because they were being crushed, but their suffering in Jesus' name yielded a sweet fragrant offering to the Lord.

Jesus' followers are told to stand in all circumstances without wavering and without renouncing our faith. This fact flies in the face of today's worship culture that expects blessings and breakthroughs. The letter to the Smyrna believers starts out with Jesus reminding them that He is the *"'first and the last, who died and came to life'"* **(Rev. 2:8)**. They and many other believers need these words of encouragement for the *"ten days"* **(Rev. 2:10)** of tribulation they are going to suffer, which is representative of a "complete" number of days, not ten literal days. The number ten represents completion. We only need to look at Paul and John's persecution and countless others throughout history to know that this does not mean ten literal days, as some camps believe.

The city of Smyrna was rich. It was located on a well-protected harbor at the end of the Hermus River—an important inland trade route—making it a vibrant business hub. It rivaled the wealth of Ephesus and other cities. There was money here, but not amongst the believers in the church. There are two words used for poverty in the Greek. One denotes having enough for your basic needs, but no extra. That's not the case here. The believers in Smyrna were *ptōcheia*—indigent, lacking even the basic necessities.[9] Jesus says to them,

---

9 *Strong's Concordance*, s.v. "πτωχεία (ptócheia)" accessed March 31, 2021, https://biblehub.com/greek/4432.htm.

"'I know your tribulation and your poverty (but you are rich)'" **(Rev. 2:9)**. The Smyrna believers had no materials goods, but they did have something much more important—the grace and favor of God. They were spiritually rich. This may sound like a strange statement in a world where today's believers expect God to make them financially comfortable—or, at the very least, where believers can't fathom that God would let them suffer in any way. The truth is believers are told to expect suffering and persecution. And persecution on top of their poverty is exactly what the Smyrna church got.

The believers in Smyrna lived amongst pagan worshipers and were commanded to worship the emperor, Caesar—both of which cause persecution. There was also a strong Jewish presence in the region. Jesus tells these precious believers in Smyrna that He knows *"the slander of those who say that they are Jews and are not, but are a synagogue of Satan'"* **(Rev. 2:9)**. Why was Jesus so harsh in His words about them? The Jews in Smyrna hated Christians, just as they did in the many cities. Smyrna was a very hostile environment for Christians. The Smyrna believers suffered harsh persecution—imprisonment, lashings so terrible that the mechanism of their flesh was visible even as far as the inward veins and arteries. Some were thrown to wild beasts to be torn apart. Some were burned at the stake like Polycarp, Bishop of Smyrna, in 156 AD. Tradition says that when he was sentenced to the fire, the Jews of the city were some of the most ardent gatherers of the wood.[10]

Smyrna's Christians hadn't wavered. Persecution always weeds out the goats from the sheep. Imagine a Sunday where the pastor of a large, stadium-sized church stands up and tells his members that unless they deny Christ, they will be destitute, sent to prison, or worse, severely tortured, maybe even to death. How many professing believers would sign up for that?

Organizations like Open Doors and others monitor persecution throughout the world today. A January 2020 report says that every day, eight Christians

---

[10] J.B. Lightfoot, Trans., "The Martyrdom of Polycarp," Early Christian Writings.com, 1990, http://www.earlychristianwritings.com/text/martyrdompolycarp-lightfoot.html.

worldwide are killed because of their faith. Every week, 182 churches or Christian buildings are attacked; and every month, 309 Christians are imprisoned unjustly. Last year, forty nations scored high enough to register "very high" persecution levels; this year, it's forty-five. And 260 million Christians are suffering severe levels of persecution—fifteen million more than last year.11 We need to pray fervently for our brothers and sisters. Pray that God would deliver them from their chains in light of the fact that Jesus prayed to the Father to let the cup of wrath pass from Him. But Jesus also prayed for God's will to be done. So, we also need to pray that they are given the words to make the Gospel known and that they declare it fearlessly like Paul, who was in chains, writes in **Ephesians 6:19-20**. We should pray that they will find God's grace sufficient in their weakness and that they rely on God's power and not on themselves, according to **2 Corinthians 12:9**. And we need to pray that despite their circumstances, their faith will reach regenerated hearts and bring others to Christ.

Any one of us could find ourselves in the same situation that believers in Smyrna were in when they got this letter. We need to remember what He told them about Himself at the beginning of the letter—that He is God eternal and that He died but rose again. Keeping those things in mind will help us put into practice the things Jesus told them. Jesus said, *"Be faithful unto death, and I will give you the crown of life. He who has an ear, let him hear what the Spirit says to the churches. The one who conquers will not be hurt by the second death"* **(Rev. 2:10-11)**. We will look in detail at the second death in later chapters. The promise of the crown of life from the King of Glory was a promise the Smyrna believers clung to, and one we should, too.

THE PERGAMUM CHURCH

The next church addressed in Revelation was located in Pergamum, described in **Revelation 2:12-17**. The city of Pergamum was the capital of the

---

11 Linda Lowry, The 10 most dangerous places for Christians," Open Doors USA.org, January 15, 2020, https://www.opendoorsusa.org/christian-persecution/stories/the-10-most-dangerous-places-for-christians.

ancient Greek kingdom of Pergamos until given over to Rome in 133 BC. Early on, it served as the seat of government for the Roman province of Asia. It was a cultural city, possessing a library estimated to have the capacity to hold over two hundred thousand papyri, making it one of the most important libraries of the ancient world. Like the rest of the province of Asia, worship of the emperor was demanded, and the site of the first temple for Imperial Caesar worship was erected here—a temple to Rome and Augustus in 29 B.C. The city was also home to multiple other pagan cults. It's no wonder Jesus refers to this city as *"Satan's throne"* **(Rev. 2:13)**.

The Word of God is the attribute of Jesus that we see at the beginning of this letter—the One who *"has the sharp two-edged sword"* **(Rev. 2:12)**, so we know what Jesus has to say to the church at Pergamum has to do with Scripture. **Ephesians 6:17** tells us we're to take *"the sword of the Spirit, which is the word of God"* when we're fighting spiritual warfare. **Hebrews 4:12** tells us how this sword does its job: *"The word of God is living and active, sharper than any two-edged sword, piercing to the division of soul and of spirit, of joints and of marrow, and discerning the thoughts and intentions of the heart."* As we study Scripture, the Holy Spirit uses the word to convict us of sin and lead us to repentance.

Some in the church at Pergamum were standing firm in the faith. The church even had one steadfast, martyred believer named Antipas, whom Jesus called *"faithful witness"* **(Rev. 2:13)**, a title used for King Jesus Himself! But some of Pergamum's church members were not standing firm. Without knowing Scripture, trusting God enough to stand against harsh persecution is almost impossible. The result was that some in the church were holding *"to the teachings of Balaam"* **(Rev. 2:14)**. This harkens back to the Old Testament book of Numbers, where pagan king Balak summoned Balaam to come and lay a curse on the Israelites (chapters 22-24). God prevented him from doing that, but Balaam did give King Balak advice on how to beat the Israelites—use the pagan women to entice the Israelites to worship their pagan gods. That worship included eating meat sacrificed to idols and sexual immorality. By mentioning this in His rebuke of Pergamum, Jesus is pointing to the fact that some in the church were using food and sex to entice faithful believers to ignore God's Word and sin by participating in trade guild feasts—feasts that included worship of false gods, food, and sex. Compromising with the world, even under harsh persecution, is not what Christians are called to do. As the apostle Paul says in **Ephesians 6:14**, we are to stand firm. Another problem for the Pergamum church was that, like the Ephesus church, there were those in this church who practiced the antinomianism of the Nicolaitans.

Christians have three enemies—the world with its temptations, our sinful flesh that always wants to give in, and the devil. We don't fight by rebuking Satan. We fight by not sinning. Our fight is against sin. Our weapon is knowing the Word of God. It's what Jesus used against the devil in His wilderness temptations. Knowing the Bible, along with prayer and the help of the Holy Spirit, helps us stand firm against sin and mortify it.

When we study the Bible, we learn about God. We learn of His attributes—things like His goodness, faithfulness, majesty, and sovereignty. Without this knowledge and the assurance it gives, Christians can waver easily. **Proverbs 9:10** says, *"The fear of the LORD is the beginning of wisdom, and the knowledge of the Holy One is insight."* As one commentator puts it, "The very first, and, indeed, the principal thing which is to be instilled into all men's minds,[sic] (without which they will make no progress in true wisdom,[sic]) is a serious sense of the Divine Majesty, and an awful regard toward him."[12] Christians cannot neglect reading and studying Scripture.

A pastor's most important job is to open the Word of God and explain the Bible in a way that his listeners grasp what God is saying and to make sure his listeners learn and understand the overarching story of the Bible, culminating in the Gospel. Expository preaching, also known as expositional preaching, is a type of preaching that explains the meaning of a particular

---

12 *Benson Commentary*, s.v., "Proverbs 9," accessed March 11, 2021, https://biblehub.com/commentaries/benson/proverbs/9.htm.

text or passage of Scripture. It seeks to unfold the original meaning of the text for the listeners and apply it to their lives. One of the benefits of teaching this way is that the verses are understood within their context. Expository preaching is the style of preaching that leads to a proper understanding of the Bible, as opposed to topical preaching, where individual verses are pulled from all over to support an idea. In topical preaching, verses can sound like they mean one thing when they actually have a totally different meaning when understood in their context.

The model for teaching in an expository fashion comes straight from the Word. As the risen Savior walked on the Road to Emmaus, He encountered two men talking about the news of the day. Jesus said to them, *"'O foolish ones, and slow of heart to believe all that the prophets have spoken! Was it not necessary that the Christ should suffer these things and enter into his glory?' And beginning with Moses and all the Prophets, he interpreted to them in all the Scriptures the things concerning himself"* **(Luke 24:25-27)**. Jesus explained Scripture. The way to interpret Scripture is with other Scripture. How fitting that Jesus is interpreting it here! As the two men say later in the passage, *"He opened to us the Scriptures"* **(Luke 24:32)**. He is the example to follow. It's not that there is never a proper way to do a topical sermon; but if topical teaching is what a congregation is getting Sunday after Sunday, they aren't getting the Scriptures opened and explained as modeled by "the Word made Flesh" **(John 1:14)**.

Jesus warns the believers in Pergamum in **Revelation 2:16**, *"Therefore repent. If not, I will come to you soon and war against them with the sword of my mouth."* A church is responsible for its erring members. Being lax in church discipline with members who are going astray isn't being kind to them; it's neglecting the duty to turn someone from their sin to repentance. The believers in Pergamum were to repent for tolerating the sinful behavior of the Nicolaitans and the compromisers. What would it look like for Jesus to war against them with the sword of His mouth? Some commentators believe the answer lies with Balaam, who is mentioned in the passage of **Revelation**

2 to the believers in Pergamum. *"Balaam . . . was killed with the sword"* **(Josh. 13:22)**. Is Jesus saying He's going to kill some of them if they don't repent? Maybe. Over and over again, God brought earthly justice to those amongst His people who pollute the Body as a warning to His chosen—the golden calf worshipers **(Exod. 32)**, Korah and his followers **(Num. 16)**, and Ananias and Sapphira **(Acts 5)**, to name a few.

Believers need to feed on the Word of God. Without it we are weak, vulnerable and unable to stand against temptation. Jesus says in **Revelation 2:17**, *"'To the one who conquers I will give some of the hidden manna, and I will give him a white stone, with a new name written on the stone that no one knows except the one who receives it.'"* All who feed on Christ, the true Manna, will live. They will be given a verdict indicated by the white stone—"not guilty."

THE THYATIRA CHURCH

The fourth church mentioned is the church in Thyatira. The city of Thyatira was located between the cities of Pergamos and Sardis; however, it was not located on a major trade route and wasn't as culturally or politically illustrious as some of the other cities mentioned. That doesn't mean they weren't wealthy. Jesus describes Himself as *"'the Son of God, who has eyes like a flame of fire, and whose feet are like burnished bronze'"* **(Rev. 2:18)**, evoking images of metalworking. Thyatira's claim to fame was its trade guilds, which dealt mainly in metals and fabrics, especially copper and fabric dyers. Lydia, whom Paul met in Philippi in **Acts 16:14**, was a Thyatiran seller of purple goods and a believer.[13]

The trade guilds were wealthy and powerful. They were organized, owned property, and contracted for work. If you wanted to use your craft to earn a living, you had to belong to a trade guild. The problem for Christians, was that the guilds held feasts honoring pagan gods that included sexual immorality, including orgies. If you wanted pay, you had to play.

---

13 Henry H. Halley, "Essay," In *Halley's Bible Handbook*, 25th ed. (Grand Rapids: Zondervan, 2000), 921.

There were some very good things going on at this church. Jesus commended them for their *"love and faith and service and patient endurance"* **(Rev. 2:19)**. Not only that, but their later works were also greater or more abundant than earlier. This says that for some in the church of Thyatira, there had been growth and evidence of real fruit, but not for everyone. Jesus rebuked the church for one of the same things for which He's rebuked others—tolerating false teaching that was leading others astray.

It's impossible to read the Bible and come away with the idea that believers are not to root out false teaching. It's imperative to the spiritual health of God's people! The Thyatira church was tolerating a self-proclaimed prophetess referred to as "Jezebel." The name Jezebel denotes a particular heinousness in the false teaching at Thyatira. Jezebel is a reference back to an evil queen in **1 Kings 21**. She was the wife of King Ahab, who imposed Baal worship on the nation of Israel and put God's true prophets to death.

Jesus says to the Thyatiran church, *"I have this against you, that you tolerate that woman Jezebel, who calls herself a prophetess and is teaching and seducing my servants to practice sexual immorality and to eat food sacrificed to idols"* **(Rev. 2:20)**. Someone in the church was telling people it was okay to join the guilds. This would have been tempting for people who could not earn a living in their craft without joining. Jezebel was enticing people to compromise what the Bible says not just for their own comfort, nor just for the sake of being tolerant, but also quite possibly to put food on the table for their family.

There are many who choose to compromise their faith just for the sake of their own comfort. There are many individuals and even whole churches who call themselves Christians who choose to compromise what the Bible says (and teach others to do so) just for the sake of being able to live their lives however they want or to be considered "tolerant." But some have to make a choice whether or not to compromise based on their needs. With Christian persecution rising year after year, more and more brothers and sisters in the faith will have to make the same type of life-or-death choices that the believers in Thyatira did.

In **Luke 9:23-26**, Jesus says:

> *"If anyone would come after me, let him deny himself and take up his cross daily and follow me. For whoever would save his life will lose it, but whoever loses his life for my sake will save it. For what does it profit a man if he gains the whole world and loses or forfeits himself? For whoever is ashamed of me and of my words, of him will the Son of Man be ashamed when he comes in his glory and the glory of the Father and of the holy angels."*

This is echoed in both Matthew's and Mark's gospels. Jesus doesn't promise that we won't suffer, nor that our children or other family members won't suffer along with us—even to death. We know from **Romans 8:16-17** that believers are *"children of God, and if children, then heirs—heirs of God and fellow heirs with Christ, provided we suffer with him in order that we may also be glorified with him."* Jesus started out in **Revelation 1:5** reminding His persecuted people that He is *"firstborn of the dead."* He does that to remind us and comfort us that there's more than just this life. Actually, there's something far better! He started the letter to the Thyatira church reminding them that He is the Son of God, reminding them of His Deity. He gets to make the rules. He never says that we will not suffer because we are believers or that we will not die as martyrs. That's a sobering thought when we think about ignoring or compromising His Word, for any reason. Jesus gives the Church comfort but also reminds us that He is God.

This false prophetess Jezebel and her "offspring," or followers, were given time to repent, but there's no repentance. The Old Testament Jezebel suffered the consequences of the curse of **Deuteronomy 28**. She and her offspring died, and she was eaten by dogs. The corpses of the wicked are often eaten by dogs and birds or beasts of the field. In fact, we're going to see them feasting on the wicked later in **Revelation 19**. What's going to happen to this Jezebel? Jesus tells us in **Revelation 2:22-23**, *"Behold, I will throw her onto a sickbed, and those who commit adultery with her I will throw into great tribulation, unless they repent of her works, and I will strike her children dead. And all the churches will know that I am he who searches mind and heart, and I will give to each of you according to your works."*

There was a remnant in the church of Thyatira that didn't hold to false teaching. Jesus says that He will not lay on them any additional burden. It's a burden to be a true believer in a church where there is false teaching going on and nothing's being done about it. The true believers in Thyatira, whose families may have been starving because of their refusal to disobey God's Truth or who were suffering the effects of persecution in some other way, were forced to watch others in the church who had no problem compromising the Truth to avoid hardship.

Encouraging them to keep standing firm until He comes, Jesus gave His steadfast remnant something to cling to. He said, *"The one who conquers and who keeps my works until the end, to him I will give authority over the nations, and he will rule them with a rod of iron, as when earthen pots are broken in pieces, even as I myself have received authority from my Father"* **(Rev. 2:26-27)**. This is a reference to **Psalm 2:9**, which says Jesus will *"'break [the wicked] with a rod of iron and dash them in pieces like a potter's vessel.'"* For anyone who suffers because of their refusal to disobey God, Jesus promises something that far outweighs any affliction—*"the morning star"* **(Rev. 2:28)**—a reference to Himself from **Revelation 22:16**.

THE SARDIS CHURCH

We find the next church, Sardis, in chapter three of Revelation. The people of Sardis felt that their city was "safe" or impregnable, because it sat up on a hill—a good vantage point to have when you stay vigilant. But Sardis got lazy. Twice in its history (547/546 and 214 B.C.), Sardis was sacked. First by Cyrus II and then by Antiochus III. Both attacks happened because their watchmen were neglecting their duties and their foes were able to sneak up on them.[14] The city also suffered a massive earthquake in 17 A.D. Part of the reconstruction included building a temple to the pagan god, Artemis. By the time of the apostle John's writing, there was an established Jewish community in Sardis. Judaism was a religion okayed by the Roman Empire during the reign of Augustus at the end of the first century. This Jewish population was granted rights to worship according to the laws of their ancestors, including the right to send money to the temple in Jerusalem.[15] This was a huge bonus to the Jewish worshipers, who wouldn't have to fear martyrdom for not worshiping Caesar. This was the backdrop for the words Jesus says to the church in Sardis in **Revelation 3:1-6**.

Out of the seven churches that received Jesus' revelation given to John, there are only two in which there is not an enemy to the church mentioned— no false teachers, no outside persecution, not even Satan is mentioned. One of those two churches is Sardis. There is no need for Satan to mess with the Sardis congregation in any of those ways. Why? Because they think they're saved, but in reality, they're spiritually dead.

The letter opens with *"'the words of him who has the seven spirits of God and the seven stars'"* **(Rev. 3:1)**. The book of Revelation introduced us to "the seven spirits of God" in chapter one—a reference to the Third Person of the Trinity, the Holy Spirit. God the Holy Spirit is the same in substance and equal in power and glory with God the Father and God the Son. He proceeds from the Father and the Son to regenerate the hearts of the elect and sanctify them through helping them know and understand the Bible and convicting them of sin. In **John 5:21**, Jesus says, *"For as the Father raises the dead and gives them life, so also the Son gives life to whom he will."* Jesus holds salvation in His hands. The opening of this letter is a fitting start to what's written to the church in Sardis, for until and unless God opens our hearts

---

14 Study Notes for Revelation 3:2-3: The Church in Sardis, *ESV Study Bible: English Standard Version* (Wheaton, IL: Crossway Bibles, 2016).
15 Josephus, Flavius, and William Whiston, "Essay," In *The Antiquities of the Jews* (McLean, Va: IndyPublish.com, 2001).

through regeneration by the Holy Spirit, we are dead in our trespasses and sins with no way to save ourselves.

The church in Sardis looked alive on the outside. But Jesus had some strong words for them: *"'I know your works. You have the reputation of being alive, but you are dead"* **(Rev. 3:1)**. The Sardis church looked vibrant and alive—partly because of their good works—but most of those in the church were spiritually dead.

A reputation of being "alive" speaks of a vibrant, thriving church that people know. From the outside looking in, a thriving body of believers who can go through their days without the burdens other churches were enduring must have certainly seemed alive. They may have even seemed to be "blessed" by God. Especially to believers from other parts of the region who, under the heavy hand of persecution, were watching their brothers and sisters be killed, were starving, or had to meet for worship in secret.

We know that there were only *"a few names in Sardis, people who have not soiled their garments"* **(Rev. 3:4)**. That means that in Jesus' eyes, a majority of the Sardis church was unbelievers. Just like the city they lived in, the people of the church in Sardis thought they were safe; but in fact, they were slumbering, unaware that they were in grave danger. Jesus tells them in **Revelation 3:2**, *"Wake up . . . for I have not found your works complete in the sight of my God."* **John 6:29** says, *"This is the work of God, that you believe in him whom he has sent."* Jesus was telling them that they weren't saved. The church in Sardis felt their good works and reputation constituted salvation. The truth is we bring absolutely nothing to the table for our salvation. Our good works and reputation have no saving power. The Sardis church looked like a bunch of believers on the outside, but Jesus told them to wake up because they were about to die! In the same way the city of Sardis had gotten too comfortable in their assurance of safety and were sacked by the enemy twice, the people in this church were in danger of being sacked by their Enemy—God! Unless God saves us, we are enemies of God **(Rom. 5:10)**, children of wrath **(Eph. 2:3)**, and alienated from God **(Col. 1:21)**.

But these people had a good reputation. How does a church full of people Jesus says were unsaved get a good reputation in a pagan community, especially in a community where they were required to bow the knee to the emperor? Perhaps the same way as many churches today—by doing good works for everyone to see, by not making waves, and by being tolerant. There is no mention of this church suffering or enduring persecution. It's likely that because *Judaism* was allowed to be practiced freely and without having to worship Caesar, that fitting in to society as a Christian in Sardis was much easier than for other churches in the region. As long as they didn't proclaim "Jesus is Lord" (at least not too loudly) nor balk at the fact that Caesar was to be proclaimed Lord according to Roman law, it would be easy to go unnoticed.

There are loads of churches with busy, vibrant, friendly members happily going to church each Sunday and serving the church and the community throughout the week. They may even meet for Bible study and prayer meeting regularly. They look good on the outside. But if you asked them to explain the Gospel message, you'd get a host of different answers, and you would find that most of them had no idea what God's plan of salvation was at all.

But there was hope for the Sardis church! Jesus told them in **Revelation 3:3**, *"Remember, then, what you received and heard. Keep it, and repent."* The Sardis church had heard the Gospel before. They needed to remember the grace, love, and forgiveness that comes only through Jesus and repent of their sin! And there were people in their midst who could help them—those *"few names in Sardis, people who have not soiled their garments"* **(Rev. 3:4)**. Hope for revival wasn't totally lost!

Jesus says, *"I will come like a thief, and you will not know at what hour I will come against you"* **(Rev. 3:3b)**. We don't know the day of our death nor when Jesus is going to return. The church of Sardis needed to wake up, as do many churches today. Some churches aren't teaching their members and attendees that they are sinners who have offended our perfectly holy God and, because of that, deserve punishment in Hell for eternity. Some churches are preaching a social justice message instead of the Gospel. Social justice issues are very important, but heart change is the only thing that leads to true and lasting change in behavior. And that only comes from the true Gospel message.

There are churches that teach that God wants you to be happy, healthy, and prosperous, or that He wants to fulfill your heart's desires and plans. There are still others who are busy serving the community with multiple projects and programs, but the leaders and the members have very little interest in having solid Bible studies or prayer meetings.

Sardis was a dead church. There are lots of them out there. A dead church isn't dead because it's one that's barely hanging on financially or because it only has a dozen members. A church isn't dead because they don't sing contemporary music or don't seem very lively. A church isn't dead because they have all older people or all Caucasians or because they don't have many children in the congregation. A church is dead because its members are not being fed the Word of God and because they aren't proclaiming the true and complete Gospel message—the only thing that can bring someone to faith and repentance. Neglecting the true preaching of the Word and preaching a false or half-truth Gospel message results in many congregants not actually being saved, and most won't even realize it until it's too late.

Will proclaiming the true Gospel message result in everyone who hears being saved? In **Luke 8:5-10**, Jesus tells a parable of the sower, where the seed (the Gospel message) fell on different kinds of soil. Jesus said:

> "And as he sowed, some fell along the path and was trampled underfoot, and the birds of the air devoured it. And some fell on the rock, and as it grew up, it withered away, because it had no moisture. And some fell among thorns, and the thorns grew up with it and choked it. And some fell into good soil and grew and yielded a hundredfold." As he said these things, he called out, "He who has ears to hear, let him hear." And when his disciples asked him what this parable meant, he said, "To you it has been given to know the secrets of the kingdom of God, but

for others they are in parables, so that 'seeing they may not see, and hearing they may not understand.'"

Only God knows *"who has an ear"* **(Rev. 3:6)** to hear. It is a church's job to obey by preaching the true and complete Gospel message that we are sinners who have offended our perfectly holy God, and there is nothing we can do to fix it on our own. We need the Savior.

THE PHILADELPHIA CHURCH

Let's move on to the words Jesus has to say to the church in Philadelphia found in **Revelation 3:7-13**. Like the city of Sardis, Philadelphia was set on a hill, making it defendable against its enemies. On one side of the city were volcanic cliffs, on the other a fertile area known for its grapevines producing high-quality, excellent wine. Also, like Sardis, it suffered greatly from the earthquake in 17 A.D. and was practically destroyed. It received help from the Roman government for rebuilding and for a short time was renamed "NeoCaesarea" (Caesar's New City).[16]

Inscriptions from the city mention worship of the Hellenistic gods Zeus, Hestia, and others in the region. Christians in the church named the city of "brotherly love" not only had to deal with pagan worshipers, they also had to deal with Jewish backlash and persecution, like their brothers and sisters elsewhere. Despite their hardships, Philadelphia is the second of only two churches not to get a rebuke from Jesus! Like the church in Smyrna, Jesus had nothing but commendation and encouragement for His people worshiping there.

Jesus began this letter stating that He is *"'the holy one, the true one, who has the key of David, who opens and no one will shut, who shuts and no one opens'"* **(Rev. 3:7)**, a reference to the prophecy in Isaiah 22:22. No one else can open or shut the door to life. Jesus told this church, *"'I know your works. Behold, I have set before you an open door, which no one is able to shut'"* **(Rev. 3:8)**. For people who

---

[16] "Philadelphia," BiblicalTraining.org, accessed April 1, 2021, https://www.biblicaltraining.org/library/philadelphia.

have little power and are suffering and who will continue to suffer, even to death, this would have been a comfort.

Jesus commends them because despite having *"little power"* **(Rev. 3:8)**, they stood firm, keeping His word and not denying Him. This church in Philadelphia truly understood the words Jesus gave to Paul in **2 Corinthians 12:9**: *"'My grace is sufficient for you, for my power is made perfect in weakness.'"* In the not-too-distant future of receiving this letter, during the time of Polycarp, they would be under extremely harsh persecution, and some would suffer martyrdom.

Once again, Jesus referred to the Jews who thought they were part of God's family but are not as the *"synagogue of Satan"* **(Rev. 3:9)**. This time, He even calls them liars. Jesus made a promise to the Philadelphia church, saying, *"I will make them come and bow down before your feet, and they will learn that I have loved you"* **(Rev. 3:9)**. Because they have been faithful to Jesus, patiently enduring trials and tribulation, the Philadelphia church would be kept *"from the hour of trial that is coming on the whole world, to try those who dwell on earth"* **(Rev. 3:10)**. Jesus wasn't saying that all believers will be "raptured" off the face of the earth before a period of great tribulation. Scripture has to have meaning for those to whom it was written. This was written to the Philadelphia church, and they weren't raptured away. We also know that believers are promised temptation, trial, and tribulation—even martyrdom—over and over again throughout the Bible, so the idea of the Church being raptured away to avoid suffering is not supported by Scripture.

Instead, these verses had two meanings. Like we said before, the city of Philadelphia resided among some of the best grapes of its time and would have been familiar with the process of making wine. Jesus was promising the believers in the church that they would not suffer the winepress of God's wrath—something that's reserved for the wicked. It's also a promise of spiritual protection. Because believers are sealed with the Holy Spirit for salvation, they cannot lose it. Jesus was telling this church that they can endure whatever suffering was coming, even suffering an intense time of tribulation brought on the world by God.

In His High Priestly prayer, Jesus prayed to the Father for believers. In **John 17:15**, Jesus says, *"I do not ask that you take them out of the world, but that you keep them from the evil one."* How did the Philadelphia church—and how do we—know that believers can endure suffering and not lose their salvation? Jesus says in **Revelation 3:10**, *"I will keep you."* It is God Who keeps us, seals us, and protects us. That's referred to as the "perseverance of the saints." We persevere because God is preserving us.

Jesus tells the Philadelphia believers, *"I am coming soon. Hold fast what you have, so that no one may seize your crown"* **(Rev. 3:11)**. Jesus' encouragement that He is coming soon is an incentive to the suffering believers in the Church. This doesn't mean His second coming was going to be in the near future for them. But in light of eternity, our time here on earth is short. Paul says in **2 Corinthians 4:16-18**, *"So we do not lose heart. Though our outer self is wasting away, our inner self is being renewed day by day. For this light momentary affliction is preparing for us an eternal weight of glory beyond all comparison, as we look not to the things that are seen but to the things that are unseen. For the things that are seen are transient, but the things that are unseen are eternal."* Christians are to hold fast to what they have—their salvation and the One Who saved them. Can someone "seize the crown" of God's elect? No. For it is God Who saves and seals us for eternity. But on the flip side of God's preservation of His people are the exhortations to the saints, given to make us diligent and watchful—one of the means of our final perseverance.

Jesus' letter to these precious believers in Philadelphia ends with this promise: *"The one who conquers, I will make him a pillar in the temple of my God. Never shall he go out of it, and I will write on him the name of my God, and the name of the city of my God, the new Jerusalem, which comes down from my God out of heaven, and my own new name"* **(Rev. 3:12)**. What does it mean that believers will be a pillar in the temple of God? We'll talk about that toward the end of the book. *"He who has an ear, let him hear what the Spirit says to the churches'"* **(Rev. 3:13)**.

THE LAODICEA CHURCH

There is one more church to look at—Laodicea. The city of Laodicea was not unlike the other cities John wrote to in that there were pagan worshipers, a Jewish population, and the requirement of emperor worship. This was a robust city known for its medical, textile, and banking industries. It sat on an important crossroads along the trade routes and was popular for its financial transactions and the soft, black wool of the sheep that grazed in the pasture beyond the city. This city was rich—so rich that when an earthquake destroyed it in A.D. 60, they declined imperial disaster relief.[17]

The city was lacking one thing, however—water. There were two sources to get it—Hierapolis, which had mineral-rich hot springs, or Colossae, which had cold water. To get water to Laodicea, it had to travel from these towns through two aqueducts of about five-to-six miles in length. By the time the water arrived from either location, it was lukewarm and not useful for anything. The cold water from Colossae was lukewarm and no longer refreshing, and the hot water from the springs in Hierapolis was no longer fit for soaking because it had lost its heat. No one likes to take a lukewarm Epsom salt bath.

Jesus addresses the letter to the Laodiceans from *"'the faithful and true witness'"* **(Rev. 3:14)**. As such, He doesn't waste time getting down to the truth of their problem. The Laodicean church was like the water—lukewarm. Jesus said to them, *"Would that you were either cold or hot!"* **(Rev. 3:15)**. Without knowing the geography of the area or anything about the sources of the city's water, many believe that Jesus was saying to either be *for* Him (all-in, hot) or *against* Him (cold, an enemy). They think He would prefer either of these to being lukewarm. But that is not what Jesus was saying at all. Laodicea didn't lay at the source of either temperature water. Jesus is telling them, "You need

---

17 Tacitus, "The Annals," Alfred John Church and William Jackson Brodribb, trans., Classics. mit, 109 A.C.E., http://classics.mit.edu/Tacitus/annals.10.xiv.html.

the Source." Only Jesus can give us Living Water, and the Laodicean church didn't have it.

This church thought they didn't need anything. They were self-reliant. They were rich; their needs were being met. They even had medicine and plenty of clothing. Looking at their prosperity, you might be inclined to think that God was blessing them. But as Jesus viewed them from a spiritual standpoint, He saw them in a totally different light and told them they were *"wretched, pitiable, poor, blind, and naked"* **(Rev. 3:17)**. Speaking to believers in the Sermon on the Mount, Jesus said, *"Blessed are the poor in spirit, for theirs is the kingdom of heaven"* **(Matt. 5:3)**. The "poor in spirit" are those who recognize that they are spiritually bankrupt before God. They realize that they have nothing to offer for salvation and that they need saving! This is certainly not where the Laodicean church members find themselves. They may be materially rich, but they are lacking the most important thing every human needs—salvation—and they don't even realize their need. Ever know someone who seemed to have it all and yet was never satisfied? The Laodiceans had material wealth, but that doesn't satisfy. They had medical resources at their disposal, but even possessing good health probably didn't satisfy them. The Laodiceans had to be thirsty. They had been drinking lukewarm water that would never satisfy. Jesus had them in the exact right place at the right time to hear Him *"counsel"* them to *"buy from me gold refined by fire, so that you may be rich, and white garments so that you may clothe yourself and the shame of your nakedness may not be seen, and salve to anoint your eyes, so that you may see"* **(Rev. 3:18)**. No amount of money can buy these things. Only by God's grace can the Laodicean church be saved.

Jesus wasn't inviting them to buy new gold and white clothes. The word "counsel" here actually means "advise."[18] He was *telling* them to buy. **Isaiah 55:1-3** says:

---

18 W. E. Vine, "Essay," In *Vine's Complete Expository Dictionary of Old and New Testament Words: with Topical Index*, (Nashville: Thomas Nelson, 2000), 49.

> *"'Come, everyone who thirsts, come to the waters; and he who has no money, come, buy and eat! Come, buy wine and milk without money and without price. Why do you spend your money for that which is not bread, and your labor for that which does not satisfy? Listen diligently to me, and eat what is good, and delight yourselves in rich food. Incline your ear, and come to me; hear, that your soul may live."*

Just like the calling of the apostles, Jesus says, "Come. Follow Me." It's not a question; it's a call. Jesus loved the Laodicean church. They are part of His elect, and as a loving father reproves and disciplines His children, so was Jesus telling them it's time to repent because judgment is coming. He told the Laodicean church, *"Those whom I love, I reprove and discipline, so be zealous and repent"* **(Rev. 3:19)**. The word "reprove" used here denotes an unbeliever being convicted of his sinful state.[19] When God convicts us of our sin, the response is repentance. There is a difference between God's wrath and God's discipline. **Deuteronomy 8:5**, **Proverbs 3:12**, and **Hebrews 12:6** are just some of the Scriptures that tell us God's discipline is for His children. **1 Corinthians 11:32** says, *"But when we are judged by the Lord, we are disciplined so that we may not be condemned along with the world."* Jesus told the Laodiceans to *"be zealous"* in repenting. The Source had come, and it was time to be saved.

Jesus says in **Revelation 3:20**, *"Behold, I stand at the door and knock. If anyone hears my voice and opens the door, I will come in to him and eat with him, and he with me."* Jesus doesn't say, "If you hear my message and *decide* to answer the door, I'll come in." He wasn't standing at the door knocking, wringing His hands and hoping that someone would open it. Jesus doesn't come to the door as a salesman, hoping His salespitch works. In **John 10:2b-4** Jesus tells us that His *"sheep hear his voice, and he calls his own sheep by name and leads them out. When he has brought out all his own, he goes before them, and the sheep follow him, for they know his voice."* Jesus comes to the door of those who were chosen before the

---

19 Blue Letter Bible, s.v. "-Elegchō," accessed March 13, 2021, https://www.blueletterbible.org/lang/lexicon/lexicon.cfm?Strongs=G1651&t=ESV.

foundation of the world; He comes as the Master of the house, Who expects His servants to open it quickly because they know His voice.

Jesus started out this letter to the Laodiceans calling Himself *"the faithful and true witness"* **(Rev. 3:14)**. He is the source of Living Water. Jesus is the One Zechariah prophesied about saying, *"On that day living waters shall flow out from Jerusalem, half of them to the eastern sea and half of them to the western sea. It shall continue in summer as in winter. And the LORD will be king over all the earth. On that day the LORD will be one and his name one"* **(Zech. 14:8-9)**. The Laodicean and every other church is supposed to be like the Source—faithful witnesses like Jesus, about Jesus. The Church proclaims the Gospel message to all, and those who've been born again—those whose hearts have been changed from stone to flesh by the Holy Spirit—hear and respond in repentance and faith.

"'He who has an ear, let him hear what the Spirit says to the churches'" **(Rev. 3:22)**.

CHAPTER 2
STUDY GUIDE

GETTING YOUR TOES WET

God, in all three Persons of the Trinity, addressed a letter to His Church about their spiritual condition. *In light of that, how does that make you feel about examining your own church?*

Jesus gives each church the remedy for their spiritual condition. *Can you see yourself helping make changes that might need to be made at your church, in light of what Jesus says?*

In this letter, Jesus has harsh rebukes if the church refuses to change. *If your church fit the profile of one of these churches and refused to change, what would your response be?*

DIVING IN DEEP

A major problem in some of the seven churches, as well as in many today, is false teaching. *What do these verses say about false teaching and false teachers?*

Galatians 1:6-9

2 Peter 2:1-3

2 Timothy 4:3-4

Romans 16:17-18

Jesus paid the penalty for our sin, in our place. But that doesn't mean we can be like the Nicolaitans and take our sin lightly. *What do these verses say about sin and our response to it?*

1 John 3:6-10

Hebrews 10:26

Galatians 5:19-21

From the outside, the Laodicean church looked like they were blessed by God. The idea that Jesus secures for Christians an easy life of prosperity and health, free of suffering, is popular today. *What did Jesus have to say about the subject?*

Matthew 5:10-12

Mark 13:13

Luke 14:27

John 16:33

The church at Thyatira had a false prophet, Jezebel, convincing the believers it was okay to join the trade guilds, even though they would have to sin against God to belong. It's easy today to find Christians who rationalize sin for certain reasons. They say things like, "God will understand why I had to," or "It will be okay because God knows my heart." *Based on Jesus' words to the seven churches and the passages you read from the last question, do you believe God is ever "okay" with sin?*

BACK ON DRY LAND

The Pergamum church had people holding on to false theology and doctrine. It's critically important for pastors to teach their congregants Scripture in a way that they know and understand the Bible. One way this is accomplished is through expository teaching and preaching. *What kind of teaching and preaching is your church getting each Sunday? Do you regularly hear a topical sermon with verses (usually one-liners) pulled from all over the Bible as support, or do you get an expository sermon with portion of Scripture explained and supported by other portions of Scripture, all taken within their context?*

Do you feel you have an overall knowledge and understanding of the Bible as a whole? If not, what are your plans to remedy the situation?

CHAPTER 3

PULLING BACK THE CURTAIN

Do you know any good news/bad news people? You know the type—they tell you they have good news and bad news. Often, they give you the good news first to soften the blow of the bad news. And if the bad news is really bad, getting some good news first gives you something to hold onto while you deal with the bad news.

To clarify, there is nothing in the book of Revelation that is bad news for believers. In the words of Albert Barnes, this book "was designed to cheer the hearts of those to whom the book was first sent, in their trials, and the hearts of all believers in all ages, with the assurance of the final triumph of the gospel."[20] For the people of God, Revelation is the good news of the culmination of the Gospel! However, chapters six through nineteen do tell us how God deals with and punishes the unbelieving world. This can be difficult for us to read, especially since we all probably have people we love who are not believers.

Sandwiched between Jesus' letter to the seven churches and the prophecy of Divine judgment on the wicked is an amazing interlude in chapters four and five—an incredible vision that is meant to fill us with sheer joy and sustain us as we deal with the judgment passages that are to follow. Jesus

---

20 Albert Barnes, "Revelation," in "Albert Barnes' Notes on the Whole Bible," StudyLight.org, accessed March 3, 2021, https://www.studylight.org/commentaries/eng/bnb/revelation.html.

pulls back the curtain and gives John a glimpse into Heaven. In chapters four and five, we, through John, are shown God's throne room in Heaven. But more than that, we are shown what goes on in that heavenly throne room. God is on the throne directing everything that has, is, and will happen on earth, while everyone in Heaven worships Him.

God is the same yesterday, today, and tomorrow. He never changes: *"For I the Lord do not change"* (**Mal. 3:6**). **Hebrews 13:8** says, *"Jesus Christ is the same yesterday and today and forever."* Chapters four and five of Revelation show us that the same is true with what goes on in Heaven. Heaven never changes. This should be a huge comfort to us! No matter how chaotic or seemingly out of control things are on earth, we know that a Heaven that has always been, is, and will always be serene, joyful, and orderly is waiting for us.

THE APPEARANCE OF GOD

Revelation 4:3 is a very descriptive passage. But when you read it, you can't help but notice something it *doesn't* describe: *"And he who sat there had the appearance of jasper and carnelian, and around the throne was a rainbow that had the appearance of an emerald."* Nowhere is there any mention of the physical appearance of God the Father. It says, *"He . . . had the appearance of jasper and carnelian"* but offers no concrete, physical description of the Almighty. Similarly, if we look back in the Old Testament, we see that both Isaiah **(Isaiah 6)** and Ezekiel **(Ezekiel 1)** were also given similar "behind the scenes" visions; and they, too, did not physically describe the Lord. Instead, John uses precious stones to convey the magnificence and majesty of God. Jasper is a quartz that is usually orange, red, yellow, or a mixture of all three. Carnelian, too, has hues of orange and red. These colors convey fire. Fire is used throughout Scripture to symbolize the presence, judgment, and power of God.

Back in the Old Testament, we see this several times. **Exodus 13:21-22** shows fire as a symbol of God's presence: *"And the Lord went before them by day in a pillar of cloud to lead them along the way, and by night in a pillar of fire to give them light, that they might travel by day and by night."* We see God's judgment depicted as fire in **Numbers 11:1**: *"And the people complained in the hearing of the LORD about their misfortunes, and when the Lord heard it, his anger was kindled, and the fire of the LORD burned among them and consumed some outlying parts of the camp."* And finally, in **1 Kings 18:38**, we see the power of God being symbolized by fire: *"Then the fire of the LORD fell and consumed the burnt offering and the wood and the stones and the dust, and licked up the water that was in the trench."*

It may seem odd that John uses these precious stones as a description of God, but it's really not. Other than a symbolic description we get of Jesus in Revelation 2 and 19, there is scant information on what Jesus looked like, and He physically walked the earth for thirty-three years and met thousands of people! Only in **Isaiah 52:14** and **53:2** do we get any indication of Jesus' appearance, and even they are very vague. John spent three years at Jesus' side. If anyone could have given us an accurate physical picture of Him, it's John. Yet, he doesn't. In fact, as we will see in upcoming verses in chapter five, John describes Jesus' appearance in that throne room much like he does God the Father's—by using metaphors. Why is that? Remember, the key to understanding the book of Revelation is to do your homework in the Old Testament. So, let's do some homework!

Exodus 20 and **Deuteronomy 5** both list the ten commandments, with **Exodus 20:4** and **Deuteronomy 5:8** citing the second commandment specifically: *"You shall not make for yourself a carved image, or any likeness of anything that is in heaven above, or that is in the earth beneath, or that is in the water under the earth."*

In the Old Testament, the biggest sin the Israelites were guilty of was idolatry and, more specifically, syncretism. Idolatry is worshipping something other than the one, true God, while syncretism is blending idolatry *with* the worship of God. The Israelites fell into both. We see the first sign of this in **Exodus 32:1-6**:

> *When the people saw that Moses delayed to come down from the mountain, the people gathered themselves together to Aaron and said to him, "Up, make us gods who shall go before us. As for this Moses,*

the man who brought us up out of the land of Egypt, we do not know what has become of him." So Aaron said to them, "Take off the rings of gold that are in the ears of your wives, your sons, and your daughters, and bring them to me." So all the people took off the rings of gold that were in their ears and brought them to Aaron. And he received the gold from their hand and fashioned it with a graving tool and made a golden calf. And they said, "These are your gods, O Israel, who brought you up out of the land of Egypt!" When Aaron saw this, he built an altar before it. And Aaron made a proclamation and said, "Tomorrow shall be a feast to the LORD." And they rose up early the next day and offered burnt offerings and brought peace offerings. And the people sat down to eat and drink and rose up to play.

This is a familiar story to many of us. Why did the Israelites ask Aaron to make them a god out of gold? They did it because Moses had been away for a while, so it had been some time since they had heard a Word from God. They wanted something concrete and tangible to worship. Their faith alone wasn't strong enough to sustain them—thus, the calf.

We see it again when the Israelites enter the Promised Land for the second time to conquer it, with instructions by God to completely destroy and/or drive out the pagan nations that were inhabiting the Promised Land. Every Israelite tribe failed to do as commanded. As a result, the Israelites were living amongst pagan civilizations and soon began to assimilate to them. These pagan groups had many gods. They crafted representations of these gods out of wood, silver, gold, and other materials and then worshipped the statues. It didn't take long before the Israelites joined in and were doing the same. They still worshipped Yahweh for the big things, like protection from enemies, but they also worshipped the pagan gods and idols for things like fertility and crops. Like the golden calf incident, the Israelites wanted something physical and concrete to worship and hold.

God, of course, knew worshipping statues and idols would be the Israelites' downfall, just as it can be a downfall to some today. Like the Israelites, we are inundated with "religious" statues, paintings, medals, and drawings. There are many who claim to be Christians who cling to these artifacts, much like one clings to a rabbit foot or lucky coin. Many of these renderings are of Mary, the mother of Jesus, or others who have been deemed saints by the Catholic, Lutheran, and Anglican churches. These worthless, material objects are often worshipped more than, or instead of, worshipping Christ! This is idolatry and syncretism. The purpose of the second commandment is to keep God's people from sinning by forbidding them to have any kind of image or representation of anything. Even a cross can be an idol if we are relying on it for some magical property we believe it has, rather than just wearing it to publicly proclaim we belong to Jesus. The point of the second commandment is that we are to focus on the spiritual, rather than on the physical, worthless things of the world, leaning on our faith in Christ. Instead of clinging to an object, we should cling to what Christ has done for us, His Word, and how we are called to respond. **John 4:23-24** and **Hebrews 11:1** reiterate this. Jesus says in **John 4:23-24**, *"But the hour is coming, and is now here, when the true worshippers will worship the Father in spirit and truth, for the Father is seeking such people to worship him. God is spirit, and those who worship him must worship in spirit and truth."* The author of Hebrews says in **Hebrews 11:1**, *"Now faith is the assurance of things hoped for, the conviction of things not seen."*

THE HEAVENLY THRONE ROOM

John goes on using colors as symbols to describe the throne room. He tells us, *"Around the throne was a rainbow that had the appearance of an emerald"* **(Rev. 4:3b)**. Going back to the Old Testament, we see the Noahic covenant in **Genesis 8:21-22**: *"And when the LORD smelled the pleasing aroma, the LORD said in his heart, 'I will never again curse the ground because of man, for the intention of man's heart is evil from his youth. Neither will I ever again strike down every living creature as I have done. While the earth remains, seedtime and harvest, cold and heat, summer and winter, day and night, shall not cease."* God set the rainbow in the clouds as a symbol of the covenant He made with Noah. Sometimes, we just see that God promised to never flood the Earth again without looking any deeper. By never again destroying the Earth, God was preserving the stability of nature. This was important because this stability was necessary if Jesus was going to enter history to save His people. Since all living things would never again be destroyed by a flood, the whole Earth was the beneficiary of this covenant. The Noahic covenant, symbolized by the rainbow that is around the throne of God, demonstrates God's love for all His creation and shows us that one day, God will set the Earth back to where it was always meant to be before the Fall.

Along the same line, John tells us that the rainbow had an appearance of an emerald. Emeralds are green. Green is used as a symbol of nature—as we see in **Psalm 23:2**: *"He makes me lie down in green pastures"*—and again points to God renewing and restoring the Earth.

John's vision continues in **Revelation 4:4-6a**:

> *Around the throne were twenty-four thrones, and seated on the thrones were twenty-four elders, clothed in white garments, with golden crowns on their heads. From the throne came flashes of lightning, and rumblings and peals of thunder, and before the throne were burning seven torches of fire, which are the seven spirits of God, and before the throne there was as it were a sea of glass, like crystal.*

There is a lot of symbolism in these verses. The twenty-four elders represent *all* of the people of God. Twelve is a number of completeness. Twelve is also the number of tribes of Israel, which is symbolic of the people of Israel God chose to save, and the number of apostles, which is symbolic of the Gospel being preached to and accepted by God's elect from among the Gentiles. So, the number twenty-four represents all of the people God has chosen to save. They are seated next to God in robes of white with gold crowns on their heads. They are enjoying fellowship with God. The white robes show the righteousness and holiness that is imputed to them by Christ. We see a reference to the gold crowns back in **Isaiah 28:5**: *"In that day the*

LORD of hosts will be a crown of glory, and a diadem of beauty, to the remnant of his people."

The crowns represent the people of God sharing in the glory of God. Remember this because we are going to see what they do with these gold crowns shortly. But first, we see that thunder and lightning are coming from God's throne with seven torches of fire, which are the seven spirits of God, before it. Again, the fire represents God's omnipotence—seven meaning it is complete, perfect omnipotence—and likewise, the seven spirits of God are His complete Spirit. Obviously, this is a reference to the Holy Spirit. The sea of glass like crystal—before the throne again—conveys the sereness and majesty of God and Heaven.

Revelation 4:6b-8 continues John's vision of the throne room and some pretty crazy creatures he sees.

> *And around the throne, on each side of the throne, are four living creatures, full of eyes in front and behind: the first living creature like a lion, the second living creature like an ox, the third living creature with the face of a man, and the fourth living creature like an eagle in flight. And the four living creatures, each of them with six wings, are full of eyes all around and within, and day and night they never cease to say, "Holy, holy, holy, is the Lord God Almighty, who was and is and is to come!"*

These verses are an example of the apocalyptic language that tends to trip up people. Here, we see various creatures described—creatures that are hard for us to envision with eyes all over the front and back of them, six wings, etc. But we don't have to be frightened or wigged out about them. These are basically the worship leaders in Heaven. Probably a little funkier than worship leaders we have encountered, but worship leaders, nonetheless. They lead everyone in Heaven in praising God, saying, *"'Holy, holy, holy is the Lord God Almighty who was and is and is to come.'"* And if you know your Old Testament, you know that this is not the first time we see creatures like this nor words of worship like this.

Once again, going back to Ezekiel's and Isaiah's visions of Heaven in **Ezekiel 1** and **Isaiah 6**, we see they saw similar creatures. Isaiah tells us they are seraphim, which are angels. Isaiah also recorded very similar words of worship used by the creatures in **Isaiah 6:3**: *"'Holy, holy, holy is the LORD of hosts; the whole earth is full of his glory.'"* This vision given to John was not something new. We will repeat this often, but it is a crucial truth. The New Testament, including Revelation, is the fulfillment of the Old Testament, not a bunch of crazy, new teachings.

We want to make a side note here before we move on. Some of you may recall that Daniel also had a vision of some wild-looking creatures in **Daniel 7**. Those creatures were not the same as the creatures seen in Isaiah, Ezekiel, and Revelation. When you put those Daniel verses into context, it becomes clear that those creatures represented evil kingdoms, not heavenly worshipers.

Revelation 4 finishes up by showing us what the elders do with those gold crowns that were given to them. Whenever those creatures we just saw worship God by giving Him glory, honor, and gratitude, the elders fall down before God and *"cast their crowns before the throne saying, 'Worthy are you, our Lord and God, to receive glory and honor and power, for you created all things, and by your will they existed and were created'"* **(Rev. 4:10-11)**.

These verses show us that the twenty-four elders (the people of God) return the glory they have been given, represented by the crowns, back to where it belongs—to God. All of God's people are giving back to God the glory in which they have been allowed to share, and all of God's people are in perfect unity! What a beautiful picture this is, especially when we see so much division in the Church right now. Can I get a hallelujah, amen?!

GOD IS BIGGER THAN THE BOOGEYMAN

We said earlier that God is giving us this glimpse into Heaven to encourage and give desperately needed hope to the Christians of John's time, as well as to Christians of all time. As we alluded to in chapter one, when the book of Revelation was written, the Roman emperors thought of themselves as gods and demanded to be worshipped. They hated Christians and Christianity because loyal followers of Jesus refused to bow down to them and to look to them as the ultimate authority. The torturing and killing of some Christians was intended to send a message to the rest. We can sympathize with how tempting it may have been for these early Christians to give in and bow their knee to Caesar—or, at the very least, water down the Gospel so that it wasn't as offensive. In fact, many Christians all over the world are in the exact same position today. But these verses tell us why we need to stand strong in our faith, no matter the cost. Our suffering can bring glory to Jesus, just as Jesus' suffering brought glory to God the Father. In Jesus' High Priestly prayer right before His crucifixion and death and after He had told His disciples that He would be leaving them and that they would have tribulation, He says, *"Father, the hour has come; glorify your Son that the Son may glorify you'"* **(John 17:1)**. From Genesis to Revelation, Scripture is all about worshipping and glorifying our Almighty God. As the Westminster Confession says, "Man's chief and highest end is to glorify God and fully to enjoy him forever."[21] We see from this vision that purpose perfected in Heaven.

Friends, there is something much bigger than us, or any governing power, at work. God the Almighty is Sovereign and on the throne. And someday, we will be at that throne worshipping Him face to face! Knowing that should help strengthen and empower us to stand against anyone or anything that opposes the things of God, regardless of the consequences. Stephen gave us a valuable lesson in **Acts 7**. When he was dragged out to be stoned, he gazed up at Heaven and saw the glory of God. Stephen knew the thing to do when in the midst of persecution is to look up.

Regardless of what has occurred on earth or what awaits us in the future, God's people will prevail! And again, this isn't new teaching. Babylonian King Nebuchadnezzar realized this very same thing. As punishment for

---

21 Westminster Divines, "The Westminster Larger Catechism (1648)," Ligonier.org, May 12, 2021, https://www.ligonier.org/learn/articles/westminster-larger-catechism.

his sins, God gave Nebuchadnezzar the mind of an animal for seven years. At the end of those seven years, the king says in **Daniel 4:34**, *"At the end of the days I, Nebuchadnezzar, lifted my eyes to heaven, and my reason returned to me, and I blessed the Most High, and praised and honored him who lives forever for his dominion is an everlasting dominion, and his kingdom endures from generation to generation."*

THE LION OF JUDAH AND ROOT OF DAVID

In chapter five, we see more apocalyptic language, numbers and symbols, as well as John's vision widening to include Jesus. **Revelation 5:1-5** says:

> *Then I saw in the right hand of him who was seated on the throne a scroll written within and on the back, sealed with seven seals. And I saw a mighty angel proclaiming with a loud voice, "Who is worthy to open the scroll and break its seals?" And no one in heaven or on earth or under the earth was able to open the scroll or to look into it, and I began to weep loudly because no one was found worthy to open the scroll or to look into it. And one of the elders said to me, "Weep no more; behold, the Lion of the tribe of Judah, the Root of David, has conquered, so that he can open the scroll and its seven seals."*

Verse one gives us a great example of why taking the approach that everything in the book of Revelation is literal causes a problem. It describes God the Father seated on the throne with a scroll in His right hand. We know that it's God the Father on the throne because—as we are going to see in the next verses in chapter five—Jesus is standing among the elders. God the Father is an Essence, a Spirit. He does not have a physical body. Jesus does, but God the Father does not. John saying God has a "right hand" is called anthropomorphism. This is a literary device used that gives God human qualities to make God and His actions more understandable to our finite minds. We see it in several places in Scripture. **Numbers 6:25** says, *"The Lord make his face to shine upon you."* And **Psalm 89:10b** says, *"You scattered your enemies with your mighty arm."*

Beginning at verse two, we get a courtroom feel. An angel is proclaiming loudly, *"Who is worthy to open the scroll?"* Again, this is nothing new. The Bible uses a courtroom setting in other places, specifically in—you guessed it—the Old Testament. **Micah 6**, for example, has this courtroom-like scenario that's used to convict the Israelites of their guilt before God and the punishment they are given for their guilt. **Daniel 7** also has a courtroom scene. It is actually a vision of what we see here in Revelation. **Daniel 7:9-10** says:

> *As I looked, thrones were placed, and the Ancient of Days took his seat; his clothing was white as snow, and the hair of his head like pure wool; his throne was fiery flames; its wheels were burning fire. A stream of fire issued and came out from before him; a thousand thousands served him, and ten thousand times ten thousand stood before him; the court sat in judgment, and the books were opened.*

The "books" in the above verse from Daniel are the same as the scrolls. Isaiah and Ezekiel, too, link the scrolls and the books. **Ezekiel 2:9-10** tells us what's in the scroll: *"And when I looked, behold, a hand was stretched out to me, and behold, a scroll of a book was in it. And he spread it before me. And it had writing on the front and on the back, and there were written on it words of lamentation and mourning and woe."*

The verses in **Revelation 5** tell us that John wept because no one is found worthy to open the seals of the scroll. When we look at the verses from Daniel and Ezekiel, we see that John's sorrow stems from his knowing that the scroll contained God's judgment on His enemies and justice for God's people. If no one opened it, then the things in it would not be brought to their full conclusion as God intended. There would be no end to the persecution for the Church, no justice for God's elect, and no complete redemption for God's people.

The elders tell John to weep not because there is One Who is worthy to open the scroll—the Lion of Judah and the Root of David. Of course, this is Jesus. Jesus' description as the Lion of Judah comes from a prophecy about

Jesus in **Genesis 49:9-10**: *"Judah is a lion's cub; from the prey, my son, you have gone up. He stooped down; he crouched as a lion and as a lioness; who dares rouse him? The scepter shall not depart from Judah, nor the ruler's staff from between his feet, until tribute comes to him; and to him shall be the obedience of the peoples."* Likewise, the depiction of Jesus as the Root of David is from Messianic prophecy seen in **Isaiah 11:1-2**: *"There shall come forth a shoot from the stump of Jesse, and a branch from his roots shall bear fruit. And the Spirit of the LORD shall rest upon him, the Spirit of wisdom and understanding, the Spirit of counsel and might, the Spirit of knowledge and the fear of the LORD."*

Dr. Joel Beeke, president of the Puritan Theological Seminary, has great insight into why only Jesus was worthy to open the scroll. He said:

> *A human person had to open the book because the promise (contained in it) was made to humanity, but no person could open it because all have sinned and stand under the judgment contained in the book. But Christ was found worthy because He suffered the final judgment as an innocent on behalf of His people whom He represented and consequently redeemed. He is able to open the scroll and our inheritance because He is the God-Man who was slain.*[22]

THE LAMB WHO WAS SLAIN

There is a lot to unpack when we get to **Revelation 5:6-8** as John uses a lot of symbolism.

> *And between the throne and the four living creatures and among the elders I saw a Lamb standing, as though it had been slain, with seven horns and with seven eyes, which are the seven spirits of God sent out into all the earth. And he went and took the scroll from the right hand of him who was seated on the throne. And when he had taken the scroll, the four living creatures and the twenty-four elders fell down before the Lamb, each holding a harp, and golden bowls full of incense, which are the prayers of the saints.*

---

22 Joel R. Beeke, *Revelation* (Grand Rapids, MI: Reformation Heritage Books, 2016).

Let's start with **Revelation 5:6**, where John sees *"a Lamb standing, as though it had been slain, with seven horns and with seven eyes, which are the seven spirits of God sent out into all the earth."* Again, this is obviously Jesus. And just like with God the Father, John uses metaphors to describe Jesus' appearance. First, He is the Lamb Who looks as though He had been slain. On Good Friday, Jesus took upon Himself the wrath of God that we deserve for our sin. Jesus' enemies thought that when He died on the cross from the wounds they had inflicted by beating Him and crucifying Him, that was the end; and it would have been for anyone else. But we know how this story ends. Jesus overcame death and resurrected. When Jesus appeared to His apostles after His resurrection, He still had the scars from His wounds to symbolize just how high a cost He had paid to overcome sin, Satan, and death for His people.

Continuing with the symbolic, and not the literal, Jesus is said to have seven horns and seven eyes. Horns are used many places in Scripture to represent authority. For example, **Deuteronomy 33:17** says, *"A firstborn bull—he has majesty, and his horns are the horns of a wild ox; with them he shall gore the peoples, all of them, to the ends of the earth."* The seven eyes are a symbol of Jesus seeing and knowing all. Since seven is a number of perfect completeness, Jesus having seven horns and seven eyes means He is omnipotent and omniscient. As before, the seven spirits of God are a reference to the Holy Spirit. This shows Jesus is fully God, part of the Trinity, and omnipresent, as demonstrated by the seven spirits of God sent out into all the Earth.

John continues, saying that Jesus takes the scroll from God the Father. When He does, the elders fall down before Him. Each of them holds a harp and golden bowls of incense. These bowls of incense represent the prayers of the saints. Most likely, these are specifically the prayers of the martyrs and of those who have been persecuted for the name of Jesus. This is a little complex to explain, but we can surmise this because the scroll contained God's judgment and God's justice, as we will see when we get to **Revelation 6**. There is one prayer that demands God's judgment and God's justice, and that is vindication for those who have been persecuted and/or killed for proclaiming Jesus as Lord.

It's not that those who have given their life for their faith are better or more important than those who have not, but remember, the entire Bible points to Jesus. Jesus is the ultimate Martyr. He, more than anyone else, deserves to see God's judgment and justice for how He was treated and killed by the wicked. These verses show us that those who remain enemies of God will be dealt with justly.

Is there anything more comforting and encouraging than knowing that those who are enemies of God—and, likewise, by our status as God's children, enemies of us—will receive justice? It's easy to look at the evil and wickedness going on in the world today and get discouraged and sick over it. We can wonder why God is allowing it. Revelation answers this question for us. God is allowing it only for a time. Those perpetrating the evil *will* be called to account if God does not bring them to salvation either before they die or Jesus comes back.

But this also means something else for those already in Christ. Because we know that God will handle the justice and judgment, we do not have to worry about it. This means that we are free to love our enemies. We don't need to be looking to avenge ourselves. God has everything well in hand. Instead, we can freely show grace and compassion to everyone—no matter how wicked they are. That doesn't mean that we don't fight against evils like abortion and gender mutilation of children, for example. We should absolutely fight against all things that are perverting and mocking the Word of God. However, while we are fighting against sinful practices, we can show grace to individuals, even those directly involved in the practices. In fact, knowing what is in store for those who do not belong to Jesus should stir our compassion and our drive to witness to them!

It's easy to get frustrated seeing people who are openly opposed to God have all the money, fame, and power they desire, while many Christians are struggling and oppressed. Even Asaph lamented this in **Psalm 73:3**: *"For I was envious of the arrogant when I saw the prosperity of the wicked."* But here's something to think about. While we hate to quote the false teaching of the Word of Faith movement who constantly tell people to "live your best life now," this is the message for unbelievers because their time on earth *is* their best life! Things are not going to be pretty for them when the end comes, as we will see in the upcoming chapters.

A CHOSEN PEOPLE

Revelation 5:9b-10 is a verse that sometimes gets misinterpreted. It says, *"'For you were slain, and by your blood you ransomed people for God from every tribe and language and people and nation, and you have made them a kingdom and priests to our God, and they shall reign on the earth.'"* Contrary to how some believe, these verses do not say that God will save everyone. They say that Jesus' blood was ransomed for the people for God. Not everyone is part of the people of God—just those God has chosen from before the foundation of the world. What this verse does say, though, is that God *has* chosen people from every tribe, every language, every people group, and every nation. Four is a number used to symbolize creation and the Earth. If you notice, there are four groups listed—tribe, language, people group, and nation. Within these four groups are *all* of the people God has chosen to save. All will reign with Christ when He returns.

This is one of the already/not-yet fulfilled prophecies. As the children of God, we are already priests and reigning with Christ through the Church. It is not the fully consummated, perfected reign that will come when Jesus returns, but it is happening now. As **Daniel 7:27** tells us, *"'And the kingdom and the dominion and the greatness of the kingdoms under the whole heaven shall be given to the people of the saints of the Most High; his kingdom shall be an everlasting kingdom, and all dominions shall serve and obey him.'"*

Let's end this chapter by finishing up chapter five of Revelation. **Revelation 5:13-14** says, *"And I heard every creature in heaven and on earth and under the earth and in the sea, and all that is in them, saying, 'To him who sits on the* *throne and to the Lamb be blessing and honor and glory and might forever and ever!' And the four living creatures said, "Amen!" and the elders fell down and worshiped."*

Things are about to get pretty harsh in chapter six when we move onto the woes. We will see just what God's judgment and justice look like. Chapters four and five are meant to encourage God's people and give us confidence, as we ground ourselves in the knowledge that God is Sovereign over everything, that He is securely on the throne, and that Jesus is ready to return and bring to completion the victory He has already won over Satan, sin, and death. Soon, He will come back to bring to consummation the Kingdom of God and His reign as the one, true King.

These chapters, along with other Scripture, show us that we serve an orderly God, Who has never and will never change—a God Who is intentional about everything and is working all things, even the most evil things, out for our good, for His purpose, and for His glory. This should give us the confidence and courage to face whatever may be ahead for us. We can endure our day-to-day life on earth, no matter how painful or miserable it is, because we know there is something magnificent going on in Heaven right now and will still be going on when we get there! May knowing that our Sovereign Lord has firmly in His grasp and firmly under His control what may seem like an uncertain and scary future to us bring you peace as you walk through your current and future trials.

CHAPTER 3
STUDY GUIDE

GETTING YOUR TOES WET

How is it comforting to know that God has never and will never change?

How does getting a glimpse into God's throne room give us hope and encouragement to hold onto and persevere through whatever our circumstances may be?

Idolatry is worshipping something other the one, true God, while syncretism is blending idolatry *with* the worship of God. *What are some examples of idolatry and/or syncretism we see today?*

DIVING IN DEEP

Other than in **Revelation 2** and **19**, only Isaiah gives us a vague glimpse of Jesus' physical appearance. These glimpses are not for us to speculate on what Jesus physically looked like. They are to convey a deeper truth. *What important truth do these passages from Isaiah tell us about the Person of Jesus?*

Isaiah 52:14

Isaiah 53:2

Revelation 4:4 says, *"Around the throne were twenty-four thrones, and seated on the thrones were twenty-four elders, clothed in white garments, with golden crowns on their heads."* This is not meant to be taken literally that there are twenty-four elders. These twenty-four represent all the people of God. *How do the following verses support this?*

Psalm 132:17-18

Isaiah 28:5

2 Timothy 4:6-8

Revelation 7:9

In **Revelation 4:11**, the twenty-four elders cast their crowns before the throne of God and said, *"'Worthy are you, our Lord and God, to receive glory and honor and power, for you created all things, and by your will they existed and were created.'"*

This picture would have shown the early followers of Christ the same thing it shows us. There is something much bigger than us, or any governing power, at work. God the Almighty is Sovereign and on the throne. The Westminster Catechism says, "The chief and highest end of man is to glorify God and fully enjoy Him forever."[23] *What do these verses say about how we are to glorify God on this side of Heaven?*

Matthew 5:14-16

1 Peter 1:14-16

Colossians 3:23-24

---

23 Westminster Divines, ibid.

Romans 12:1-2

1 Peter 4:10-11

We can wonder why God is allowing evil. Revelation answers this question for us. God is allowing it only for a time. The judgments God begins to unleash in chapter six are not something new or unforewarned. *What do the following verses say about God allowing evil and His judgment?*
Ezekiel 18:19-24

Matthew 12:36-37

Romans 14:10-12

2 Peter 2:4-10

BACK ON DRY LAND

Let's be honest, there's a lot to make us angry: abortion, gender mutilation of children, destruction of the family, churches abandoning the biblical Gospel for a social justice gospel. But Scripture makes it clear that God has justice and judgment well in hand. For those of us who are in Christ, this is great news! We do not have to be angry looking to avenge all the social wrongs and all of the personal wrongs done to us. This does not mean we do not speak out against social evils—we absolutely should! But since we are not the ones responsible to dispense justice, we can show grace to individuals—even those involved in the most heinous of acts. This is hard! However, as we move along in the book of Revelation and see what is in store for those who are not in Christ, our compassion for unbelievers should be stirred to a new high.

Jesus calls us to love everyone, even our enemies. In Scripture, when we are called to "love our enemies," the Greek word used is agape. Agape love is not the emotional, warm, fuzzy feeling we often equate with love. Agape love is an unconditional love; it is an in-spite-of love. In spite of what someone has done publicly or personally to us, we still put that person's best interests first. It is the love that God the Father showed us when we had absolutely nothing to offer Him but our sin, yet He chose to show us mercy and grace and save us. This is the radical love we are to show unbelievers—even those who are perpetrating evil. *In the following verses, the original Greek word used for "love" is agape. What do these verses tell us about agape love?*

Matthew 5:43-48

Romans 5:1-5

1 John 4:7-11

It is easy to get frustrated seeing people who openly mock God have all the money, fame, and power they desire, while many Christians are struggling and oppressed. But, Friends, the unbelieving world is to be pitied. And even if we are struggling with that, we are commanded by Jesus to love our enemies—not to tolerate them, but to full-on, agape love them. *What is one feasible thing you can do to live out this command?*

CHAPTER 4

ALL HELL'S GONNA BREAK LOOSE

Talk with most anyone who paints with oil or acrylics and they'll tell you their paintings often take days and sometimes longer to finish. One of the reasons for that is layering. Layering is the technique of painting a picture, letting it dry, then painting over the same picture again (or at least part of it), and repeating this process a number of times. The result is the same landscape, or still-life, or person that was originally painted, but now it's a multi-faceted, multi-dimensional piece that's grown in intensity with each layer.

The book of Revelation is similar in some ways. The visions John received are not to be lined up chronologically, as if they were multiple sketches for a storyboard. Those who take a historist approach view them this way and try to link them with history to create a timeline. Futurists also look at them as being in a chronological timeline but of future events near the Second Coming of Christ. But each of John's seven visions is the same picture—a picture of the conflict between Christ's Church and their enemy Satan and his followers. The visions retell the story of the same conflict but viewed from different vantage points. And since they are recapitulations and not chronologically ordered pictures, the things they tell us can have multiple fulfillments throughout this time period or these "last days." And like the layering of paint on the same picture, there is some building of intensity with each of the views. So, as each vision is unfolded, keep in mind that each is telling of the Church battling Satan and his minions from the time of the apostles until Jesus comes again. Christ has already won the battle. Victory is already a done deal. Revelation was written to strengthen and encourage you. So, *"Fear not, little flock, for it is your Father's good pleasure to give you the kingdom"* **(Luke 12:32)**.

Revelation 6 is the first of three cycles of God's judgment on unbelievers: the seals, the trumpets, and the bowls. The visions of the seal, trumpet, and bowl judgments are each a retelling, of course, of history during this interadvent period but from different perspectives. These recapitulations are depictions of all wars in this period, as well as all famines and plagues and all kinds of upheavals that come on earth until Jesus returns. The visions are "layered" in that they occur throughout the Church Age, overlapping and increasing in intensity, each of them culminating in the return of Christ to earth and the end of the world. There are seven judgments in each cycle, symbolizing the complete perfection of God's judgment.

Jesus explains this best when He likens the end times to birth pains in **Matthew 24:4b-8**. He says:

> *"See that no one leads you astray. For many will come in my name, saying, 'I am the Christ,' and they will lead many astray. And you will hear of wars and rumors of wars. See that you are not alarmed, for this must take place, but the end is not yet. For nation will rise against nation, and kingdom against kingdom, and there will be famines and earthquakes in various places. All these are but the beginning of the birth pains."*

Taking Jesus' example, the birth of a baby is one event, yet it has different stages. Contractions begin; they ebb and flow in intensity as the woman's uterus expands and the baby makes his way down the birth canal. Right before the baby is born, contractions are extremely intense, and painful pushing needs to occur. After all of this trauma, a precious, beautiful baby is born. The baby is the culmination of the event. And while there are different layers and stages of the birth, it is still one event. This is exactly how we should view the seal, trumpet, and bowl judgments.

For those who hold to a futurist view of Revelation, the start of the opening of the seals has not happened yet. Futurists believe that at some point in the future, the first seal will be opened and will mark the beginning of the time referred to as the Great Tribulation. The other six seals, seven trumpets, and seven bowls will follow in succession. However, since each of the cycles culminates in Christ's return, lining them up end-to-end chronologically does not make sense. The other camps agree with the futurists that the opening of the seals is what inaugurates God's judgments but believe that it has already *been* inaugurated. In other words, some of the seals and trumpets have already been opened, and these instruments of God's judgment were already in progress at the time of John's writing and continue to be.

Satan already knows he is defeated. Since neither Satan nor his demonic army can attack or indwell Christians directly, he will work against them through persecution brought by beastly, anti-Christian governments; through false teaching by some within the Church, as well as through false religions; and through the temptations of the world. Throughout this inter-advent period described in the seals, trumpets, and bowls, the Church is to preach the Gospel to the nations, despite these hardships and persecutions. Interludes are inserted within the cycles of judgments, giving us assurance that God's people are being kept spiritually safe in that they cannot and will not lose their salvation during these hard times; and although they will endure suffering by Satan brought through the beast, the false prophet, and temptations of the harlot, they will not suffer God's wrath and eternity in Hell.

The vision of the seals being opened is viewed from the heavenly throne room, where we left off in chapter five. We see worship abounding as Jesus begins to open the seals. He is the only One worthy to open the seals because it was with His blood He redeemed people from every tribe, language, people, and nation, reconciling them to God. He's with the four living creatures, which are angels.

THE HORSEMEN OF THE APOCALYPSE

In **Revelation 6:1-8**, Jesus explains further and in more detail what He had been saying to His disciples in **Matthew 24** about the opening of the seals. The first four seals opened contained colored horses, each with riders. These four horses and their riders harken back to the imagery from the vision in **Zechariah 6:1-8**, where four colored horses and chariots are sent out by God *"to the four winds of heaven, after presenting themselves before the Lord of all the earth"* **(Zech. 6:5b)**. The number four symbolizes creation. Just as those four horses and chariots were sent throughout all the earth, these four horsemen in Revelation were bringing God's judgment on the wicked—all of them—throughout the whole earth. It includes all unbelievers—from those who don't even give Jesus a moment's thought, to those who are actively persecuting His Church. The horses and riders represented (in order) are conquest, war, famine, and death.

THE WHITE HORSE

We're told about the first horse and rider in **Revelation 6:1-2**, which says, *"Now I watched when the Lamb opened one of the seven seals, and I heard one of the four living creatures say with a voice like thunder, 'Come!' And I looked, and behold, a white horse! And its rider had a bow, and a crown was given to him, and he came out conquering, and to conquer."*

The first rider is often thought to be Jesus taking the Gospel out to the nations. Although Jesus is pictured riding a white horse in **Revelation 19**, in that instance, Jesus is wearing *many* crowns (not just one) and has a sword (the sword of His mouth), not a bow. Here, Jesus was the One opening the seals and unleashing the horses and riders. This rider on the white horse in **Revelation 6** represents one of God's agents for judgment.

White horses were often used as symbols of conquest in the ancient world.[24] When interpreting the Bible, we have to keep in mind that it would have made sense to those to whom it was written at that time. A rider carrying a bow would have been familiar to the people of John's time since the Parthians, Rome's most formidable foe both militarily and economically, carried bows. The Parthians were well-suited to counter the concentrated troop movements of the Roman army using riders on horseback to provide a steady stream of arrows. The Parthians were so adept at using their bows while riding, they developed the "Parthian shot"—the ability to shoot backward at full gallop, delivering kill shots. The visions given would have brought the persecuted hearers of this letter hope. They wouldn't have thought of this rider as Jesus. But putting ourselves in the shoes of these brothers and sisters of the faith, we can start to imagine what hearing this meant—there was Someone able to stand firm against their enemy, who had the ability to conquer them. For first century Christians, that enemy was the seemingly invincible Roman Empire.

To believers throughout the rest of the Church Age, the rider on the white horse symbolizes various realms desiring and trying to obtain conquest of parts of the Earth; and with conquest comes war, famine, and death. This goes right along with the *"wars and rumors of wars"* Jesus told his disciples about on the Mount of Olives in **Matthew 24:6**.

THE RED HORSE

Next, Jesus opened the second seal, and John heard a second creature say, *"'Come!' And out came another horse, bright red. Its rider was permitted to take peace from the earth, so that people should slay one another, and he was given a great sword"* **(Rev. 6:4)**.

This time, it is a red horse, signifying bloodshed and warfare, with a rider who takes peace from the Earth, causing people to slay one another. Some

---

24 "Sermons on the Book of Revelation #12," transcript of sermon delivered at Christ Reformed Church, 2002, http://kimriddlebarger.squarespace.com/downloadable-sermons-on-the-bo.

believe that this rider persecutes the saints. But the text says they are slaying *"one another"* **(Rev. 6:4)**, so we know that it means all wars, not just the wicked killing the righteous. We should take note that this rider is given a great sword. These are not nations acting outside of God's control or outside of His decree! In **Matthew 10:34**, Jesus says, *"Do not think that I have come to bring peace to the earth. I have not come to bring peace, but a sword."* God is sovereignly in control of every single thing and is working out His decreed will through these conquering nations all through history. The people going to war with one another (or the rulers who make them) are doing it for their own reasons. That is the reason they are responsible for any sinfulness that is in those decisions. But God is using it for His purposes.

THE BLACK HORSE

The next opened seal unleashes a black horse with a rider holding a pair of scales. *"And I heard what seemed to be a voice in the midst of the four living creatures, saying, 'A quart of wheat for a denarius, and three quarts of barley for a denarius, and do not harm the oil and wine'"* **(Rev. 6:6)**.

Scales were used for weighing out grain, which was a big commodity. In the first century, a quart of wheat was a day's food supply for a soldier and would cost about one-eighth of a day's wage, which was one denarius. By the time the black horse and its rider are finished their rampage, it is going to cost the whole denarius just to eat that day. That is an inflation rate of eight hundred percent! Barley—the food of the poor because it was not as nutritious—was going to be outlandishly expensive, too. Inflation of that nature brings severe economic hardship. But God is merciful and longsuffering, as **Exodus 34:6** tells us: *"The LORD, the LORD, a God merciful and gracious, slow to anger, and abounding in steadfast love and faithfulness."* **Revelation 6:6** shows God's patience with man. He does not touch the prices of the oil or the wine. It is not a total famine. In 92 A.D., Emperor Domitian ordered the vineyards cut down during a grain shortage to make room for more wheat fields. But the outcry from the people was so great, he canceled that order, sparing the wine! It is likely the people of John's time would have connected this imagery to protecting the wine.

Imagery of God not releasing a total famine on the Earth is a picture of God's common grace—grace given to *all* men—the unsaved as well as the elect. But God's patience and longsuffering will come to an end someday. Paul talks about God's longsuffering with the wicked hypocritically judging sin in others in **Romans 2:4-5**, saying, *"Do you presume on the riches of his kindness and forbearance and patience, not knowing that God's kindness is meant to lead you to repentance? But because of your hard and impenitent heart you are storing up wrath for yourself on the day of wrath when God's righteous judgment will be revealed."* God is certainly patient, loving, and kind; but judgment is coming.

THE PALE HORSE

John saw Jesus open the fourth seal, bringing out a pale horse. We're told in **Revelation 6:8**, *"And I looked, and behold, a pale horse! And its rider's name was Death, and Hades followed him. And they were given authority over a fourth of the earth, to kill with sword and with famine and with pestilence and by wild beasts of the earth."*

As some translations say, this horse was green, as in the color of sickness, according to the Greek. On its back was a rider named Death, and Hades was following close behind. We learned earlier in Revelation that Jesus holds the keys of death and Hades. Here, Jesus gives this horse and rider power and authority to kill through sword, famine, pestilence—and this time, also by wild beasts.

Death by wild beasts is something we do not often think of as God's judgment. In **Genesis 1:28**, God told Adam and Eve to *"'be fruitful and multiply and fill the earth and subdue it, and have dominion over the fish of the sea and over the birds of the heavens and over every living thing that moves on the earth.'"* But their sin affected all of creation—even the animals—and God used animals as a form of punishment on the wicked throughout history.

During one of the travels of Elisha, God's prophet, *"Some small boys came out of the city and jeered at him, saying, 'Go up, you baldhead! Go up, you baldhead!' And he turned around, and when he saw them, he cursed them in the name of the LORD. And two she-bears came out of the woods and tore forty-two of the boys"* **(2 King 2:23b-24)**.

In later times, both before and after John recorded these visions, *Damnatio ad bestias* (Latin for "condemnation to beasts") was a way to kill Christians and others, usually slaves, in the Roman arenas. One of the most famous killings in this manner was under Emperor Trajan, when Ignatius, bishopric of Antioch, was sentenced to die at the mouths of wild beasts. It is said that when he heard the roar of the lions, he said, ""I am the wheat of Christ: I am going to be ground with the teeth of wild beasts, that I may be found pure bread."[25] And, of course, these beasts could represent the beastly wicked rulers of the nations who devour not only God's people, but also each other.

Judgment of the wicked has been going on throughout history, right alongside God's people, the righteous, living their lives. More judgment is coming. And it does not discriminate by race, or gender, or even age. The fact that we are told Jesus gave the four horses and their riders only the authority to kill a fourth of the Earth's population is a picture of God restraining His own wrath through restraining humanity's violent actions toward one another.

The judgments represented by the first four seals echo judgments on Jerusalem for breaking the covenant curses, as prophesied by Ezekiel in **Ezekiel 14:12-21**. As we'll see, later judgments echo the judgments of God upon the Egyptians when He freed His people from slavery and brought them to the Promised Land.

THE FIFTH SEAL

When Jesus opened the fifth seal, we get a glimpse into Heaven, where we see *"the souls of those who had been slain for the word of God and for the witness they had borne"* **(Rev. 6:9)**. These believers stood strong for the Lord, despite persecution, without denying their faith. These martyred saints are pictured

---

25 John Foxe, "Chapter II: The Ten Primitive Persecutions," in *Foxe's Book of Martyrs*, Christian Classics Ethereal Library, accessed March 19, 2021, https://www.ccel.org/f/foxe/martyrs/fox102.htm.

under the temple altar, where the blood of the animals slain for sacrifice was poured out. *"They cried out with a loud voice, 'O Sovereign Lord, holy and true, how long before you will judge and avenge our blood on those who dwell on the earth?'"* **(Rev. 6:10)**. They are not crying out for justice for their own sakes. God's judgment is just and perfect. These saints are not only clothed with *"a white robe"* **(Rev. 6:11)**, which signifies their Savior's righteousness; they have also been perfected to be like Him in their desires. They want God's perfect judgment because they are like Him. Saints being glad at God's judgment on the wicked was foretold in **Psalm 58:10a**, which says, *"The righteous will rejoice when he sees the vengeance."*

The vision of the souls of the saints in Heaven shows us that when Christians die, their souls are alive and with Christ, clothed in the righteousness of Christ, waiting *"until the number of their fellow servants and their brothers should be complete, who were to be killed as they themselves had been"* **(Rev. 6:11)** as they wait for the day when Jesus returns to earth. It is at that point, our bodies are raised and perfected, and we go to live with Him in the new heavens and earth. Christ will come after the last of God's elect comes to faith. Until then, the martyrs are crying out.

THE SIXTH SEAL

The opening of the sixth seal brings a great earthquake. From the first century until now, people understand what a great earthquake can be like—entire cities crumble to the ground, and then there is rebuilding. But there is no rebuilding in this vision in **Revelation 6:12-17**. The sixth seal begins the deconstruction of the first heavens and earth. The description of the sixth seal being opened begins, *"When he opened the sixth seal, I looked, and behold, there was a great earthquake, and the sun became black as sackcloth, the full moon became like blood, and the stars of the sky fell to the earth as the fig tree sheds its winter fruit when shaken by a gale. The sky vanished like a scroll that is being rolled up, and every mountain and island was removed from its place"* **(Rev. 6:12-14)**.

The words used at the opening of the sixth seal reflect more of Jesus' teaching from the Olivet Discourse in **Matthew 24:29-31**:

> *Immediately after the tribulation of those days the sun will be darkened, and the moon will not give its light, and the stars will fall from heaven, and the powers of the heavens will be shaken. Then will appear in heaven the sign of the Son of Man, and then all the tribes of the earth will mourn, and they will see the Son of Man coming on the clouds of heaven with power and great glory. And he will send out his angels with a loud trumpet call, and they will gather his elect from the four winds, from one end of heaven to the other.*

When the Old Testament speaks of God coming to earth, the ground shakes. Mount Sinai trembled when the Lord descended in **Exodus 19:18**; the mountains melt, and valleys split open at the Lord's coming in **Micah 1:4**; and *"the earth is violently shaken"* in **Isaiah 24:18**.

There are seven types of people mentioned in the passage—*"the kings of the earth and the great ones and the generals and the rich and the powerful, and everyone, slave and free"* **(Rev. 6:15)**. The number seven symbolizes perfect completeness and tells us that God's perfectly complete judgment is on all of humanity.

For all of the unsaved who are on earth at this time, God's sixth seal judgment will be so bad, John's vision shows that they *"hid themselves in the caves and among the rocks of the mountains, calling to the mountains and rocks, 'Fall on us and hide us from the face of him who is seated on the throne, and from the wrath of the Lamb, for the great day of their wrath has come'"* **(Rev. 6:15-17)**. If you've ever stood beside a large mountain, think about that! The wicked will be so distraught, they would rather be buried underneath the rubble than to stand in the presence of God. None of the wicked will be able to deny God is real any longer.

The wicked will be asking one thing: *"'Who can stand?'"* **(Rev. 6:17)**. Standing under God's righteous judgment is a theme throughout the Bible. **Malachi 3:2** says, *"But who can endure the day of his coming, and who can stand*

ALL HELL'S GONNA BREAK LOOSE 95

when he appears? For he is like a refiner's fire and like fullers' soap." In **Psalm 130:3-4a**, the psalmist writes, *"If you, O LORD, should mark iniquities, O Lord, who could stand? But with you there is forgiveness."* No one can stand before God without having Jesus as their Savior.

THE 144,000

Turning to **Revelation 7**, we see those who are able to stand—the 144,000. Chapter seven is referred to as an interlude. There are two more interludes in Revelation. These interludes are between each of the sixth and the seventh seal trumpet and bowl judgments. The interludes are there so the saints can be assured that God is looking after them throughout all of the trials and tribulations that are happening. God's people can be sure that they will not lose their salvation during this period of intense suffering—they can stand regardless of what comes—because they are *sealed*. **Revelation 7:1-3** says:

> *After this I saw four angels standing at the four corners of the earth, holding back the four winds of the earth, that no wind might blow on earth or sea or against any tree. Then I saw another angel ascending from the rising of the sun, with the seal of the living God, and he called with a loud voice to the four angels who had been given power to harm earth and sea, saying, "Do not harm the earth or the sea or the trees, until we have sealed the servants of our God on their foreheads."*

The four angels holding the four corners of the Earth does not mean that the Earth is flat. Although some people say so, the early church did not teach that. As we have seen, the number four is symbolic for all the Earth. Under the direction of God, these four angels have been and will continue to hold back His full wrath until all of the elect are sealed from all parts of the earth.

When someone believes, they receive the Holy Spirit—their seal and guarantee of salvation. The idea of being sealed is like a signet ring signifying ownership. The fact that it is symbolically "on the forehead" is taken from **Ezekiel 9:4**, where God's people who were groaning over the sinfulness of the wicked in Jerusalem were marked on their foreheads, and the rest were slaughtered because they were wicked. Take notice that it is God's angels doing the work of the sealing as He commands. God knows whom He's going to seal. **Ephesians 1:3-6** says:

> Blessed be the God and Father of our Lord Jesus Christ, who has blessed us in Christ with every spiritual blessing in the heavenly places, even as he chose us in him before the foundation of the world, that we should be holy and blameless before him. In love he predestined us for adoption to himself as sons through Jesus Christ, according to the purpose of his will, to the praise of his glorious grace, with which he has blessed us in the Beloved.

God chose the elect long before creation, and God will keep those He seals as they endure the tribulation. They will not lose their salvation.

All of God's elect will be sealed before Jesus returns. This vision is an already/not-yet vision. God has been sealing His people by the Holy Spirit regenerating their dead hearts, making them "born again" so they can respond to the Gospel message and believe. This will continue throughout the whole Church Age. Jesus' words to the Laodacean church were that the time had come! They thought they were okay, but they didn't have the Source! Just like the apostles left what they were doing and immediately followed Jesus when He bid them "Come!," when the Holy Spirit is tugging at your heart, don't delay!

The number 144,000 is symbolic. It refers to the complete number of the people of God from both the Old Testament and the New Testament and beyond. This number is twelve times twelve times one thousand (the number ten signifying completion, and one thousand being ten times ten times ten—the number of *complete completion*). **Revelation 7:4-8** says:

> And I heard the number of the sealed, 144,000, sealed from every tribe of the sons of Israel: 12,000 from the tribe of Judah were sealed, 12,000 from the tribe of Reuben, 12,000 from the tribe of Gad, 12,000 from the tribe of Asher, 12,000 from the tribe of Naphtali, 12,000 from the

tribe of Manasseh, 12,000 from the tribe of Simeon, 12,000 from the tribe of Levi, 12,000 from the tribe of Issachar, 12,000 from the tribe of Zebulun, 12,000 from the tribe of Joseph, 12,000 from the tribe of Benjamin were sealed.

Some claim that this is a list (perhaps literal or symbolic) of ethnic Jews, who will be saved right after Jesus comes back because they think this is a list of the twelve tribes of Israel. But it is not. The tribes of Israel got their names from Jacob's (who God later named "Israel") sons, with Joseph's two offspring (Ephraim and Manasseh) getting his share of the inheritance. The list of the tribes in **Revelation 7** is not a list of Jacob's sons. The list here still includes Joseph and omits Ephraim yet names Manasseh, and the tribe of Dan is not mentioned at all. In addition, this list is out of birth order. Each time the Bible lists the tribes of Israel and it does not match the original, there is a reason. As **Romans 9:6** says, *"not all who are descended from Israel belong to Israel."* Jewish ethnicity does not save in the future any more than it has in the past. This altered list of the tribes of Israel is symbolic of all of those for whom Christ died for—the true Israel—comprised of both Jews and Gentiles who once were not included and now are *"fellow heirs, members of the same body, and partakers of the promise in Christ Jesus through the gospel"* **(Eph. 3:6)**. The tribal list in **Revelation 7** is symbolic of all of God's people throughout all of history, something also referred to as the Universal Church.

GOD'S ELECT, SAFE AT HOME

The rest of the verses in chapter seven emphasize that the Gospel has gone out to the ends of the Earth and brought God's elect from every tribe, tongue, people group, and nation into Jesus' Church. One day, believers with all their vast array of differences, from every corner of the globe, will worship Jesus together. One of the elders in John's vision spoke to him, saying, *"'Who are these, clothed in white robes, and from where have they come?'"* **(Rev. 7:13)**. But John knows it's a rhetorical question—the elder knows who they are. *"These are the ones coming out of the great tribulation. They have washed their robes and* *made them white in the blood of the Lamb'"* **(Rev. 7:14)**. Verse fourteen makes it abundantly clear that God's people do go through what some refer to as the Great Tribulation. We are in the period of tribulation right now. The things talked about in the seal judgments are happening right now! They have been happening all throughout history. How bad will it get before Jesus comes back? We have no idea! But if you are trusting in Jesus' death on the cross as payment for your sin, you have been *"sealed for the day of redemption"* by the Holy Spirit, according to **Ephesians 4:30**. In light of that, you have no reason to fear, for when believers die, as **Revelation 7:15-17** says:

> *"Therefore they are before the throne of God, and serve him day and night in his temple; and he who sits on the throne will shelter them with his presence. They shall hunger no more, neither thirst anymore; the sun shall not strike them, nor any scorching heat. For the Lamb in the midst of the throne will be their shepherd, and he will guide them to springs of living water, and God will wipe away every tear from their eyes."*

CHAPTER 4
STUDY GUIDE

GETTING YOUR TOES WET

The four horsemen released from the first four seals symbolize conquest, war, famine, and death. They mark the beginning of God's judgment on the Earth—something that has already begun. *Give some examples of these that are going on currently.*

In light of the fact that this is going on now, what problem does this present for futurists who believe the church will be raptured before they have to suffer in the tribulation?

DIVING IN DEEP

God shows His "common grace" to all men. *What do these verses say about it?*
Psalm 145:15-16

Matthew 5:45

Luke 6:35

God elected some to salvation before the beginning of the world. **Ephesians 1:4-5** says, *"Even as he chose us in him before the foundation of the* world, that we should be holy and blameless before him. In love, he predestines us for adoption to himself as sons through Jesus Christ, according to the purpose of his will."

How do these verses support the doctrine of election?
Mark 13:20

John 17:6

Acts 13:48

Romans 8:28-30

God is patient, but His patience will not last forever. *What do the following verses say about God's patience and longsuffering?*
Numbers 14:18

2 Peter 3:9

Romans 2:4

BACK ON DRY LAND

People often wonder what happens to our souls and to our bodies when we die. What do these verses tell us?
Daniel 12:2

Luke 23:43

John 11:25

1 Thessalonians 4:13-18

Philippians 1:23

Does reading these verses comfort you? Why or why not?

CHAPTER 5
SOUND THE TRUMPETS!

Christians have been suffering for the sake of Christ since Jesus' ascension. They have been crucified, dragged to death by horses, beaten to death, burned alive, run through with spears, thrown to wild animals to be torn apart for sport, starved, ostracized, decapitated, and more. Not sure how futurists or dispensationalists can say that *in the future* things get really bad.

Scripture is clear that Christians are going to suffer some horrific things. For example, **2 Timothy 2:3** says, *"Share in suffering as a good soldier of Christ Jesus."* Jesus says about Paul in **Acts 9:16**, *"'For I will show him how much he must suffer for the sake of my name.'"* Paul learned this lesson well and tells us in **Philippians 1:29**, *"For it has been granted to you that for the sake of Christ you should not only believe in him but also suffer for his sake."*

Revelation is not meant to discourage us but, instead, to encourage us and give us a picture of how God is going to bring to fulfillment His judgment and Jesus' victory over sin, Satan, and death. And since He is Sovereign over everything and we already know the ending, we can live our lives in confidence and without fear, no matter what the future holds.

With the seal judgments, we were given a big picture view; and now, with the trumpets and, later, the bowl judgments, we will see the same judgments from a different, more up-close perspective.

This literary tool may not be familiar to us, but it was a common practice in ancient Jewish literature and is used in some of the minor prophetic books of the Bible. Readers first get the big picture, and then the writer recapitulates with a zoomed-in look of the same account. Micah is a great example of this. In chapter one of the book of Micah, Micah told the people of the northern nation of Israel and the southern nation of Judah that God was going to punish them for their sin and disobedience by their being overthrown and exiled. Then in chapters two and three, Micah recounts this coming punishment in more specificity.

SILENCE IN HEAVEN

When we left off in the last chapter, we finished up chapter seven of Revelation, which was the opening of six of the seven seals. The first six seals were a lot to take in! So much so that Revelation 8 starts with a pause. **Revelation 8:1** says, *"When the Lamb opened the seventh seal, there was silence in heaven for about half an hour."* As we will see, Jesus shows John the culmination of God's judgment plan for the wicked and the redemption plan for the saved in this seventh seal. So, why the long silence?

Have you ever been told or shown something really shocking or stunning, and you just needed to step back and take a deep breath to process it? That might be what is going on with the silence after opening the seventh seal. What John and the angels saw in the seventh seal was so incredible, they needed time to take it all in. Now, thirty minutes may seem like just a blip in light of eternity, but think of it from a human standpoint. Can you imagine showing or telling someone something, and afterward, they are silent for half an hour?! The seventh seal is God's final judgment on the wicked. Seeing it would have definitely been overwhelming.

THE DAY OF THE LORD

The first six seals contained tribulation that is already occurring or will occur before Jesus comes back. The seventh seal is the completion of the judgment cycle, so the events in this seal have yet to occur. But again, Revelation is not saying anything brand new. The seventh seal—and God's final judgment contained in it—coincides with "the day of the Lord," which is prophesied about in many of the books of the prophets. **Isaiah 13:9**, for example, says, *"Behold, the day of the Lord comes, cruel, with wrath and fierce anger, to make the land a desolation and to destroy its sinners from it."* And **Joel 2:1-2** says:

> *Blow a trumpet in Zion; sound an alarm on my holy mountain! Let all the inhabitants of the land tremble, for the day of the LORD is coming; it is near, a day of darkness and gloom, a day of clouds and thick darkness! Like blackness there is spread upon the mountains a great and powerful people; their like has never been before, nor will be again after them through the years of all generations.*

"The day of the Lord" is also talked about in the New Testament. Paul speaks of it in several of his letters. In **1 Thessalonians 5:1-5**, he says:

> *Now concerning the times and the seasons, brothers, you have no need to have anything written to you. For you yourselves are fully aware that the day of the Lord will come like a thief in the night. While people are saying, "There is peace and security," then sudden destruction will come upon them as labor pains come upon a pregnant woman, and they will not escape. But you are not in darkness, brothers, for that day to surprise you like a thief. For you are all children of light, children of the day. We are not of the night or of the darkness.*

It is safe to say that besides everyone who saw the vision of the seventh seal being overwhelmed, the silence also represents a separation between the first six seals, which were already happening or would be happening sometime before Jesus comes back, and the coming final seventh seal, which is the culmination of God's judgment on the wicked and the full redemption of His people. In other words, the seventh seal contains what will happen at the day of the Lord, which is Jesus' Second Coming.

SOUND THE TRUMPETS!

We continue with **Revelation 8:2-5**:

> "Then I saw the seven angels who stand before God, and seven trumpets were given to them. And another angel came and stood at the altar with a golden censer, and he was given much incense to offer with the prayers of all the saints on the golden altar before the throne, and the smoke of the incense, with the prayers of the saints, rose before God from the hand of the angel. Then the angel took the censer and filled it with fire from the altar and threw it on the earth, and there were peals of thunder, rumblings, flashes of lightning, and an earthquake."

There is some serious weather going on here! We will get to that shortly, but first, let us deal with the trumpets. You might wonder, why trumpets and not, say, violins? The trumpets are, once again, harkening back to the Old Testament. Trumpets are used in many places to signify a call. This call could be a warning call, a call for God's people to assemble, or a call to war for God's people, which God would ultimately fight *for* them and defeat the enemy. We see an example of the trumpet being used as a warning call in **Ezekiel 33:1-6**:

> *The word of the Lord came to me: "Son of man, speak to your people and say to them, If I bring the sword upon a land, and the people of the land take a man from among them, and make him their watchman, and if he sees the sword coming upon the land and blows the trumpet and warns the people, then if anyone who hears the sound of the trumpet does not take warning, and the sword comes and takes him away, his blood shall be upon his own head. He heard the sound of the trumpet and did not take warning; his blood shall be upon himself. But if he had taken warning, he would have saved his life."*

It is used as a call for God's people to assemble in **Isaiah 27:13**, which says, *"And in that day a great trumpet will be blown, and those who were lost in the land of Assyria and those who were driven out to the land of Egypt will come and worship the Lord on the holy mountain at Jerusalem."* And, finally, trumpets are used as a call to Holy War, in which God fought for His people in **Joshua 6:20**: *"So the people shouted, and the trumpets were blown. As soon as the people heard the sound of the trumpet, the people shouted a great shout, and the wall fell down flat, so that* the people went up into the city, every man straight before him, and they captured the city."

The symbolism of trumpets continues in the New Testament. Jesus talks of trumpets in His Olivet Discourse as a call to assembly in **Matthew 24:30-31**: *"Then will appear in heaven the sign of the Son of Man, and then all the tribes of the earth will mourn, and they will see the Son of Man coming on the clouds of heaven with power and great glory. And he will send out his angels with a loud trumpet call, and they will gather his elect from the four winds, from one end of heaven to the other."* Paul, too, uses trumpets as a call to Holy War in **1 Thessalonians 4:16**: *"For the Lord himself will descend from heaven with a cry of command, with the voice of an archangel, and with the sound of the trumpet of God. And the dead in Christ will rise first."*

ANOTHER ANGEL

Revelation 8:3 introduces us to another angel that is different from the seven angels with trumpets. This angel is given incense to offer the prayers of the saints, who are God's people. Again, we need only look back to the Old Testament to understand that this angel was doing exactly what the priests in the Old Testament did for Israel. We see this in **1 Samuel 2:28**: *"Did I choose him out of all the tribes of Israel to be my priest, to go up to my altar, to burn incense, to wear an ephod before me? I gave to the house of your father all my offerings by fire from the people of Israel."*

This angel is lifting up the prayers of all of God's people for all time, including the prayers of Christians who go through tribulation. All of the prayers of God's people are heard, but specifically, God promises retribution for His people who have suffered persecution and martyrdom. In other words, believers who have suffered for standing up for God's Word and for their faith in Jesus. They are looking for Divine justice on the enemies of God. This picture we are given here, complete with thunder, lightning, and an earthquake, is the complete judgment of God on the unbelieving world. It also shows complete vindication for God's elect who have suffered for their faith, complete redemption of all who belong to Jesus, and the complete victory of Christ. This is why there are seven angels, seven seals, seven trumpets, and seven bowls. The thunder, lightning, and earthquake show that God's judgment is going to be something to be feared by those opposed to God.

THE FIRST FOUR TRUMPET JUDGMENTS

> *The first angel blew his trumpet, and there followed hail and fire, mixed with blood, and these were thrown upon the earth. And a third of the earth was burned up, and a third of the trees were burned up, and all green grass was burned up. The second angel blew his trumpet, and something like a great mountain, burning with fire, was thrown into the sea, and a third of the sea became blood. A third of the living creatures in the sea died, and a third of the ships were destroyed. The third angel blew his trumpet, and a great star fell from heaven, blazing like a torch, and it fell on a third of the rivers and on the springs of water. The name of the star is Wormwood. A third of the waters became wormwood, and many people died from the water, because it had been made bitter. The fourth angel blew his trumpet, and a third of the sun was struck, and a third of the moon, and a third of the stars, so that a third of their light might be darkened, and a third of the day might be kept from shining, and likewise a third of the night* **(Rev. 8:7–12)**.

As we have said, the trumpet judgments correspond with the seal judgments. There is one difference, though. While they are the same, the trumpets increase in intensity and are more widespread. The seal judgments are unleashed on one-fourth of mankind, the trumpet judgments on one-third. Neither of these numbers are meant to be taken literally. They are meant to show the increasing intensity, frequency, and consequences suffered by unbelievers.

So, here we have the first four trumpet judgments. If you remember the first four seals, they contained the four horsemen whom Jesus set loose onto Earth. In order, they represented conquest, war, famine, and death. Here in the first four trumpets, we see exactly what their unleashing on the Earth looks like. And again, it doesn't mean that all of the things listed have already happened or are happening now, but they will happen before Jesus comes back. In fact, as we get closer and closer to the time of Jesus coming back, we will see more and more of the things mentioned occurring.

In the first trumpet, there are hail and fire, mixed with blood, hurled to the Earth. One-third of the Earth burns up; a third of the trees burn up; and all the green grass burns up. We can all recall seeing on the news hailstorms or watching wildfires that burn up thousands of acres. And certainly, people have died in them. But we should not limit ourselves to just thinking that God has allowed these things to occur only through "natural disaster" or climate change. God is God, and He can cause any or all of this to happen anytime He chooses.

The second trumpet contains something like a mountain burning and being thrown into the sea. John does not say this is an actual mountain but *"like a mountain."* This could be a giant glacier melting into the sea or a fire so big, it looks like a mountain is burning. He goes on to tell us that one-third of the sea becomes blood; one-third of the living creatures die; and a third of the ships are destroyed. Again, God can and has caused all of these things to happen throughout history by seemingly "human or natural means," like warmer climates causing glacier mountains to melt, water pollution or warm ocean temps killing sea life, or wars destroying ships. But He can also just as easily make them happen anytime He chooses or however He chooses. *"The sea becoming blood"* in verse eight may mean the blood from all of the dead sea life; but God has turned the sea to blood before, so there's certainly a possibility He could do it again.

It is the same with the third and fourth trumpets. John talks about a great star falling from heaven, blazing like a torch, causing the waters to become bitter and causing people to die from drinking it and one-third of the sun, moon, and stars being struck, so there is darkness. This could be talking about asteroids, acid rain, eclipses, smog, air pollution, or other things that have already happened and continue to happen. And, again, that doesn't mean that

God cannot or will not literally do what John says sometime before Jesus comes back.

Joel and Jesus warned us about these very same things. **Joel 2:30-31** says, *"'And I will show wonders in the heavens and on the earth, blood and fire and columns of smoke. The sun shall be turned to darkness, and the moon to blood, before the great and awesome day of the LORD comes.'"* And in **Matthew 24:29**, Jesus says, *"'Immediately after the tribulation of those days the sun will be darkened, and the moon will not give its light, and the stars will fall from heaven, and the powers of the heavens will be shaken.'"* Jesus was telling us that sometime after His ascension when the tribulation began and before He comes back, this darkness on the Earth will happen. Again, God may use some "natural" means to do this, and/or He may just do it.

One last thing on the first four trumpets. Notice that it is one-third of the Earth burned up; one-third of the living creatures in the sea die, etc. As horrible as these things are, God is still being merciful. This is not yet complete judgment. This is God still putting up with the wickedness and sin on Earth.

The last verse of chapter eight serves as a transition between the first four trumpet judgments and the fifth and sixth trumpet judgments that we will see in chapter nine. **Revelation 8:13** says, *"Then I looked, and I heard an eagle crying with a loud voice as it flew directly overhead, 'Woe, woe, woe to those who dwell on the earth, at the blasts of the other trumpets that the three angels are about to blow!'"* This is signaling to us that things are about to get a lot worse.

THE FIFTH TRUMPET JUDGMENT

Revelation 9:1-6 says:

> And the fifth angel blew his trumpet, and I saw a star fallen from heaven to earth, and he was given the key to the shaft of the bottomless pit. He opened the shaft of the bottomless pit, and from the shaft rose smoke like the smoke of a great furnace, and the sun and the air were

darkened with the smoke from the shaft. Then from the smoke came locusts on the earth, and they were given power like the power of scorpions of the earth. They were told not to harm the grass of the earth or any green plant or any tree, but only those people who do not have the seal of God on their foreheads. They were allowed to torment them for five months, but not to kill them, and their torment was like the torment of a scorpion when it stings someone. And in those days people will seek death and will not find it. They will long to die, but death will flee from them.

These verses sound like something out of a horror movie! If we were historians who assigned a specific event in history to everything in Revelation, maybe we attribute the murder hornets that we were all told were coming to kill us to this. Since we are not historians and we do not believe that everything in Revelation is a specific event, instead, we will look back to the fifth seal to begin to understand the meaning of these verses.

The fifth seal was the martyrs crying out to God, *"'O Sovereign Lord, holy and true, how long before you will judge and avenge our blood on those who dwell on the earth?'"* **(Rev. 6:10)**. If you recall, they were told that they would not be completely avenged until all those who were still to be martyred were with them. This means *complete* retribution for them would not come until the last seal, the last trumpet, and the last bowl.

However, God is passing judgment on some of the wicked right now, just as He always has—like on Assyria, Babylon, Rome, and others. We see this in the fifth trumpet. This judgment is on those who are not sealed on their foreheads by God. So, this judgment is on God's enemies or those who do not belong to God, including those who have killed God's people. The first four trumpets, like the first four seals, were perpetrated on all the Earth, but now, God is directly targeting the wicked with the fifth and sixth trumpets. This goes directly back to Exodus and the plagues. Remember, the first three plagues were on everyone, but the last seven were aimed only at the Egyptians. God's people were spared. As **Exodus 8:21-23** says:

> "Or else, if you will not let my people go, behold, I will send swarms of flies on you and your servants and your people, and into your houses. And the houses of the Egyptians shall be filled with swarms of flies, and also the ground on which they stand. But on that day I will set apart the land of Goshen, where my people dwell, so that no swarms of flies shall be there, that you may know that I am the LORD in the midst of the earth. Thus I will put a division between my people and your people."

Revelation is the ultimate fulfillment of the book of Exodus. Both books are intended to show a stark division between the godly and ungodly. As with the fourth plague and beyond in Exodus, the fifth trumpet is only unleashed on the ungodly. This punishment being inflicted on the unbelievers in the trumpet judgments is and will be so bad, those people will wish they were dead. This is very similar to what we saw in Egypt after the last plague of the death of the firstborn in **Exodus 12:33**: *"The Egyptians were urgent with the people [Israelites] to send them out of the land in haste. For they said, 'We shall all be dead.'"* It is also a recapitulation of the sixth seal, where people wished for the mountains to fall on them rather than stand before God.

THE LOCUSTS ARE COMING!

Before we talk about these locusts that come out of the bottomless pit, let's read how Scripture describes them. **Revelation 9:7-11** says:

> *In appearance the locusts were like horses prepared for battle: on their heads were what looked like crowns of gold; their faces were like human faces, their hair like women's hair, and their teeth like lions' teeth; they had breastplates like breastplates of iron, and the noise of their wings was like the noise of many chariots with horses rushing into battle. They have tails and stings like scorpions, and their power to hurt people for five months is in their tails. They have as king over them the angel of the bottomless pit. His name in Hebrew is Abaddon, and in Greek he is called Apollyon.*

Okay, so maybe even historists would not think these are the murder hornets. The description of these locusts is crazy, but guess what? It is not new. The prophet Joel talked about locusts similar to these. Joel 1 prophecies about swarms of different locusts that will appear on the Earth. Chapter two describes these locusts. Here is a sampling of how Joel describes them: *"Their appearance is like the appearance of horses, and like war horses they run. As with the rumbling of chariots, they leap on the tops of the mountains, like the crackling of a flame of fire devouring the stubble, like a powerful army drawn up for battle. Before them peoples are in anguish; all faces grow pale. Like warriors they charge; like soldiers they scale the wall"* **(Joel 2:4-7a)**.

Scholars are split on what the locusts in Revelation mean, just as they are split on what the locusts in Joel mean. Some think they are a metaphor for being attacked; others think it is a literal locust invasion; and some think it is both. But here is the side on which we land. Besides not looking like actual locusts, these locusts do not eat the plants or grass. Now, can God make actual locusts that look like this and attack people instead of greenery? Of course, He can. So, while we will not say this is absolutely not a literal attack, we lean more toward this symbolizing an attack.

And since these locusts are let out of a bottomless pit, Scripture points to them being demons. A bottomless pit is very the definition of abyss.[26] Four other times in Revelation **(11:7, 17:8, 20:1-3, and 20:7)**, the abyss is attributed to the place where Satan, the beast, and demons dwell. In fact, the secondary definition of abyss is "the infernal regions, hell."[27] What we see in the fifth trumpet is God giving unbelievers over to Satan and his demons. This is reiterated by naming the leader. The name of the leader is Abaddon, in Hebrew, and Apollyon, in Greek. These names mean destruction and destroyer.[28] God has been giving people over to Satan for all time—not just since Jesus' ascension, but this seems to be a more intense, intentional demonic influence that will overtake the wicked.

---

26 *Dictionary.com*, s.v. "Abyss," accessed March 20, 2021, https://www.dictionary.com/browse/abyss?s=t.
27 Ibid.
28 *Easton's Bible Dictionary*, s.v., "Abaddon," accessed March 20, 2021, from https://www.biblestudytools.com/dictionary/abaddon.

It is a reality that there is absolute spiritual blindness and that throughout history, God has allowed Satan to pull the strings of some people, institutions, and governments. Paul confirms this in his letter to the church in Ephesus, where he is speaking of our condition before God chose to save us—in other words, when we were unbelievers. *"And you were dead in the trespasses and sins in which you once walked, following the course of this world, following the prince of the power of the air, the spirit that is now at work in the sons of disobedience—among whom we all once lived in the passions of our flesh, carrying out the desires of the body and the mind, and were by nature children of wrath, like the rest of mankind"* **(Eph. 2:1-3)**. Satan is the prince of the power of the air. These verses tell us that there are only two masters one can follow. If God is not your master, then Satan is. As things intensify with the fifth trumpet, Satan will have his way more and more with unbelievers.

In the plague in **Exodus 10:15**, God unleashed locusts on Egypt, *"They covered the face of the whole land, so that the land was darkened ... Not a green thing remained, neither tree nor plant of the field, through all the land of Egypt."* You can bet that when God gives the go-ahead to Satan and his demons to fully target unbelievers, they will swarm in to destroy all that they can just like the locusts in **Exodus 10**. The result will be misery, anguish, and pain so horrific, they will wish they were dead.

THE SIXTH TRUMPET

Then the sixth angel blew his trumpet, and I heard a voice from the four horns of the golden altar before God, saying to the sixth angel who had the trumpet, "Release the four angels who are bound at the great river Euphrates." So the four angels, who had been prepared for the hour, the day, the month, and the year, were released to kill a third of mankind ... By these three plagues a third of mankind was killed, by the fire and smoke and sulfur coming out of their mouths ... The rest of mankind, who were not killed by these plagues, did not repent of the works of their hands nor give up worshiping demons and idols of gold and silver and bronze and stone and wood, which cannot see or hear or walk, nor did they repent of their murders or their sorceries or their sexual immorality or their thefts **(Rev. 9:13-15, 18, 20-21)**.

These verses tie directly to the seals talking about the four angels, who were held back from destroying people and things on Earth until God's people were all sealed. So, again, this judgment is on unbelievers. This also shows an escalation from the demons in the fifth trumpet, who were allowed to torment unbelievers but not kill them. Now we see angels being given a license to kill one-third of mankind. Like with the first four trumpets, "one-third" is probably not a literal one-third, but symbolic of "a portion" of mankind. Does this mean that these angels are demonic angels? Maybe, maybe not. Scholars are split, but it does not really matter because both are under the complete Sovereignty and authority of God. Throughout Scripture, God has used both His obedient angels and evil angels to serve His purpose, as we see in verses like **2 Kings 19:35**: *"And that night the angel of the LORD went out and struck down 185,000 in the camp of the Assyrians. And when people arose early in the morning, behold, these were all dead bodies."* Likewise, he can use evil angels to accomplish His will, as **1 Samuel 16:14** shows: *"Now the Spirit of the LORD departed from Saul, and a harmful spirit from the LORD tormented him."*

We mentioned earlier about complete spiritual blindness. Wow! This is certainly evident in **Revelation 9:20-21**. Despite all that unbelievers suffer and are put through, they continue to worship their false gods and do not repent of their evil. Jesus gives us a clue as to how this can be. In **John 12:40**, Jesus quotes what was told to the prophet Isaiah, *"'He has blinded their eyes and hardened their heart, lest they see with their eyes, and understand with their heart, and turn, and I would heal them.'"* Paul reiterates the same truth in **2 Corinthians 4:3-4**: *"And even if our gospel is veiled, it is veiled to those who are perishing. In their case the god of this world has blinded the minds of the unbelievers, to keep them from seeing the light of the gospel of the glory of Christ, who is the image of God."* These verses tell us that God has hardened the hearts and closed the minds of those who are not His elect. This is a hard truth to hear, but it is the truth, nonetheless. And this does not mean that people who are not God's elect have an excuse for their refusal to see God and His works. God has given what is called "common grace" to everyone—both believers and unbelievers—so that no one is without excuse when it comes to seeing the truth about God. Finally, understand that just because someone is hardened to God's Word now does not mean that the Holy Spirit will not, at some point, regenerate their hearts. This is why we need to witness the Gospel and all of God's Word to as many as we can. We never know what seed we may be planting that God will use later in that person's life!

Right now, as you read this, God is judging the wicked and bringing partial justice to earth. Those who are His can never be taken out of His grasp because of what Jesus sacrificed and accomplished for us. And while we may suffer and even be killed for our faith, our future is secure; and God will work everything out for our good and for His glory. Instead of being depressed by what we read in Revelation, use it to live in gratitude to our Lord and Savior! Use it to motivate you to preach the Gospel to every unbeliever you know. What is at stake for those who do not know Jesus is monumental!

CHAPTER 5
STUDY GUIDE

GETTING YOUR TOES WET

Scripture warns us that persecution and, perhaps, martyrdom is not just a possibility; according to Paul in **2 Timothy 3:12**, it is a given. Paul says, *"Indeed, all who desire to live a godly life in Christ Jesus will be persecuted."* Jesus tells His apostles outright that they will be martyred in **Matthew 24:9** when He says, *"'They will deliver you up to tribulation and put you to death, and you will be hated by all nations for my name's sake.'"* And in fact, they were. Every one of Jesus' apostles, except John, were executed. James, John's brother, was beheaded; Philip was scourged and crucified; Matthew was impaled with a halberd (a spear/ax combo); James, Jesus' brother, was beaten, stoned, and thrown off of the temple roof; Matthias was stoned and beheaded; Mark, the writer of the Gospel of Mark, was dragged to pieces behind a horse; Peter was crucified upside down; Paul was beheaded; Jude, Bartholomew, and Andrew were crucified; Thomas was run through with a spear; and Luke, the writer of Luke and Acts, was hung from a tree.

Does what we have studied in Revelation eight and nine make you feel emboldened like the apostles and others throughout history to stand firm in your faith, even in the face of persecution or death? Why or why not?

How do you think God is glorified through our suffering?

THE FINAL EXODUS

DIVING IN DEEP

We said the seventh seal, and God's final judgment contained in it, coincides with "the Day of the Lord," which is prophesied about in many of the books of the prophets. What do these verses from the prophetic books say about "the day of the Lord?"

Zephaniah 1:14-18

Isaiah 13:9-11

Jeremiah 46:10

Matthew 7:22-23

There is strong imagery in Revelation about the prayers of God's people rising before God. Sometimes, we may feel like God is not listening. *How do these verses reinforce what we are told in Revelation about God and our prayers?*

Psalm 145:18-19

Jeremiah 29:12-13

Matthew 6:5-13

1 John 5:14-15

Revelation is the ultimate fulfillment of the book of Exodus. *How do these plagues of Exodus correspond with the trumpet judgments?*

Exodus 7:17-18

Exodus 9:18-19

Exodus 10:4-5

Exodus 10:21-23

Exodus 11:4-6

BACK ON DRY LAND

Jesus' Sovereignty extends to being Sovereign over Satan and his demons. *How does this passage depict this truth?*

Matthew 8:28-32

We never need be afraid or worried about our future. God has everything well-in-hand and will work everything out for the good of His people. We serve a mighty God, a God even the darkest forces fear! As Martin Luther so brilliantly penned:

> *And though this world with devils filled should threaten to undo us*
> *We will not fear, for God hath willed*
>
> *his truth to triumph through us.*
> *The Prince of Darkness grim, we tremble not for him*
> *His rage we can endure, for lo, his doom is sure.*
> *One little word shall fell him.*[29]

---

[29] Martin Luther, "A Mighty Fortress is Our God," Public Domain, https://sovereign-gracemusic.org/music/songs/a-mighty-fortress-is-our-god.

CHAPTER 6
"EAT YOUR SCRIPTURE!"

What we ingest matters. The color of salmon in the supermarket can be white, have just a tinge of orange, or be vibrant red. Overwhelmingly, this difference in color is because of what they eat! Like flamingos, wild salmon get their deep red color from their food—carotenoid-rich crustaceans such as shrimp and krill. Farm-raised salmon, on the other hand, do not have access to those. They are fed diets of corn, soy, and fishmeal; and if their diet was left that way, they would naturally be gray. To give them a pink color, farmers add synthetic astaxanthin, a naturally occurring compound in carotenoids, to their feed.[30] While it might sound healthier to eat only wild salmon, both kinds of salmon have health benefits.

That is not the case with the plethora of Bible teaching and preaching that is out there for Christians to devour. Unlike the salmon that look different but are still salmon, teaching can be labeled "Christian" but, in reality, be anything but! God's people have always been infiltrated by false prophets and teachers, like the false prophet Jezebel in the church at Thyatira. There is no benefit when we feed on false teaching. In fact, it can be downright harmful or deadly. What can we do to protect ourselves? Feed on the Word of God! Daily reading and studying gives us the ability to recognize a counterfeit gospel when we hear one *"so that we may no longer be children, tossed to and fro*

---

[30] "Salmon Color Guide: Why Salmon are Pink, Orange or Red," Wild Alaskan Company, April 16, 2018, https://wildalaskancompany.com/blog/heres-why-salmon-are-pink-orange-or-red.

by the waves and carried about by every wind of doctrine, by human cunning, by craftiness in deceitful schemes" **(Eph. 4:14)**. Taking in the Word of God daily not only helps us know and understand the Bible for ourselves; it also prepares us to take the message to a sin-filled world that needs to hear it. So, feed on it daily, Church! Bon appétit!

THE BIG ANGEL HOLDING THE LITTLE BOOK

We open to **Revelation 10**, which is the beginning of another interlude, like the one between the sixth and seventh seals in **Revelation 7**. Like that one, this interlude is also a picture showing God keeping His people spiritually safe through this time of Great Tribulation. No matter what comes against them, all who are spiritually united with Christ are eternally secure. They will not lose their salvation.

This interlude comes between the sixth and seventh trumpet judgments. **Revelation 10:1-3** says:

> *Then I saw another mighty angel coming down from heaven, wrapped in a cloud, with a rainbow over his head, and his face was like the sun, and his legs like pillars of fire. He had a little scroll open in his hand. And he set his right foot on the sea, and his left foot on the land, and called out with a loud voice, like a lion roaring. When he called out, the seven thunders sounded.*

In this vision, John sees another mighty angel, different than the mighty angel from **Revelation 5:2**. Like God's throne in **Revelation 4:3**, this angel is surrounded by a rainbow. Just like the descriptions of Jesus, the Son of Man, this angel comes in a cloud; his face shines like the sun; and his legs are like pillars of fire. He also has a voice like one might expect from the Lion of Judah. Because of this imagery associated with Jesus, some commentators believe that this is not an angel but is, in fact, Jesus Himself.

The problem with this idea lies in the fact that nowhere else in Revelation is Christ called an angel. Additionally, whoever this is came down from Heaven, and we are not told that Jesus comes at any other time in the future, except for the Second Coming. Furthermore, angels are described similarly in other places in the Bible—like in **Daniel 10:6**, where the angel had *"arms and legs like the gleam of burnished bronze."* Most importantly, we have to remember from **Revelation 1:1** that the Father gave Jesus this revelation; Jesus gave it to an angel; and the angel delivered it to John. In light of these things, it is most likely this angel has the *characteristics* of God because he is an angel *representing* God. In his commentary on the book of Daniel, Ian Duguid says, "The angelic messengers reflect the image of the glorious God whom they serve, so to look on the angel is tantamount to viewing God Himself."[31]

SOMETHING REVEALED AND SOMETHING CONCEALED

The angel in John's vision is huge—so huge, he is straddling land and sea. This signifies God's control over all creation. He is carrying a "little scroll"—or, in other words, a little book—in his hand. The words *little scroll* in the original Greek is the same word that we get the word "Bible" from.[32] We are not told exactly what is in this little book, but the book is open. What it says is not hidden; it is something that has already been revealed.

This big angel has a voice to go with his size. He thunders out words that John is just about to write down until a voice from Heaven stops him, saying, *"'Seal up what the seven thunders have said, and do not write it down'"* **(Rev. 10:4)**. Unlike the little book that was opened, this Divine revelation is concealed. We do not know what words were thundered. In the Old Testament, the prophets spoke of God's voice thundering or roaring at times of pronouncing judgment, like in **Amos 1:2**, where he says, *"The LORD roars from Zion and utters his voice from Jerusalem; the pastures of the shepherds mourn, and the top of Carmel withers."* Or like the prophet Joel writes in **Joel 3:16**, *"The LORD roars from Zion, and utters his voice from Jerusalem, and the heavens and the earth quake.*

---

31 Iain M. Duguid, "Daniel/Chapter 13/Prepared for Battle," in *Daniel*, (Phillipsburg: P & R Publishing, 2008), 181.
32 *Strong's Exhaustive Concordance*, s.v. "biblaridion," accessed April 1, 2021, https://biblehub.com/strongs/greek/974.htm.

But the LORD is a refuge to his people, a stronghold to the people of Israel." These words from Joel are fitting for the context of this interlude. At the seventh trumpet, judgment will come and will not be delayed any longer. Swearing an oath about this and confirming it by the sea, land, and Heaven, the angel announces in **Revelation 10:6-7**, *"There would be no more delay, but that in the days of the trumpet call to be sounded by the seventh angel, the mystery of God would be fulfilled, just as he announced to his servants the prophets."*

When something is referred to as a *mystery* in the Bible, it is not something we track down the meaning of, like a detective. A mystery is something which has not been revealed yet. The "mystery" of God yet to be fulfilled is the culmination of God's unfolding plan to *"unite all things"* **(Eph. 1:10)** in Christ bringing together people from all tribes and tongues and nations, in perfect harmony, under our King. We won't experience the full reality of this until the plan is consummated at Christ's second coming; something that will happen at the sounding of the seventh trumpet. But until that happens, believers have work to do.

THE GREAT COMMISSION CONTINUES

Once again, the "little book" is brought to John's attention, and he is told to go and take the open scroll from the hand of the angel. John doesn't get to hold on to the book for long, though. The angel says, *"'Take and eat it; it will make your stomach bitter, but in your mouth it will be sweet as honey'"* **(Rev. 10:9)**. And John did eat it, and things were exactly as the angel told him. And then he was told, *"'You must again prophesy about many peoples and nations and languages and kings'"* **(Rev. 10:11)**.

This isn't the first time in Scripture someone talks about eating a book. When lamenting his mistreatment by the wicked for being a servant of God, Jeremiah said, *"Your words were found, and I ate them, and your words became to me a joy and the delight of my heart"* **(Jer. 15:16)**. God told Ezekiel:

> "Son of man, eat whatever you find here. Eat this scroll, and go, speak to the house of Israel." So I opened my mouth, and he gave me this scroll to eat. And he said to me, "Son of man, feed your belly with this scroll that I give you and fill your stomach with it." Then I ate it, and it was in my mouth as sweet as honey. And he said to me, "Son of man, go to the house of Israel and speak with my words to them" **(Ezek. 3:1-4)**.

Taking the scroll and eating it symbolizes internalizing the Word of God. Like these prophets, speaking God's Word to rebellious people is what John is told to do. Jeremiah and Ezekiel proclaimed the sweet promises of blessing for obedience and the bitter warnings of mourning and woe for disobedience to the sinful people in their day. John's message is to preach the sweet news of the Gospel *and* the bitter demands of the Law. In other words, he is to take this message of the requirements of the Law—something no mere human can possibly fulfill perfectly—coupled with the salvific message of Christ's blood shed for forgiveness to *"'many peoples and nations and languages and kings.'"* Without sharing both parts of this message, John and anyone else would be sharing a half-truth gospel, which is no Gospel at all.

False prophets have always been around preaching a sweet message that their hearers wanted to hear. Jesus rebuked the Ephesus church for allowing it to happen. There's a reason for that! A Scripture diet of preaching and teaching from prosperity preachers will leave us with a sweet taste in our mouth, but not with a saving Gospel message. A rules-based, legalistic, diet of teaching that says we have to keep the Law ourselves in order to be saved will leave us with a bitter taste in our mouths. Neither of these is the true and complete Gospel message—that we are sinners separated from God, deserving His wrath because we have broken His Law, but that He has provided a way to fix that relationship and forgive us our sin through His Son. You need the Word. Others need to hear the Word. Eat your Scripture. Eat all of it. *"Every word of God proves true; he is a shield to those who take refuge in him"* **(Prov. 30:5)**.

THE STANDING CHURCH

Over the past few years, we have seen a large part of our society worship at the altar of health and safety. We live in a world willing to shut down economies, stay separated from loved ones, and be denied ability to gather for worship because of a virus. There is nothing wrong with desiring health or safety—they are good things that are blessings from God when we have them. But to a world obsessed with *physical* safety, the idea that God does not promise to keep His people from physical harm may seem jolting. It is one of the reasons a large chunk of believers wants to believe in the idea of a pre-tribulation rapture of the Church. But think of the Christian martyrs who have gone ahead of us. Numerous saints have been burned at the stake, never denying their faith, and singing hymns of praise to God as the flames licked their feet.

In Myanmar, Buddhist monks have invaded church compounds and built their Buddhist shrines inside, many Christians are enduring persecution from their communities and even from their families, and many are facing hardship from a lack of resources, some suffering even while living in IDP camps for internally displaced persons where humanitarian access has been blocked.[33] Yet still they endure without losing their faith.

In July of 2020, John MacArthur of Grace Community Church in California stood firm, while being threatened with legal actions for resuming in-person worship services despite coronavirus regulations—regulations that were unjustifiable in light of other establishments being open. In February 2021, Pastor James Coates of Grace Life Church in Edmonton was imprisoned for holding a church service against these same types of regulations. Persecution is abounding and may be coming to a church near you soon!

Taking the message to the nations is the mission of Christ's Church, even in times of terrible persecution or martyrdom. The Church may suffer while

---

[33] "Myanmar," Open Doors USA, January 12, 2021, https://www.opendoorsusa.org/christian-persecution/world-watch-list/myanmar.

on earth, but God promises to be a refuge for her as she goes about her work. We will see this more than ever as we look at the next section of Revelation.

FAULTY VIEWS

Revelation 11 has some very familiar imagery in it, and the different views people have of the book of Revelation come into play in several areas in the coming verses. Before we dive into what is really going on, there are some aspects of the varying views that need discussion. First, those who hold to a partial preterist view (the one saying most of Revelation's prophecy was already fulfilled by the fall of Jerusalem in 70 A.D.) say that the "great city" being trampled on by Gentiles for forty-two months is Jerusalem because that is what happened when the Romans destroyed it in 70 A.D. While some of the imagery is very compelling and partial preterism is a valid view of Revelation, there is a problem with it. This view cannot link the Roman Empire and the sacking of Jerusalem being the fulfillment of most of the prophecy of the book with the prophecies of worldwide judgment and the destruction of all of God's enemies, which is yet to come.

Futurists, or dispensationalists, also have issues that they cannot resolve in this section. **Revelation 11:1** says, *"Then I was given a measuring rod like a staff, and I was told, "Rise and measure the temple of God and the altar and those who worship there."* Futurists, or those who believe the visions of Revelation in the way the *Left Behind* books portray them, take John's measuring rod literally, saying that sometime during the Great Tribulation, the Jewish temple will be rebuilt in Jerusalem. They refer to this temple as the "third temple." That is why many were excited about Israel being made an actual nation again in 1948. To dispensationalists, that started paving the way.

They also believe that when the temple is finished, Jewish worship will be reinstituted in it. But there are two problems with that. After Jesus overturns the tables in the temple and says the Pharisees have defiled the house of His Father, we read in **John 2:18-19**, *"So the Jews said to him, 'What sign do you show us for doing these things?' Jesus answered them, 'Destroy this* *temple, and in three days I will raise it up.'"* Jesus is talking about His crucifixion and resurrection in that passage. He is the ultimate Sacrifice that will atone for the sins of God's people. To think that God wants the temple sacrifices reinstituted after Jesus has already been the final and complete Sacrifice for sin makes no sense at all.

The second problem is that dispensationalists believe in a third temple era because they think that God's plan for Israel and the Church are two different plans. They believe the Church was an afterthought—or, in other words, a Plan B—brought about by ethnic Israel's rejection of Christ. They claim that **Romans 11** speaks of an ethnic Jewish remnant that is going to be brought in, with whom God is going to do something special. They do not define the name Israel as being the true people of God throughout all time.

In reality, all through the Bible, you see God having *one* set of people who are His—not two. Take note, however, that God is not *replacing* Israel with the Church, as some believe. The biblical view (which is sometimes mistakenly called "replacement theology") affirms that the *true* Israel always was, always is, and always will be comprised of all of God's chosen people, "the elect"—all those who are saved through faith—throughout all of time. There is only one people of God because there is only one way of salvation, and that is through *faith*!

GOD IS OUR REFUGE

Getting back to what we believe Revelation is actually saying, **Revelation 11:1-2** says, *"Then I was given a measuring rod like a staff, and I was told, 'Rise and measure the temple of God and the altar and those who worship there, but do not measure the court outside the temple; leave that out, for it is given over to the nations, and they will trample the holy city for forty-two months.'"* The temple and the holy city are God's people. The Old Testament background for these verses is **Ezekiel 40-48**, where Ezekiel is shown the temple. The last line says, *"The name of the city . . . shall be 'The LORD Is There'"* **(Ezek. 48:35)**. We saw this in **Revelation 1:12-13** when Jesus was standing amidst the Church. We see it also in **1 Corinthians 3:16**, which says, *"Do you not know that you are God's temple and that God's Spirit dwells in you?"* God's people are referred to as a temple and city later in Revelation, too.

Revelation 11:1 indicates that the saints are *spiritually* protected during this time because God is with His people. But as verse two indicates, they will be physically trampled on, meaning persecuted. Therefore, it begs the question, "For how long?" How long are these "last days" going to last? Verse two says, *"For forty-two months."* This is not a literal forty-two months. Instead, it is "for some period of time of suffering." John is echoing a timeframe from **Daniel 7** and **Daniel 12**—"time, times, and half a time" **(Dan. 7:25, 12:7)**—three-and-a-half years, forty-two months, or 1260 days. When you do the math, you see that they are all the same amount of time.

Most dispensationalists regard these as an exact three-and-half years of intense persecution right before Jesus comes. But John used these numbers because the Jews hearing it would automatically recognize it as a time of trial for God's people and with good reason. In 167 B.C. Antiochus Epiphanes IV came into Jerusalem and sacrificed a pig in the temple, which is referred to as *"the abomination that makes desolate"* **(Dan. 11:31)**. That lasted for about three-and-a-half years. The sacking of Jerusalem started between 66 and 67 A.D. and ended in 70 A. D. when Jerusalem was demolished. To the hearers of this letter, that was another example of three-and-a-half years of trial and tribulation. We can see why John uses this length of time as a metaphor for suffering. The people in the seven churches would have recognized it right away.

THE TWO WITNESSES

Revelation 11:3 says, *"And I will grant authority to my two witnesses, and they will prophesy for 1,260 days, clothed in sackcloth."* The two witnesses are metaphors for the Church. We see that later in verse seven, where the beast attacks them after they finish their witness, something that is reiterated in **Revelation 13:7**, where it says the beast attacked the saints. This is symbolic of the visible Church shining the light of the complete Gospel message—the bitter demands of the Law coupled with the sweet message of the Gospel salvation—to a dark world. The Church is fueled by the Holy Spirit, represented by the oil from the olive trees in **Revelation 11:4**. The witnesses symbolizing the visible Church are clothed in sackcloth, clothing that showed mourning over sin and need for repentance. That is what is pictured here. Just as the true prophets of the Old Testament mourned over the sin of the people in their midst while calling them to hear God's words and repent, here the Church is mourning over the sinfulness of mankind while faithfully preaching and teaching the true Gospel message, trying to lead others to repentance. These two witnesses are the two faithful churches (Smyrna and Philadelphia) from **Revelation 2**. They are also the two faithful lampstands.

The reference to the two olive trees harkens back to the Old Testament to Zechariah's vision, where the two olive trees represented two men who were anointed by God—Zerubbabel (who was royalty) and Joshua (a priest). This is John referencing that Jesus has made us a kingdom of priests and kings, as it says in **Revelation 1:6** and **5:10**. Again, John is telling us the two witnesses represent the Church.

Revelation 11:5-6 says about these witnesses, *"And if anyone would harm them, fire pours from their mouth and consumes their foes. If anyone would harm them, this is how he is doomed to be killed. They have the power to shut the sky, that no rain may fall during the days of their prophesying, and they have power over the waters to turn them into blood and to strike the earth with every kind of plague, as often as they desire."* These are references to Moses and Elijah. Moses (who turned the Nile to blood and brought the plagues to Pharaoh) represents the Law, and Elijah (who shut up the sky so it would not rain during Ahab and Jezebel's time) represents the Prophets. They represent the bitter and sweet messages of the Gospel that comes with power to save sinners.

There are even more parallels with Moses and Elijah that go with the number forty-two. In **Numbers 33:3-48**, we saw the forty-two locations where the Israelites camped as Moses led them in the wilderness. The wilderness was their time of testing and trial while God kept them safe. When Elijah shut up the sky so it would not rain, the drought he brought lasted for three-and-a-half years (forty-two months) according to **Luke 4:25**.

You can see all of this imagery fits perfectly together. There's no need to try to make it fit a special timeline any more than there is reason to believe that someday two people—the two witnesses— will literally breathe fire from their mouths, according to some dispensationalists. That imagery is taken from **Jeremiah 5:14**, where the Lord tells says to Jeremiah about disobedient, unrepentant Israel, *"Behold, I am making my words in your mouth a fire, and this people wood, and the fire shall consume them."* This was picturing God's prophet proclaiming God's Word to unrepentant people, who did not listen. John is showing the Church fulfilling her prophetic role.

Revelation 11:7 continues, *"And when they have finished their testimony, the beast that rises from the bottomless pit will make war on them and conquer them and kill them."* The Church will be spiritually protected during this time. True believers will not lose their salvation. They cannot because God is holding onto them. Satan and his beast cannot touch their souls. But when the Church's witness on earth is finished, there will be a time when things will get much worse. The Beast is freed to kill Christians. To signify just how much the world hates Christ and hates the Church and its message, John says, *"Their dead bodies will lie in the street"* **(Rev. 11:8)**. Back then, refusing to bury the corpse of your enemy was the ultimate sign of contempt. Several cities representing godlessness are mentioned for where this will happen. This means it is likely to happen throughout the whole earth. *"For three and a half days some from the peoples and tribes and languages and nations will gaze at their dead bodies and refuse to let them be placed in a tomb, and those who dwell on the earth will rejoice over them and make merry and exchange presents, because these two prophets had been a torment to those who dwell on the earth"* **(Rev. 11:9-10)**. Satan and his followers will think they have won for a short time, until the dead saints are raised to life, like the army of dry bones in **Ezekiel 37:1, 10**: *"The hand of the LORD was upon me, and he brought me out in the Spirit of the LORD and set me down in the middles of the valley; it was full of bones . . . So I prophesied as he commanded me, and the breath came into them, and they lived and stood on their feet, an exceedingly great army."* When that day comes, the wicked will be terrified.

The three-and-a-half *days* of the wicked's revelry and partying and the three-and-a-half *years* of God's Church standing their ground victoriously are both symbolic. But when you compare the "days" of the wicked's revelry to the "years" of the Church's victorious standing, you see just how shallow and short-lived the wicked's celebration will be. After being raised to life again, the Church will hear *"a loud voice from heaven saying to them, 'Come up here!'"* **(Rev. 11:12)** and be caught up to Heaven in a cloud—raptured! But this will not occur *before* the Great Tribulation, like the dispensationalists say. The Church goes through the tribulation and, at the last trumpet, goes home to Jesus. *"And at that hour there was a great earthquake, and a tenth of the city fell. Seven thousand people were killed in the earthquake, and the rest were terrified and gave glory to the God of heaven. The second woe has passed; behold, the third woe is soon to come"* **(Rev. 11:13-14)**.

Revelation 11 ends with the sounding of the seventh trumpet. In Heaven, the saints and angels praise and magnify God. They praise Him because the world's kingdoms are finished and Christ's kingdom has come, and He will reign forever—through all eternity. They thank Him, saying, *"The nations raged, but your wrath came, and the time for the dead to be judged, and for rewarding your servants, the prophets and saints, and those who fear your name, both small and great, and for destroying the destroyers of the earth"* **(Rev. 11:18)**.

"Then God's temple in heaven was opened, and the ark of his covenant was seen within his temple. There were flashes of lightning, rumblings, peals of thunder, an earthquake, and heavy hail" **(Rev. 11:19)**. We get a picture of Heaven opened up in this text, just as the final trumpet is sounding. The wicked get a full

picture of what the heavenly throne room is like and how wonderful it is. They can see what they are missing. Some commentators say that part of their suffering eternally in Hell will be regret from knowing what they are missing out on for eternity because they did not repent of their sin. They get to see the universal Church—the whole Church of all times throughout history (represented by the twenty-four elders)—worshiping and enjoying their Creator. The picture here is of Heaven opened up showing all of the beauty and God being worshipped, while in the meantime, earthquakes and hail and dread and fear and lightning and thunder are going on below. For a book that is meant to give persecuted people hope in times of suffering, that seems to be a very fitting picture.

CHAPTER 6
STUDY GUIDE

GETTING YOUR TOES WET

Have you seen Christian persecution happen in the country you live in? How?

If no, from the political situation you are in right now, do you think it is possible it will happen in your lifetime?

If yes, does what you are seeing politically make you think it is going to worsen or get better?

DIVING IN DEEP

The rewards of the book of Revelation are for believers who stand firm in their faith regardless of what they may face. *What do these verses say about standing firm in our faith?*

1 Corinthians 16:13

Matthew 10:22

James 1:2-4

Taking the message of the Gospel to the nations is the mission of Christ's Church, even in times of terrible persecution or martyrdom. The Church may suffer while on earth, but God promises to be a refuge for her as she goes about her work. *What do the following verses say about persecution that comes from spreading the good news of the Gospel?*

Matthew 10:16-18

Matthew 10:21

Matthew 10:25b

Matthew 10:28

Read Luke 14:25-33. *Why do you think Jesus gives this and other similar warnings about the cost of discipleship to His Church?*

BACK ON DRY LAND

If you feared that within the next three years all Bibles and any books pertaining to the Bible were going to be confiscated and destroyed, what is the first thing you would do?

What would your long-term plan be?

In some countries, just owning a Bible or attending church is punishable by imprisonment and/or death. *If that was the case in your country, would you keep your Bible? Would you attend an underground church?*

CHAPTER 7

RELEASE THE KRACKEN

Back in chapter four of this book, we used Jesus' example of birth pains to show how the big picture of the stages of labor and delivery can help us better understand the seal, trumpet, and bowl judgments. If we zoom in for a closer look, we see that this is also an excellent picture of enduring through tribulation.

If you have ever birthed a baby or seen a baby being born, you know that there is a lot of pain involved in the process. On average, a newborn baby weighs seven-and-a-half pounds and has a head circumference of almost fourteen inches. A woman's uterine canal, which is normally around two inches wide, has to expand to four or five times that width while also pushing the baby along. Contractions are her body doing all these things. And as we all know, contractions become more intense and more painful as the time of birth approaches. When it is finally time to push the baby out, the pain is almost unbearable. She may feel like she is going to be split in two and die, but then . . . The doctor holds up that precious little one and instantly, all memory or thoughts of the pain and torment she just experienced vanish. Many women go on to have multiple children—not because they are sadists who like to be in pain and anguish, but because any amount of pain that must be endured is worth the final prize.

We left off in the last chapter at the end of **Revelation 11** with flashes of lightning, rumblings, peals of thunder, an earthquake, and heavy hail.

As we continue on with chapters twelve and thirteen of Revelation, we will delve into some well-known scenes—the woman and the dragon, Satan being thrown down to earth, and the first and second beasts.

Some of you may recognize the phrase, "Release the Kracken," from the 2010 movie, *Clash of the Titans*.³⁴ "Release the Kracken" is defined in the *Urban Dictionary* as, "To own or kick the [butt] of whomever you are releasing the Kracken on."³⁵

We can probably guess Who is the one who will be doing the butt-kicking in the next verses we are going to study, but let us dig in and find out all the details.

Revelation 12:1-6 says:

> *And a great sign appeared in heaven: a woman clothed with the sun, with the moon under her feet, and on her head a crown of twelve stars. She was pregnant and was crying out in birth pains and the agony of giving birth. And another sign appeared in heaven: behold, a great red dragon, with seven heads and ten horns, and on his heads seven diadems. His tail swept down a third of the stars of heaven and cast them to the earth. And the dragon stood before the woman who was about to give birth, so that when she bore her child he might devour it. She gave birth to a male child, one who is to rule all the nations with a rod of iron, but her child was caught up to God and to his throne, and the woman fled into the wilderness, where she has a place prepared by God, in which she is to be nourished for 1,260 days.*

There is a lot to unpack in these six verses. The first thing we should notice is that in the first verse, John says, *"A great sign appeared."* John clearly sets up that what he is about to describe is symbolic and not literal. It is a sign. We will get to the woman and dragon in a minute, but let us talk about this baby, this male child, who *"will rule all nations with rod of iron"* **(Rev. 12:5)**. There can be very little doubt that this baby boy is Jesus, but since we always

---

34　*Clash of the Titans*, directed by Louis Leterrier (Warner Brothers, 2010), 1:46:00, Video file.
35　*Urban Dictionary*, s.v. "Kracken," accessed March 21, 2021, https://www.urbandictionary.com/define.php?term=Release%20the%20kraken.

want to make sure Scripture is interpreting Scripture, let us look at a couple of verses that confirm this.

Psalm 2:7-9 says, *"I will tell of the decree: The LORD said to me, 'You are my Son; today I have begotten you. Ask of me, and I will make the nations your heritage, and the ends of the earth your possession. You shall break them with a rod of iron and dash them in pieces like a potter's vessel.'"* **Revelation 19:15** says, *"From his mouth comes a sharp sword with which to strike down the nations, and he will rule them with a rod of iron."* Every credible camp agrees that this baby is Jesus.

Let us now turn our attention to this woman John described. He said, she is *"clothed with the sun, with the moon under her feet and on her head a crown of twelve stars."* She is crying out in pain because she is about to give birth. There are a few opinions about whom this woman symbolizes. We are not even going to look at what those who believe this is a literal picture because, as we said, John refutes that in the first verse of chapter twelve. To some, this woman represents Mary, Jesus' mother. It may seem to make sense as she is the one who physically gave birth to Jesus. But this is not Mary. Nowhere in Scripture do we see Mary being described as anything like being *"clothed with the sun,"* having *"the moon under her feet,"* or having a *"crown of twelve stars"* on her head. And when we unpack what all those symbols mean, we think you, too, will see that this cannot be Mary.

Then there are some who think this woman represents Israel. This is a more realistic belief, since we can tie the symbols to the nation of Israel. The reasoning is that Joseph, from the book of Genesis, tells his family of a dream he had. He says in **Genesis 37:9b**, *"'Behold, the sun, the moon and eleven stars were bowing down to me.'"* In Joseph's dream, his father, Jacob, was the sun; his mother, Rachel, the moon; and his eleven brothers, the stars. This image in **Revelation 12** almost mirrors Joseph's dream using the same imagery. But if you notice, there are twelve stars, not eleven. Proponents who believe this is Israel theorize that the extra star is Joseph, who is now one of the tribes, since this woman encompasses all of Israel.

The argument of the woman representing Israel has some logic; but when you put in the fifty percent perspiration and fifty percent orientation, as seminary professor Dr. McDonough advises,[36] you get a clear picture of whom this woman represents. She is the Church. There is a lot to back this up. The first place we look to is—you guessed it—the Old Testament. If we go way back to **Genesis 3:15**, we find God pronouncing the punishments on Adam, Eve, and Satan. To Satan, He said, *"I will put enmity between you and the woman, and between your offspring and her offspring; he shall bruise your head, and you shall bruise his heel."* This verse is the first Gospel in Scripture and the major theme of the entire Bible! Satan is contemptuous of God and His people. Thus begins the cosmic struggle between the devil and the Church that is played out throughout Scripture and recapitulated in the book of Revelation. And, of course, Satan's offspring are his demons and unbelievers, while the woman's (the Church's) offspring is Jesus. Satan will bruise Jesus' heel at the crucifixion, but it will prove to be merely a flesh wound. Meanwhile, Jesus will bruise Satan's head, a blow that will be fatal. By dealing that fatal blow, Jesus redeems all who are His for all eternity.

Further proof is that after the woman's child is caught up to God and His throne (a picture of Jesus' ascension), the woman goes to a place in the wilderness prepared by God, where she is nourished for 1,260 days. If you recall from the last chapter, the two witnesses in **Revelation 11** represent the Church. God granted them authority to prophesy for 1,260 days while they were clothed in sackcloth, meaning they were mourning over the evil of the world. Here in chapter twelve, we see that during those 1,260 days, God has them in the wilderness. We have said this before, but it is worth repeating. The book of Revelation is not a chronological order of events and often uses the literary device of giving the big picture view, then zooming in. These verses in chapter twelve are a zooming in of chapter eleven.

---

36 Dr. Sean McDonough, "New Testament Survey II—The End of All Things," Lecture, Gordon Conwell Theological Seminary, Jacksonville, Florida, May, 2017.

Let us give further evidence of why this woman is the Church. If you go back to the Old Testament once again, the Israelites were made to wander in the wilderness for forty years as punishment for their sin of not trusting God to give them success in the taking of the Promised Land **(Numbers 13-14)**. However, they were also there so that the younger generation, everyone under the age of twenty, who *would* be permitted to enter the Promised Land at the end of those forty years, could be strengthened and prepared for that entry by communing with God and learning about God through Moses' teachings. Fast forward to the New Testament and we see Jesus going into the wilderness for forty days to get strengthened and prepared for His mission while He communed with God the Father. So, while the wilderness is not a fun place to be, it is a place God uses to strengthen His people and draw them close to Him. John shows us this exact thing when he says that God nourished the woman in the wilderness. Again, this easily translates to the Church. It could mean that they are being strengthened and prepared by feeding on God's Word and/or communing with God. And we know that God is protecting them spiritually because we saw that in the big picture with the two witnesses.

We are not done with the proof yet! **Revelation 12:1** says, *"[She is] clothed with the sun."* **Psalm 84:11** says, *"For the Lord God is a sun and shield; the LORD bestows favor and honor. No good thing does he withhold from those who walk uprightly."* Also, **2 Corinthians 4:6** says, *"For God, who said, 'Let light shine out of darkness,' has shone in our hearts to give the light of the knowledge of the glory of God in the face of Jesus Christ."* These verses show us that the Church being clothed in the sun represents them being clothed with the Gospel of Christ. So, the woman being clothed in the sun means the Church is grounded in and protected by the light of the Gospel. The twelve stars represent all the people of God, as we have seen throughout this book.

And we will say one last thing about this woman. The interpretations of this woman representing Israel and the Church do not necessarily contradict one another. The true "Israel" in the Old Testament was not the geographical nation of Israel but all who put their faith in the promise of the coming Messiah. Parallel to that, the true "Church" in the New Testament is comprised of all of those who have put their faith in what the Messiah has done. The true Israel and the true Church are the same group of people. They are both God's people, both believers, and represented by the twenty-four elders and the 144,000 sealed.

Moving onto the moon in this vision, we see *"the moon under her feet."* This gives the indication that she is above the moon. This makes perfect sense when we understand that the moon represents the Law. The Church is able to bask in the light of the sun (the Gospel) and is no longer dependent upon the moon (the Law). The light of the Gospel does not blot out the light of the Law, but the light of the Gospel does outshine the light of the Law. **Isaiah 9:2** shows us this in the prophecy about the coming Christ: *"The people who walked in darkness have seen a great light; those who dwelt in a land of deep darkness, on them has light shone."*

Let's finish up these first six verses by delving into this *"great red dragon, with seven heads and ten horns, and on his heads seven diadems"* **(Rev. 12:3)**. Again, there is little doubt about who this is. This is Satan. The way Satan is described here harkens again back to the Old Testament to a beast known as the Leviathan. The Leviathan is mentioned in several passages in Scripture. For example, **Psalm 74:13-14**, which says, *"You divided the sea by your might; you broke the heads of the sea monsters on the waters. You crushed the heads of Leviathan; you gave him as food for the creatures of the wilderness."* The name Leviathan comes from the Hebrew meaning, "twisted or coiled."[37] The definition of its name, along with passages where it is mentioned in Scripture, indicate that it was a very large and very strong monster that was feared.

There is a lot of speculation as to what the Leviathan actually was. Some think it was an actual, now extinct, ancient sea creature that terrorized

---

37 "What was the leviathan the Bible talks about?," Got Questions Ministries, accessed March 21, 2021, https://www.compellingtruth.org/leviathan.html.

the people; others think it was a really big and nasty crocodile; and still, others think it was an allegory for Satan. There is no way to know for sure, but Scripture makes the argument that it is probably an allegory for Satan. For instance, **Job 40:19** says, *"He is the first of the works of God; let him who made him bring near his sword."* Everywhere the Leviathan is mentioned, Scripture makes clear that only God can tame this monster. As **Isaiah 27:1** tells us, *"In that day the LORD with his hard and great and strong sword will punish Leviathan the fleeing serpent, Leviathan the twisting serpent, and he will slay the dragon that is in the sea."* If you flip back to **Isaiah 26:21**, you can discern that **Isaiah 27** is speaking of the day of the Lord: *"For behold, the LORD is coming out from his place to punish the inhabitants of the earth for their iniquity, and the earth will disclose the blood shed on it and will no more cover its slain."* Given that only the Lord can kill this beast, it seems clear that the Leviathan is an allegory for Satan.

SATAN THROWN DOWN TO EARTH

Revelation 12:7-12 continues with the struggle between Satan and the church:

> Now war arose in heaven, Michael and his angels fighting against the dragon. And the dragon and his angels fought back, but he was defeated, and there was no longer any place for them in heaven. And the great dragon was thrown down, that ancient serpent, who is called the devil and Satan, the deceiver of the whole world—he was thrown down to the earth, and his angels were thrown down with him. And I heard a loud voice in heaven, saying, "Now the salvation and the power and the kingdom of our God and the authority of his Christ have come, for the accuser of our brothers has been thrown down, who accuses them day and night before our God. And they have conquered him by the blood of the Lamb and by the word of their testimony, for they loved not their lives even unto death. Therefore, rejoice, O heavens and you who dwell in them! But woe to you, O earth and sea, for the devil

has come down to you in great wrath, because he knows that his time is short!"

First, these verses are confirmation that the dragon is, in fact, Satan. We started chapter twelve by talking about how Satan wanted to devour Jesus, which is a picture of Satan trying to destroy Jesus at His crucifixion; but of course, he failed miserably. This passage is one of those already/not-yet passages. The already happened part of it is that Satan and the angels who followed him were cast out of Heaven and thrown to the Earth, which we see a full picture of in **Ezekiel 28**. Jesus became fully Man, ushered in His Kingdom, declared Himself King, and then completely defeated Satan at His resurrection. But as we know, Jesus has not brought that victory to full completion yet. So, in the meantime, God is allowing the devil and his demons to prowl around the Earth, messing with believers and enslaving unbelievers.

Since the Garden of Eden, Satan has been trying to get at God by destroying His people. And he continues to try and trip up believers in this interim period between Jesus' victory on the cross and resurrection and His Second Coming. There is a cosmic battle going on between Satan and his dominions and God's angels, who are protecting the Church. Again, this isn't new information. We see this same picture in **Daniel 10**. The angel Gabriel told Daniel that he had come from fighting the prince of Persia, who resisted him for twenty-one days, so Gabriel needed to call in Michael, the archangel, to help. This prince of Persia was not the human leader of the kingdom of Persia. He was not even a man. Gabriel was telling Daniel about a cosmic, spiritual battle that was going on. This prince was a fallen angel (one of Satan's minions). This battle between Satan's demons and God's angels will continue until Jesus comes back and delivers Satan and all his followers their ultimate fate.

Make no mistake—Satan knows Scripture. That is exactly why he was able to ensnare Adam and Eve into sinning. He quoted just enough of God's Word to *seem* credible, but he twisted them, wrapped them in a lie, leading

Adam and Eve into rebellion against God. This is the same thing he does to believers today. Since the devil knows Scripture, he knows he is on borrowed time. This is the reason that John says in **Revelation 12:12**, *"'Woe to you, O earth and sea, for the devil has come down to you in great wrath, because he knows that his time is short!'"* All through the tribulation (meaning now), until Jesus comes back, Satan will continue to attack as much as God allows him to, trying to take as many people down with him as he can, knowing that he will *"'come to a dreadful end and shall be no more forever'"* **(Ezek. 28:19)**.

ON THE WINGS OF EAGLES
Revelation 12:13-17 ends the chapter by saying:

> *And when the dragon saw that he had been thrown down to the earth, he pursued the woman who had given birth to the male child. But the woman was given the two wings of the great eagle so that she might fly from the serpent into the wilderness, to the place where she is to be nourished for a time, and times, and half a time. The serpent poured water like a river out of his mouth after the woman, to sweep her away with a flood. But the earth came to the help of the woman, and the earth opened its mouth and swallowed the river that the dragon had poured from his mouth. Then the dragon became furious with the woman and went off to make war on the rest of her offspring, on those who keep the commandments of God and hold to the testimony of Jesus. And he stood on the sand of the sea."*

Here again, we are getting a zoomed-in picture. This is another view of the first six verses of **Revelation 12**. Now that we have worked so hard to put verses into context and interpret the symbolism, understanding the first few verses of this passage is not difficult. The dragon pursues the woman, who had given birth to the male child. This is another picture of the cosmic war between Satan and the Church. We see that the Church is protected from the serpent in the wilderness for *"time, times, and half a time"*—which, if you remember, is the same as three-and-a-half years, forty-two months, and 1,260 days. So, this corresponds with **Revelation 12:6**, which said she had a place for her prepared by God for 1,260 days.

One difference in these verses compared to the first six verses in chapter twelve is that here, the woman is given eagle's wings. Throughout Scripture, the eagle is a symbol of the power of God. **Isaiah 40:31**, a very familiar verse, says, *"But they who wait for the LORD shall renew their strength; they shall mount up with wings like eagles; they shall run and not be weary, they shall walk and not faint."* Just like the woman is symbolic of the Church, soaring on eagle wings is symbolic of being strengthened and empowered by God. This makes perfect sense because God is using the 1,260 days that the Church is in the wilderness to refine her and commune with her as He protects her spiritually.

The next verses are not quite as easy to interpret. *"The serpent poured water like a river out of his mouth after the woman, to sweep her away with a flood"* **(Rev. 12:15)**. To gain an understanding of what the water pouring out of Satan's mouth is, we have to look ahead to **Revelation 17:15**, which says, *"And the angel said to me, 'The waters that you saw, where the prostitute is seated, are the peoples and multitudes and nations and language.'"*

Since Satan cannot destroy the woman—again, meaning the Church—because God is strengthening and protecting her, he will use unbelievers, who are already enslaved to him, to try and get at her. The next line in **Revelation 12:16** says, *"But the earth came to the help of the woman, and the earth opened its mouth and swallowed the river that the dragon poured from his mouth."* This is another picture of God protecting His Church from Satan and anyone else trying to destroy it. "The earth" is another allusion to God putting the Church in the wilderness. And what follows next in verse seventeen is predictable: *"Then the dragon became furious with the woman and went off to make war on the rest of her offspring, on those who keep the commandments of God and hold to the testimony of Jesus. And he stood on the sand of the sea."* Satan cannot destroy the Church, so he will try and mess with its individual believers instead. His standing *"on the sand of the sea"* is a segue into chapter thirteen.

THE FIRST BEAST

And I saw a beast rising out of the sea, with ten horns and seven heads, with ten diadems on its horns and blasphemous names on its heads. And the beast that I saw was like a leopard; its feet were like a bear›s, and its mouth was like a lion›s mouth. And to it the dragon gave his power and his throne and great authority. One of its heads seemed to have a mortal wound, but its mortal wound was healed, and the whole earth marveled as they followed the beast. And they worshiped the dragon, for he had given his authority to the beast, and they worshiped the beast, saying, "Who is like the beast, and who can fight against it?" **(Rev. 13:1-4)**.

We said that Satan standing *"on the sand of the sea"* was the segue into chapter thirteen. And here in **13:1**, we see why he was standing there. He, like John, was watching a beast rise out of the sea. The beast was part leopard, part bear, and part lion, with ten horns and seven heads. Once again, we go back to the Old Testament, this time to the book of Daniel, to find out about this beast.

Daniel sees a vision very similar. **Daniel 7:1-8** says:

In the first year of Belshazzar king of Babylon, Daniel saw a dream and visions of his head as he lay in his bed. Then he wrote down the dream and told the sum of the matter. Daniel declared, "I saw in my vision by night, and behold, the four winds of heaven were stirring up the great sea. And four great beasts came up out of the sea, different from one another. The first was like a lion and had eagles' wings. Then as I looked its wings were plucked off, and it was lifted up from the ground and made to stand on two feet like a man, and the mind of a man was given to it. And behold, another beast, a second one, like a bear. It was raised up on one side. It had three ribs in its mouth between its teeth; and it was told, 'Arise, devour much flesh.' After this I looked, and behold, another, like a leopard, with four wings of a bird on its back. And the beast had four heads, and dominion was given to it. After this I saw in the night visions, and behold, a fourth beast, terrifying and dreadful and exceedingly strong. It had great iron teeth; it devoured and broke in pieces and stamped what was left with its feet. It was

> *different from all the beasts that were before it, and it had ten horns. I considered the horns, and behold, there came up among them another horn, a little one, before which three of the first horns were plucked up by the roots. And behold, in this horn were eyes like the eyes of a man, and a mouth speaking great things.*

If you have studied the book of Daniel, you know that the four beasts Daniel saw were four earthly, evil kingdoms—Babylon, Medo-Persia, Greece, and Rome (respectively)—with the fourth beast also symbolizing Satan's kingdom. And if you know your history, you know that Babylon was once the most powerful kingdom on the Earth until it was conquered by the Medo-Persian Empire, who was conquered by the Greek Empire, who was overtaken by the Roman Empire. Each subsequent empire got more powerful, and each subsequent empire was more evil. All four of them oppressed God's people. This first beast that we see in **Revelation 13** is a combination of the four beasts in Daniel and the manifestation of the symbolism of the fourth beast. In other words, this beast represents all the evil rulers and governments of the world who have had Satan as their master and who have persecuted and oppressed God's people.

There is one difference between this beast and the one in Daniel, and that is that the beast in Revelation is wearing diadems, or crowns, on its ten horns. These crowns could be an indication that there will be times when it appears as if evil is winning and ruling the Earth. These verses are just as relevant today as they were to John's original audience! Aren't we dumbfounded to see people enthusiastically and passionately supporting some of the evil things being taught to our children or made into laws? Do we not cringe when we see just how corrupt some who are in positions of power are? Have there not been times, maybe as recent as today, throughout history, where it seemed as if evil was winning?

In verse three, John says, *"The whole earth marveled as they followed the beast."* John is talking about unbelievers, not believers. We will see that is the case when we get to verse eight. But first, look at the last verse in this section—verse four. Those who worship the beast say, *"'Who is like the beast and who can fight against it?"* These are not a troubled people crying out for help. These are an arrogant people saying smugly, "You can never win against us!" Does that have a familiar ring?!

Finishing out the verses pertaining to the first beast, **Revelation 13:5-8** says:

> *And the beast was given a mouth uttering haughty and blasphemous words, and it was allowed to exercise authority for forty-two months. It opened its mouth to utter blasphemies against God, blaspheming his name and his dwelling, that is, those who dwell in heaven. Also it was allowed to make war on the saints and to conquer them. And authority was given it over every tribe and people and language and nation, and all who dwell on earth will worship it, everyone whose name has not been written before the foundation of the world in the book of life of the Lamb who was slain.*

These verses reiterate what we just said. There will be evil leaders and governments whom God will allow to have authority over every tribe, people, language, and nation for a time. There is that number four again—tribe, people, language, nation. God will allow evil to have authority over the whole earth. And notice for how long it will have authority—forty-two months, which we have seen over and over symbolizes a period of suffering for Christians between Jesus' ascension and His Second Coming. Again, not a literal forty-two months, three-and-a-half years, or 1,260 days but a *"period of some time"* represented by these numbers.

ENDURANCE THROUGH PERSECUTION

We have all seen evil and corrupt governments blaspheme God and persecute Christians. This has been going on since Jesus' ascension. And just as things in Revelation get more and more intense as we get closer to Jesus' Second Coming, the persecution of Christians is definitely getting worse.

150 THE FINAL EXODUS

More than seventy million Christians have been martyred for their faith since the time that Jesus walked upon the Earth, according to an article in *Christianity Today*. Statistician David Barrett estimates that in the twentieth century, over three hundred thousand Christians a year were martyred. That means almost half of all Christians martyred throughout history were martyred during the twentieth century![38]

But there is great encouragement, as this book is meant to give. In verse eight, we see the proof that we mentioned earlier that John was speaking about unbelievers when he said in verse three of chapter thirteen, *"The whole earth marveled as they followed the beast."* Verse eight says, *"All who dwell on earth will worship it, everyone whose name has not been written before the foundation of the world in the book of life."* Obviously, those whose names have not been written in the book of life are those God has not elected to save. These are unbelievers, whose condition will not change. They will not have their hearts regenerated at some point by the Holy Spirit. These are a direct contrast to those who have their names written in the book of life, those God has saved or will save either before their death or when Jesus comes back. As **Ephesians 1:4** says, *"Even as he chose us in him before the foundation of the world, that we should be holy and blameless before him."* While things might get almost intolerable here on Earth, we will be able to endure it because God has sealed those who are His. Even if we are physically killed, we can rest in the knowledge that we will be with Jesus for all eternity.

This passage ends with a call for the endurance and the faith of the saints. God will protect His people spiritually. If we belong to Him, there is nothing Satan or any government can do to us that can take us from God's grasp. We need to know this and ingest it, like we talked about in the last chapter. That is how martyrs throughout history have endured and kept their faith amidst horrific persecution, and that is how we will do the same.

---

38 Christof Saver and Thomas Schrirrmacher, "Father forgive them," *Christian History Magazine* online, Issue 109, 2014, https://christianhistoryinstitute.org/magazine/issue/109-persecuted-church.

THE SECOND BEAST

Revelation 13 finishes up by describing another beast that will appear. **Revelation 13 11-18** says:

> Then I saw another beast rising out of the earth. It had two horns like a lamb and it spoke like a dragon. It exercises all the authority of the first beast in its presence, and makes the earth and its inhabitants worship the first beast, whose mortal wound was healed. It performs great signs, even making fire come down from heaven to earth in front of people, and by the signs that it is allowed to work in the presence of the beast it deceives those who dwell on earth, telling them to make an image for the beast that was wounded by the sword and yet lived. And it was allowed to give breath to the image of the beast, so that the image of the beast might even speak and might cause those who would not worship the image of the beast to be slain. Also it causes all, both small and great, both rich and poor, both free and slave, to be marked on the right hand or the forehead, so that no one can buy or sell unless he has the mark, that is, the name of the beast or the number of its name. This calls for wisdom: let the one who has understanding calculate the number of the beast, for it is the number of a man, and his number is 666.

There is so much to "decipher" here! First, notice that this second beast's purpose seems to be to point people to the first beast. Since the Garden of Eden, Satan has set up a counterfeit kingdom—one that mimics God's kingdom in many ways, but is in direct opposition with it. Just as Christians are to point people to Jesus, who does the will of Father, this second beast is being used to point people to the first beast, which are evil leaders, who do the will of Satan.

Something that is different in the two beasts is that the first beast rose out of the sea, and this second beast rises out of the earth. This tells us that this is a different beast. As verse twelve indicates, this second beast exercises all the authority of the first beast. These two beasts are working together. Pastor Joe Anaday from Emmaus Reformed Baptist Church has a great take on the second beast:

> If the first beast symbolizes political powers that persecute, the second beast symbolizes the political, religious, and economic entities that serve as agents who carry out the persecution of the church and the deception of the ungodly. These two powers should not be hard for us to identify in the world. It really is quite simple to understand the way in which these two powers, though different from one another, do indeed correspond to one another and cooperate.[39]

Since this second beast controls the economy, is it any wonder that it requires complete devotion in order for people to be able to buy and sell? As we discussed earlier, this was a huge problem in the trade guilds in the Roman Empire in the first century. We saw it in Nazi Germany in the 1930s and forties. We have seen it with some requiring people to show their Covid vaccination cards to be able to work in their jobs, attend college, or even eat in a restaurant in some cities. There are even calls to deny healthcare or the ability to shop in a grocery store to anyone who refuses to get the vaccine.

How about the beast's power in the political realm? Amy Coney Barrett was told she should not be a Supreme Court judge merely because she is Catholic and pro-life. Kamala Harris and others were vocal in saying that Christians and Christian organizations should be forced to provide funding for abortion and other things that go against their biblical beliefs under the guise of health care. We have seen people fired, doxed, canceled, prosecuted, and persecuted merely for their political affiliation. And, of course, we all watched the summer of 2020, as businesses were burned and looted by domestic terrorist organizations just for not "falling in line" with their mantras. And as of the writing of this book, there is no end in sight for any of this.

---

39   Joe Anaday, "The Beast Rising From The Earth: Revelation 13:11-18," Sermon, Emmaus Reformed Baptist Church, Hemet, California, September 24, 2017, http://emmausrbc.org/2017/09/24/sermon-beast-rising-earth-revelation-1311-18.

DARK POWERS

The passage tells us that this second beast *"performs great signs, even making fire come down from heaven to earth in front of people, and by the signs that it is allowed to work in the presence of the beast it deceives those who dwell on earth, telling them to make an image for the beast that was wounded by the sword and yet lived"* **(Rev. 13:13-14)**. Once again, we go back to the book of Exodus. If you recall, the Egyptian magicians were able to replicate the first two plagues God sent on Egypt. **Exodus 7:22** tells of the first plague of Nile turned to blood: *"But the magician of Egypt did the same by their secret arts."* And again, with the second plague of the frogs, **Exodus 8:7** says, *"But the magicians did the same by their secret arts and made frogs come up on the land of Egypt."*

Satan does have supernatural powers. He is not omniscient; he is not omnipotent; and he is not omnipresent. But God does allow him to have some dark powers. These dark powers enable him and his minions to possess unbelievers, whisper lies in the ears of believers, and perform some signs and wonders. This is what we saw in the verses from Exodus and what Paul warns us about in **2 Thessalonians 2:9-10a**: *"The coming of the lawless one is by the activity of Satan with all power and false signs and wonders, and with all wicked deception for those who are perishing."* And if we wonder why God allows this, Paul goes on to tell us in **2 Thessalonians 2:10b-12**, *"Because they [those perishing] refused to love the truth and so be saved. Therefore God sends them a strong delusion, so that they may believe what is false, in order that all may be condemned who did not believe the truth but had pleasure in unrighteousness."*

In a nutshell, Satan is able to perform signs and wonders so he can deceive unbelievers. John tells believers how to combat this in **1 John 4:1-6**:

> *Beloved, do not believe every spirit, but test the spirits to see whether they are from God, for many false prophets have gone out into the world. By this you know the Spirit of God: every spirit that confesses that Jesus Christ has come in the flesh is from God, and every spirit that does not confess Jesus is not from God. This is the spirit of the*

> antichrist, which you heard was coming and now is in the world already. Little children, you are from God and have overcome them, for he who is in you is greater than he who is in the world. They are from the world; therefore they speak from the world, and the world listens to them. We are from God. Whoever knows God listens to us; whoever is not from God does not listen to us. By this we know the Spirit of truth and the spirit of error.

Whether it is the false teaching of "Christian" preachers and teachers or the false teaching of Satan, we are called to discernment. The only way we will be able to recognize and stand against the lies of Satan and those who follow him is to know the Truth. We need to know God and know His Word.

Verse fifteen of chapter thirteen may give us pause. It says, *"And it was allowed to give breath to the image of the beast, so that the image of the beast might even speak and might cause those who would not worship the image of the beast to be slain."* Standing firm in our faith may lead to our death. Certainly, millions of Christians have paid those consequences. But not standing firm in our faith and denouncing Jesus just to save our physical life has much more dire consequences as we will see in the coming chapters.

666

We will finish out this chapter with the famous number, "666." People have speculated that this is the mark mentioned in verse seventeen that people will have to receive in order to buy and sell. But the verse says, *"This calls for wisdom: let the one who has understanding calculate the number of the beast, for it is the number of a man, and his number is 666"* **(Rev. 13:18)**. Once again, we need to put the work in to understand this. The number three is a number of completeness that has a Trinitarian reference. The number seven is a number of perfect completeness. So the number 777 would be perfect perfection. In other words, the Trinity. The number six, on the other hand is a number of incompleteness. So a number comprised of three sixes is perfect incompleteness, or as incomplete as you can possibly get. This is the number used for the beast. It shows just how evil it is, and that it is the anti-Trinity, or the counterfeit Trinity. Another example of Satan's counterfeit kingdom trying to mimic God's kingdom.

We see Satan's counterfeit kingdom throughout Scripture. He uses fake gods, fake worship, fake sacrifices, fake promises, and even a fake bride. All are meant to draw God's people away from Jesus and draw them into sin. We will take a closer look at this fake kingdom—and especially the fake bride—as we move on in the book of Revelation, but all of this is why it is crucial that believers do not fall in line and follow the beasts or any other false teaching, regardless of the price we may have to pay.

CHAPTER 7
STUDY GUIDE

GETTING YOUR TOES WET
What are some examples of when it looks like evil is winning?

What are some things our government, or other governments, are trying to force believers to comply with, even though they go against God's Word? What consequences have you seen for those who refuse?

More than seventy million Christians have been martyred for their faith since the time that Jesus walked upon the Earth, according to an article in *Christianity Today*. David Barrett, a statistician, estimates that in the twentieth century, over three hundred thousand Christians a year were martyred. That means almost half of all Christians martyred throughout history were martyred during the twentieth century! *Can you think of someone who has been martyred for their faith in the twentieth or twenty-first centuries?*

DIVING IN DEEP
The woman clothed in the sun in **Revelation 12:1** represents the Church. The sun she is clothed with represents the Gospel. The Church is grounded in and protected by the light of the Gospel. The twelve stars represent all the

people of God. *How do these verses show that the Church and believers are clothed, grounded in, and protected by the Gospel?*

Isaiah 9:2-7

Romans 10:9-13

Ephesians 1:7-14

1 John 4:9-19

The fall of Satan is recorded in Ezekiel 28 under the heading, *"Prophecy against the Prince of Tyre."* The city of Tyre was the recipient of some of the strongest prophetic condemnations in the Bible. God often uses real empires as symbols for evil (e.g. the whore of Babylon). The same is the case here. Read **Ezekiel 28**. You will quickly realize that this could not be talking about an earthly prince but is, instead, about the prince of darkness. *What does **Ezekiel 28** tell us about Satan?*

In **Revelation 12:14**, we are told that the woman is given the two wings of the great eagle so that she might fly from the serpent. Throughout Scripture, the eagle is used a symbol of the power of God. *How do these verse show that?*

Exodus 19:4-6

Deuteronomy 28:47-50

Jeremiah 48:40-43

Psalm 103:1-8

BACK ON DRY LAND

Make no mistake—Satan knows Scripture. That is exactly why he was able to ensnare Adam and Eve into sinning. He quoted just enough of God's Word to *seem* credible; but he twisted them, wrapped them in a lie, and thus, led Adam and Eve into rebellion against God. This is the same thing he does to believers today. Sometimes, he uses false teachers to cause believers to believe lies and to sin. These false teachers can seem like they are teaching the Bible, but they are not. They may claim to love Jesus, but they do not. False teaching is epidemic, with much of it coming from inside the Church. *How do these verses say we can protect ourselves from false teachers?*

Matthew 7:15-20

2 Corinthians 11:12-15

Colossians 2:6-8

1 John 4:1-6

CHAPTER 8
THE LORD'S DAY OF VENGEANCE

Warning signs are a part of everyday life. Cars come with warning signals for just about everything. The tire pressure monitor light is one of the most common yet most ignored because it does not just appear when you are about to have a totally flat tire or even when you have actually got a puncture. The light tends to come on rather frequently, caused by things like an outside temperature change that is noticeable or when one or more tires is just out of the optimal range. It is easy to get complacent to the point that we do not even notice the light is on anymore; and because we see it every day, it has lost its effectiveness as a warning. While we may be able to ignore the tire pressure warning light without encountering any major issues, there are warnings we should not ignore, like the coolant level warning light. Ignore that long enough or continue being complacent, never checking your coolant level, and at some point, you will encounter a flashing red warning light telling you that your engine is overheated, and you must stop immediately. At that point, it is too late. You have ruined your engine, and your car is dead on the road.

The church at Sardis became complacent and did not keep a watch out for their enemies. There was no warning that the enemy was on their doorstep, and because of it, they got sacked twice. No one knows the day Jesus is going to return. **First Thessalonians 5:2** says, *"For you yourselves are fully aware that* *the day of the Lord will come like a thief in the night."* At that point, it will be too late. Just like Noah warned the people of his day of the impending flood, mankind is not left without warnings of Jesus' return and their need of a Savior. **Revelation 14** contains warnings for both believers and unbelievers. No one is without excuse when it comes to heeding the warnings in the Bible.

God has made Himself known through the world He created. **Romans 1:18-23** says:

> *For the wrath of God is revealed from heaven against all ungodliness and unrighteousness of men, who by their unrighteousness suppress the truth. For what can be known about God is plain to them, because God has shown it to them. For his invisible attributes, namely, his eternal power and divine nature, have been clearly perceived, ever since the creation of the world in the things that have been made. So they are without excuse. For although they knew God, they did not honor him as God or give thanks to him, but they became futile in their thinking, and their foolish hearts were darkened. Claiming to be wise, they became fools, and exchanged the glory of the immortal God for images resembling mortal man and birds and animals and creeping things.*

Since nature itself reveals to us that there is a Creator, no one is without excuse.

ON THE MOUNTAINTOP

Revelation 14 starts out with a vision of Jesus with the 144,000, the symbol of the Church from chapter seven. **Revelation 14:1** says, *"Then I looked, and behold, on Mount Zion stood the Lamb, and with him 144,000 who had his name and his Father's name written on their foreheads."*

This is a picture of those *"could stand"* from **Revelation 7**. Now, they are standing on Mount Zion with their victorious Savior, Who won their victory for them through His shed blood. It is a picture of the already-victorious saints who have made it through and symbolizes all the saints one day. **Obadiah 1:17** says, *"But in Mount Zion there shall be those who escape, and* *it shall be holy, and the house of Jacob shall possess their own possessions."* Mount Zion is a picture of Heaven from the Old Testament. It is the place of the believers' inheritance and where *"the LORD will reign . . . from this time forth and forevermore"* **(Micah 4:7)**.

HOLY WAR

This view from the mountain is from an army's vantage point—the high point—the place of looking down on your enemies. **Revelation 14** shows the fulfillment of **Psalm 2**, a Messianic Psalm called, *"The Reign of the LORD's Anointed,"* where the nations and their kings are raging and plotting against Jesus, the King, while He is reigning from on high.

There is a lot of war imagery in the Bible. But unlike the idea popularized by memes on social media of Christians in old-school battle armor, Jesus does not need people to fight for Him. He has already won the battle! Even in Old Testament Holy War, it was God Who won the battle. His people were just the "mop-up crew" taking care of the terrified and often few enemies of God who were left. Christians are not now or in the future physically fighting with a sword for Jesus.

Satan and his demons will fight by trying to impede the spiritual growth of believers through several tactics—by accusing them of their sin when they are already forgiven, using deception through false teaching, and also through temptation. **James 4:7** says, *"Submit yourselves therefore to God. Resist the devil, and he will flee from you."* A Christian's main battle is against his or her own sin. It is by saying no to ourselves and obeying God that we fight. That includes both sins of *commission*—sin we take action to commit (whether intentional or not)—and sins of *omission*—those things we know we should do, but do not, as **James 4:17** warns: *"So whoever knows the right thing to do and fails to do it, for him it is sin."* Our battle is against the world's temptations and our sinful flesh. These two enemies need no help from our third enemy, Satan, to get us to act ungodly. In light of that, most Christians should not give Satan or his demons an inordinate amount of thought. We need to be alert, but not looking for the boogeyman around every corner. Our most persistent enemy looks back at us from the mirror.

Another of Satan's designs is to oppose evangelism and ministry work. Martin Luther, father of the Protestant Reformation, claims he was under severe attack. It makes sense that Martin Luther would be under personal attack. His work and the work of the other Reformers was going to help rescue countless people from the dominion of darkness from the 1500s throughout the rest of history.

However, the picture Revelation largely shows us is Satan trying to derail the Gospel going forth through deception, oppression, and persecution of whole groups of believers—churches, cities, and nations. How do these groups of believers fight? The same way they fight individually! By resisting the devil, keeping free from sin, standing firm in their faith without wavering, and marching forward with the true and complete Gospel message without compromise. To quote James C. Osman II, pastor of Kootenai Community Church in Kootenai, Idaho:

> We are not called to go crashing and smashing down the gates of hell, claiming dominion, winning back territory, exorcising demons, binding the devil, casting him down, away, or out, or ordering him to the pit of hell. Scripture does not teach us to develop a strategy of spiritual warfare based upon personal experience, anecdote, or conversations with demons. We are not to pursue a strategy that is marked by rebuking, binding, insulting, or arguing with Satan and his demons. We are not involved in a war for territory, but for truth.[40]

Fighting sin, standing for biblical truth, and spreading the Gospel may not seem nearly as fun as picturing yourself in battle gear with a real sword. To some, it may not seem as spiritual to fight Satan and his demons with Truth

---

40   James C. Osman, "The Posture of a Soldier," in *Truth or Territory: A Biblical Approach to Spiritual Warfare* (Kootenai: James C. Osman II and Kootenai Community Church Publishing, 2015), 203.

rather than pleading the blood, putting up hedges of protection, binding demons, rebuking Satan, or any of the ways Pastor Osman mentioned. But we have to fight the way that Scripture tells us, and none of those tactics mentioned are biblical. In fact, even rebuking Satan should be left for God to do, as **Jude 1:9** tells us: *"But when the archangel Michael, contending with the devil, was disputing about the body of Moses, he did not presume to pronounce a blasphemous judgment, but said, 'The Lord rebuke you.'"* If the archangel Michael did not rebuke Satan, we should not presume to think it is our job. Satan and his demons are real, but they are totally under God's sovereign control. They cannot do anything without His permission. We need to fight how He tells us to in Scripture.

WHO DO I BELONG TO?

Why all this talk about sin and fighting Satan? **Revelation 14:1** says the Church will have the name of Jesus and the Father marked on their foreheads by the Holy Spirit. Just like the "mark of the beast" does not signify an actual tattoo or other marking, this is not an actual mark either. It is a sign meaning *ownership*, and in this case, the Owner is God. This mark stands in direct contrast to the mark of the beast from the last chapter. The mark of the beast—666—symbolized perfect *incompleteness*; this mark is the mark of *perfect completeness*.

Taking the "mark of the beast" for the people in the seven churches would have been doing things like confessing Caesar as Lord or joining the trade guilds that required them to sin like the church in Pergamum or the one in Thyatira. Even though refusing these things could result in extreme hardship or even death, doing them was sinful. Having what seems like (from a human perspective) good reasons or valid reasons for sin never changes the fact that it is sin.

In 2020, when the Covid-19 pandemic became worldwide, a lot of people were asking if getting the vaccine was "getting the mark of the beast." Taking the mark of the beast is doing something that requires compromising your faith. Many vaccines, including at least some of the Covid ones, use fetal cells obtained through abortion in various steps of vaccine-making and testing. However, they are not all the same. If we are required to get a vaccine to shop, or fly on a plane, or as requirement to work to feed our families, it is something to research and consider.

The question we should be asking ourselves when we read about these marks is, "Who am I owned by—Satan or God?" You either worship Satan and the things of the world, or you worship God, which means saying no to any compromise. To quote Jesus from the Sermon on the Mount in **Matthew 5-7** and from **Luke 12:34**, *"For where your treasure is, there will your heart be also."* That is not just a lighthearted one-liner from Jesus reminding us not to love our money too much. In context, Jesus was asking for single-minded devotion; and further in the text, He lays out the realities of following Him, which include possibly losing your life!

THE SOUND OF VICTORY

Revelation 14:2-5 says:

> *And I heard a voice from heaven like the roar of many waters and like the sound of loud thunder. The voice I heard was like the sound of harpists playing on their harps, and they were singing a new song before the throne and before the four living creatures and before the elders. No one could learn that song except the 144,000 who had been redeemed from the earth. It is these who have not defiled themselves with women, for they are virgins. It is these who follow the Lamb wherever he goes. These have been redeemed from mankind as firstfruits for God and the Lamb, and in their mouth no lie was found, for they are blameless.*

The "voice" John hears thundering *"like the roar of many waters"* are the voices of the great multitude of the redeemed. They are the *"firstfruits,"* but the number 144,000 tells us that they symbolize all believers. They are praising and singing as one voice. We will see them worshiping again when we get to **Revelation 19:6**, crying out, *"Hallelujah! For the Lord our God the Almighty* *reigns.'"* According to **Revelation 18:22**, these sounds will be silenced for the wicked. The beauty of music will not be heard. Neither will the sound of victory—only the sounds of the agony of defeat.

This "new song" sung by the saints is the celebration of God's triumph, through Jesus, over sin, Satan, and death. God's people always celebrate His victories over His enemies. They are not gloating; they are praising God for His salvation, as when Miriam led the Israelites in song after God brought the Israelites through the Red Sea, closing it over Pharaoh and his army, singing, *"'Sing to the LORD, for he has triumphed gloriously; the horse and his rider he has thrown into the sea'"* **(Exod. 15:21)**. John wrote about the new song to remind the seven churches of Christ's victory that was already won.

WARNING. WARNING. WARNING!

Believers in Heaven are pure. They are exclusively devoted to Jesus. For them, there is no more having one foot in the world and one foot with God. In Heaven, believers will not even have one pinky toenail devoted to the world anymore. The saints—these *"virgins"* who *"have not defiled themselves with women"* **(Rev. 14:4)**—are a contrast to wicked Babylon, who is often referred to using derogatory sexual terms. The idea comes from God's rules for Holy War when Israel was taking over and/or protecting the Promised Land. Israel's army was not to "defile" themselves by having sex during times of Holy War. It was a sign of specially devoting themselves to God, in contrast to Babylon, who is referred to as the harlot in Revelation. There is no spiritual adultery or idolatry found in these sanctified saints.

John saw in his vision three angels giving warnings to everyone throughout the Earth. The first angel is going out through all the Earth with the eternal message of the good news of the Gospel and a warning: *"'Fear God and give him glory, because the hour of his judgment has come, and worship him who made heaven and earth, the sea and the springs of water'"* **(Rev. 14:7)**. The hour for judgment is here, but God is merciful. Like the passage from **Romans 1:20** says, no one is *"without excuse"* because God has made Himself evident through His creation. This first angel is telling unbelievers throughout the world to acknowledge what they know is true. As **Proverbs 9:10** says, *"The fear of the LORD is the beginning of wisdom, and the knowledge of the Holy One is insight."* It is time to give God the glory and honor He deserves, repent, and believe in His Son, Whom He sent, because time is running out.

This is also an admonition to churches—the leaders and congregants—to fear God, not the beast! Pattern yourselves after the Philadelphia and Smyrna churches. Do not take the mark just to feed your belly! Do not bow to the emperor just to save your life. Do not concede that it is okay for people to pick which gender they want to be when Scripture clearly says, *"For **you** formed my inward parts; you knitted me together in my mother's womb"* **(Psalm 139:13**, emphasis added**)**. Do not succumb to the tolerance of worldly ideas that go against Scripture, becoming spiritually adulterous. As **James 4:4** says, *"Do you not know that friendship with the world is enmity with God? Therefore whoever wishes to be a friend of the world makes himself an enemy of God."*

Trust God, the Creator of Heaven and earth and everything in it! This is a real call to perseverance under tribulation—a call to obey God, not cave to worldly pressures or temptations, like Moses, who—though raised by Pharaoh's daughter—*"when he was grown up, refused to be called the son of Pharaoh's daughter, choosing rather to be mistreated with the people of God than to enjoy the fleeting pleasures of sin. He considered the reproach of Christ greater wealth than the treasures of Egypt, for he was looking to the reward"* **(Heb. 11:24-26)**.

The second angel is taking what the first one said even further, saying, *"'Fallen, fallen is Babylon the great, she who made all nations drink the wine of the passion of her sexual immorality'"* **(Rev. 14:8)**. First century Christians would have recognized Babylon as the city that opposes God. It is the personification of sin and indulgence. Like the imagery of a spotless virgin, this is not talking about sexual immorality in and of itself. The words "sexual immorality" are used here to mean anything we love more than God, which is committing spiritual adultery. The angel's words also remind them of the truth—Babylon has fallen.

She may have been a great city at one time—she may have looked really, really awesome from the outside—but she is gone! In light of that, do not fall for her! Do not fall for the lie that there is freedom in having sex with whomever or whenever you want outside of marriage. Do not fall for the lie that the baby inside your womb is just a ball of flesh and not a real human who is capable of feeling pain until after he or she is born. Both are sin that will have earthly and spiritual consequences. There is no victory in sinful, worldly pleasures—only agony. Babylon has fallen. Fear God and give Him glory.

We come to a third angel in **Revelation 14:9-11**:

> *And another angel, a third, followed them, saying with a loud voice, "If anyone worships the beast and its image and receives a mark on his forehead or on his hand, he also will drink the wine of God's wrath, poured full strength into the cup of his anger, and he will be tormented with fire and sulfur in the presence of the holy angels and in the presence of the Lamb. And the smoke of their torment goes up forever and ever, and they have no rest, day or night, these worshipers of the beast and its image, and whoever receives the mark of its name."*

HELL

Jesus gives believers a reason to have hope and to endure—God is going to bring judgment on the wicked. Some people struggle with the fact that God's going to bring judgment on anyone, but God is not only kind and merciful—He is also just! Once the Babylon wine is gone, the wicked will drink the wine of God's wrath. That is the cup of wrath Jesus drank for all of those who trust in Him for the forgiveness of their sin. The wicked will drink that cup themselves.

The notion of Hell being a place without God is untrue, according to verse ten. That notion comes from **2 Thessalonians 1:9** because some versions say something similar to *"will suffer eternal destruction, away from the presence of the Lord"* (emphasis added), but the idea of being away from God's presence does not mean that He will not be there. It means the opposite of "seeing the face of the Lord," which is an expression denoting *blessedness*. The wicked certainly will be away from God's blessing. Instead, they will get God's full-strength anger and wrath and be tormented *"in the presence of the holy angels and in the presence of the Lamb."* There is no escaping God and being left alone! God is omnipresent—He is everywhere at all times!

All those who do not belong to God *"will drink the wine of God's wrath, poured full strength into the cup of his anger"* and will be *"tormented with fire and sulfur"* **(Rev. 14:10)**. Is Hell going to be literally burning sulfur? Maybe and maybe not. But even if the description is totally symbolic, it is obviously going to be excruciating, and there will not be any rest from it day or night, *forever and ever*. However, despite the fact that this and many other verses speak of unending torment for the wicked, there are some theologians who believe in something called "annihilationism," sometimes called "conditional immortality."

Annihilationism is the belief that you are immortal if you are a believer, but all unbelievers are "snuffed out" or, in other words, "annihilated," meaning that they cease to exist. This idea comes from the wicked *"going to destruction"* in **2 Peter 3:7**, but the word for "destruction" comes from the word *apóleia* meaning, "eternal ruin, loss, perishing, causing someone or something to be completely severed—cut off entirely from what could or should have been."[41] Some also say annihilationism is supported from **Isaiah 1:28**, which says, *"But rebels and sinners shall be broken together, and those who forsake the LORD shall be consumed."* But the verses following make it clear that it does not mean "destroyed." **Isaiah 1:31** ends the passage about the wicked, saying, *"And the strong shall become tinder, and his work a spark, and both of them shall burn together, with none to quench them."* The passages used to support the notion of annihilationism do not teach that the wicked will cease to exist. That is why it is important for pastors to clarify if they say things like, "Come

---

41 *Strong's Concordance*, s.v., "Apóleia," Bible Hub.com, accessed March 24, 2021, https://biblehub.com/greek/684.htm.

to Jesus for eternal life." We all have eternal life; the difference is where we will spend it.

Annihilationism can be a comforting thought to the unsaved. To believe that you can live life in whatever manner pleases you, knowing you will suffer wrath for a while but eventually just cease to exist, does not sound nearly as bad as eternal suffering. Some believers like the idea of annihilationism, too, because to them, it gets God "off the hook" somehow; it seems more kind and loving that He does not make someone be punished for all of eternity. But we cannot change what the Bible says to suit our own ideas. Hell is real, and it is forever.

The warning of the three angels in **Revelation 14** ends with the second of the seven beatitudes. *"'Blessed are the dead who die in the Lord from now on.' 'Blessed indeed,' says the Spirit, 'that they may rest from their labors, for their deeds follow them'"* **(Rev. 14:13b)**.

THE HARVEST OF THE RIGHTEOUS

Someday, the warnings will end. **Revelation 14:14** says, *"Then I looked, and behold, a white cloud, and seated on the cloud one like a son of man, with a golden crown on his head, and a sharp sickle in his hand."*

This is Jesus coming with His sharp sickle to reap all the elect who are still living on the Earth at the time of His Second Coming. These saints are the wheat in the parable of the wheat and the tares. God the Father uses a fourth angel in this passage to tell the His Son, *"Put in your sickle, and reap, for the hour to reap has come, for the harvest of the earth is fully ripe"* **(Rev. 14:15)**. This is in accordance with **Matthew 24:36-44**, which says,

> *"But concerning that day and hour no one knows, not even the angels of heaven, nor the Son, but the Father only. For as were the days of Noah, so will be the coming of the Son of Man. For as in those days before the flood they were eating and drinking, marrying and giving in marriage, until the day when Noah entered the ark, and they were unaware until the flood came and swept them all away, so will be the*

> coming of the Son of Man. Then two men will be in the field; one will be taken and one left. Two women will be grinding at the mill; one will be taken and one left. Therefore, stay awake, for you do not know on what day your Lord is coming. But know this, that if the master of the house had known in what part of the night the thief was coming, he would have stayed awake and would not have let his house be broken into. Therefore you also must be ready, for the Son of Man is coming at an hour you do not expect."

Then John tells us Christ *"swung his sickle across the earth, and the earth was reaped"* **(Rev. 14:16)** taking the remaining members of His Church up to Heaven to join the "first fruit" saints already there on Mount Zion, right before the final judgment and the new heavens and earth.

THE GRAPES OF WRATH

"Let the nations stir themselves up and come up to the Valley of Jehoshaphat; for there I will sit to judge all the surrounding nations. Put in the sickle, for the harvest is ripe" **(Joel 3:12-13)**.

There is another harvest—the harvest of the wicked. This is the harvest Jesus explained in **Matthew 13:38-42**:

> The weeds are the sons of the evil one, and the enemy who sowed them is the devil. The harvest is the end of the age, and the reapers are angels. Just as the weeds are gathered and burned with fire, so will it be at the end of the age. The Son of Man will send his angels, and they will gather out of his kingdom all causes of sin and all law-breakers, and throw them into the fiery furnace. In that place there will be weeping and gnashing of teeth.

By the time of Jesus' Second Coming, the wicked grape clusters will be fully ripe. They will have drunk their wine of wickedness to the very dregs and are full, ready to be thrown into the winepress of God's wrath. In his vision, John saw another angel come from the heavenly temple with a sharp sickle, and another come from the altar. At His command, the sickles were put to the clusters of grapes fully ripe with sin and wickedness, and they were harvested.

TRAMPLING OUT THE VINTAGE

"Go in, tread, for the winepress is full. The vats overflow, for their evil is great" **(Joel 3:13)**.

Revelation 14:20 says, *"And the winepress was trodden outside the city, and blood flowed from the winepress, as high as a horse's bridle, for 1,600 stadia."* The amount of blood that flows from the winepress is equivalent to being 184 miles. This is a picture of Jesus from **Isaiah 63:1-6**:

> *Who is this who comes from Edom, in crimsoned garments from Bozrah, he who is splendid in his apparel, marching in the greatness of his strength? "It is I, speaking in righteousness, mighty to save." Why is your apparel red, and your garments like his who treads in the winepress? "I have trodden the winepress alone, and from the peoples no one was with me; I trod them in my anger and trampled them in my wrath; their lifeblood spattered on my garments, and stained all my apparel. For the day of vengeance was in my heart, and my year of redemption had come. I looked, but there was no one to help; I was appalled, but there was no one to uphold; so my own arm brought me salvation, and my wrath upheld me. I trampled down the peoples in my anger; I made them drunk in my wrath, and I poured out their lifeblood on the earth."*

The nations trampled Christ's Church; now, He's trampling them. Is this hyperbole? Probably. Regardless, it is a picture of horrible suffering under the wrath of God. Is it actually a human winepress? Probably not. But it is the example used, so we can assume the pain and suffering will be horrendous.

NO EXCUSES, NO ESCAPE

Regardless of whether or not they are believers, most people believe there is some sort of Hell or punishment for the wicked. They *want* to believe that because they want to see the "really bad" people go there and suffer. People like Hitler but not people like themselves. But no one is righteous enough to please God. **Romans 3:23** says, *"All have sinned, and fall short of the glory of God."*

Believers understand this truth and realize that the only way of salvation is to have Jesus' perfect record of sinlessness stand in place of their own. Someday, God will say, "Enough." We do not know when that day is.

And if you are thinking, "There is no God," **Psalm 14:1** says you are a fool. You are corrupt, and your acts are vile. There is no excuse and no escape.

CHAPTER 8

STUDY GUIDE

GETTING YOUR TOES WET

How would you explain to someone what constitutes belonging to God or to Satan?

To whom would others around you say you belong? What proof would they cite?

DIVING IN DEEP

The first angel represented the Gospel going throughout the whole earth. The parable of the soils in **Matthew 13:3b-9** gives us a complete look at the human condition in regard to salvation. *Based on those verses, what remains the same throughout the parable?*

What do these corresponding verses show us is the spiritual condition of the different groups in the parable?

Matthew 13:10-12; 2 Corinthians 4:4

Matthew 5:11-12; Galatians 1:6

Matthew 6:19-24; 1 Timothy 4:10

John 15:5; Colossians 1:5-6

Read **Matthew 13:18-23.** *What does Jesus say about the soils?*

A Christian is not saved because of his or her own works, or based on behavior, yet we are warned over and over throughout the Bible about sin. *What do these verses say about this?*
Psalm 32:5

1 John 1:9

1 John 3:4

Hebrews 10:26

BACK ON DRY LAND

How would you argue that annihilationism is not biblical to someone who is a proponent of the concept?

How would you stand against things you are confronted with in the world that are contrary to Scripture?

How about within your church?

CHAPTER 9

TIME'S UP! THE BATTLE OF ARMAGEDDON

In the study guide for chapter four, we looked at some verses that spoke about God's patience and long suffering. **Numbers 14:18** provides us with a good summary of what God's patience looks like. *"'The Lord is slow to anger and abounding in steadfast love, forgiving iniquity and transgression, but he will by means clear the guilty, visiting the iniquity of the fathers on the children, to the third and fourth generation.'"* God destroyed the Earth by a flood in approximately 2500 B.C. Add those twenty-five hundred years to the over two thousand years since Jesus' time, and you have over forty-five hundred years of God withholding His full judgment on the wicked. If that does not define *"slow to anger and abounding in steadfast love,"* we are not sure what does! God's patience has a purpose.

In the first fourteen chapters of Revelation, we have seen God's purpose in patience being played out. As **Romans 2:4** tells us, *"Do you presume on the riches of his kindness and forbearance and patience, not knowing that God's kindness is meant to lead you to repentance?"* Parts of what we have read thus far may have been difficult for some to digest, but the judgments God has and will release in the seals and trumpets is not complete judgment. They are partial judgments. They only destroy a portion of people, land, sea life, etc. And of course, this is to give those remaining a chance to repent of their sins against our holy, almighty God. But as we have also seen, many have not and will not repent.

The verse in **Romans 2:4** has a follow-up in **Romans 2:5**: *"But because of your hard and impenitent heart you are storing up wrath for yourself on the day of wrath when God's righteous judgment will be revealed."* God will not be patient forever. There will come a time when He says, "Time's up!" We see how this plays out in chapters fifteen and sixteen of Revelation through the bowl judgments.

In contrast to the seal and trumpet judgments, which are partial judgments, the seven bowl judgments that we will look at in this chapter are complete. They represent God's final wrath on the wicked. Again, these are all the same set of judgments, just at different intensities. The seal judgments were unleashed on one-fourth of the population, the trumpets on one-third, and the bowls on all.

Revelation 15:1 says, *"Then I saw another sign in heaven, great and amazing, seven angels with seven plagues, which are the last, for with them the wrath of God is finished."* Here is another big picture view. In one sentence, John has summarized that God's patience has run out and He will complete His judgment and wrath using these angels as his agents.

As always, after the big picture is given, a zoomed-in look of specificities follows. John is giving a summary of what he is about to zoom in on later in chapter fifteen and in chapter sixteen.

Although the bowl judgments are the same set of judgments as the seals and trumpets, they are a little more complex because they are the completion of the judgments, meaning they are unleashed on one hundred percent of the unbelieving world. Scholars are split as to whether any believers will be on earth during this time. There is just no solid evidence either way, so we are going to take the route of every brilliant theologian we look to for insight and say that we just do not know. What we do know, though, is that even if believers are on earth when God unleashes His complete wrath on the wicked, they will be protected.

Revelation is the ultimate fulfillment of Exodus—it is the final exodus. We will see a lot of similarities between the bowl judgments and the plagues that God sent to Egypt. If you recall, during the last seven plagues, God kept His people safe, and no harm came to them. That is how it will be if believers are still on earth when the bowl judgments are unleashed.

One last note before we dive in; John starts by saying, *"I saw another sign."* Just as at other times in this book, John is signaling that what he is about to describe is symbolism, not literal. This does not mean that some of what he will describe might not happen as he describes—we would never put God in a box like that—but for the most part, Jesus, through John, has given us pictures to help us understand things our finite minds cannot fully grasp.

PULLING BACK THE CURTAIN AGAIN

Before we get to the bowl judgments, we get another "behind the curtain" glimpse into Heaven. These glimpses into Heaven have occurred before John being shown each of the set of judgments. As with everything with God, there is a purpose for this. Remember, Revelation is meant to encourage persecuted believers. These glimpses into Heaven before depictions of all three sets of judgment serve two purposes to that end. First, they show those of us on earth that this life is not all there is. Whatever we may be going through right now, the reality is that there is something so phenomenal waiting for us, our minds can barely grasp it. The other purpose is to show a stark contrast between those who belong to God and those who do not. While that contrast may not be evident in this earthly realm, it certainly is in the spiritual realm. And someday, either by death or Jesus' Second Coming, it will be evident to all.

This heavenly interlude is described in **Revelation 15:2-3**:

> *And I saw what appeared to be a sea of glass mingled with fire—and also those who had conquered the beast and its image and the number of its name, standing beside the sea of glass with harps of God in their hands. And they sing the song of Moses, the servant of God, and the song of the Lamb, saying, "Great and amazing are your deeds, O Lord God the Almighty! Just and true are your ways, O King of the nations!*

With all the references back to the Old Testament, you might think the preceding verses are a quote from **Psalm 90** written by Moses or perhaps from Moses' song in **Deuteronomy 32**. But they are not, at least not exactly. These verses in **Revelation 15** are actually a fulfillment of Moses' song and psalm. Moses' Old Testament narratives looked forward to the day when all nations would bow down and worship God, when the perfect justice of God would be accomplished, and when God's holiness would be revered by all. For example, **Deuteronomy 32:43** says, *"'Rejoice with him, O heavens; bow down to him, all gods, for he avenges the blood of his children and takes vengeance on his adversaries. He repays those who hate him and cleanses his people's land.'"* Moses is prophesying that this scene will occur someday, and here it is in Revelation being fulfilled.

One more note on this passage before we move on. These believers that John gets a glimpse of are standing beside a sea of glass mingled with fire. If you remember, the throne of God was described as a sea of glass. God's people are worshipping at God's throne.

ALREADY/NOT-YET OCCURRED

Revelation 15:6-8 shows us things are about to get real:

> *And out of the sanctuary came the seven angels with the seven plagues, clothed in pure, bright linen, with golden sashes around their chests. And one of the four living creatures gave to the seven angels seven golden bowls full of the wrath of God who lives forever and ever, and the sanctuary was filled with smoke from the glory of God and from his power, and no one could enter the sanctuary until the seven plagues of the seven angels were finished.*

The seven angels have received the seven bowl judgments that they will pour out on the Earth. But do not miss a very significant thing that happens in verse eight. **Revelation 15:8** says, *"And the sanctuary was filled with smoke from the glory of God and from his power, and no one could enter the sanctuary until the* *seven plagues of the seven angels were finished."* At first read, we might be tempted to think this is just God protecting believers—His Church—from what the angels are about to unleash, but that is not the only thing going on. This verse is a picture of Jesus removing His intercession from mankind. Remember, for those who are saved, Jesus is the Intercessor between us and God. This is God's judgment on unbelievers coming to fulfillment. This means Jesus will not be interceding for anyone else. God has completed separating the wheats and tares—His people from those who are not. For those who have not already repented and made Jesus their Lord and Savior, time is up. There is no chance for them to repent and be saved anymore.

This scenario is ultimately what some of the prophets spoke about, like Jeremiah in **Jeremiah 13:16** when he said, *"Give glory to the L*ORD *your God before he brings darkness, before your feet stumble on the twilight mountains, and while you look for light he turns it into gloom and makes it deep darkness."* This is an example of an already/not-yet verse like we have seen throughout Revelation. Jeremiah was writing about something that was currently going on—the nation of Judah was steeped in idolatry and syncretism. He warned them to repent before God sent them into exile like He had the northern nation of Israel. However, as with much of Scripture, there is a bigger message that makes these verses applicable to all. Jeremiah's warning is a warning to all unbelievers that the time for them to repent and come to God will run out. Obviously, this has not yet occurred.

We see the same thing in John 12 during Jesus' last week on earth, when He was speaking to His disciples. He says in **John 12:35-36**, *"'The light is among you for a little while longer. Walk while you have the light, lest darkness overtake you. The one who walks in the darkness does not know where he is going. While you have the light, believe in the light, that you may become sons of light.'"* Again, Jesus was addressing the current situation—that He would soon be crucified, ascend into Heaven, and would no longer be physically with His apostles. But Jesus is also speaking prophetically to all people that there will come a time when the world no longer has the Light (meaning His intercession), and it will be in complete darkness.

It can be hard to read that there will come a time when God will no longer give people a chance to repent and turn to Him. However, there are a few things we need to keep in mind. First, as we have seen throughout Revelation and as we see throughout the Bible, God continually gives people the chance to repent and turn to Him. Over and over, we see God's mercy, and over and over, we see the wicked openly defying and mocking God. This is a mysterious and complex issue. On the one hand, God has chosen those He will save before He created the world, and everyone He has chosen has or will turn to Him. This is a guarantee we see in many places throughout Scripture, including **Ephesians 1:4-6**: *"Even as he chose us in him before the foundation of the world, that we should be holy and blameless before him. In love he predestined us for adoption to himself as sons through Jesus Christ, according to the purpose of his will, to the praise of his glorious grace, with which he has blessed us in the Beloved."*

That being the case, we can conclude that those who have refused, continue to refuse, or will refuse to repent and turn to the Lord are doing so because they were or are dead in their sin and have not had or will not have their hearts regenerated. They were or are a slave to their sin and to Satan. This is a concept that can make us scream, "That's not fair!" And the truth is, it is not fair; it is not fair that God would choose anyone to save! With the exception of Jesus, every single person who has ever lived or will ever live is deserving of all of the judgment we have seen so far in Revelation and deserving of what we are about to see.

Paul sheds some light on this in **Romans 1:20**, where he says, *"For his invisible attributes, namely, his eternal power and divine nature, have been clearly perceived, ever since the creation of the world, in the things that have been made. So they are without excuse."* God has given everyone in the world what is called "general revelation." This general revelation is the evidence of God's existence that everyone can see—sunsets, the complex, delicate balance of nature, the seasons, the birth of babies, etc. These things, and so much more, should make it glaringly obvious to all that our world could have only been created by the intelligent design of an almighty and loving God. This is why no one is without excuse to know that God exists.

Apart from Christ, we are all evil and morally bankrupt. God chose some, His elect, to be reconciled to Him and saved. He did not choose anyone because of who they were or are; He chose them because of who *He* is. In light of that, our response when we read about the judgments in Revelation should be two-fold. First, we should fall to our knees in gratitude that God has chosen to save us and seal us for all eternity and that the only reason we do not have to face what is written in this book is not because we do not deserve it but because Jesus has already endured it for us. And since Jesus has paid the price for us, our second response should be to mourn for those in our lives who are not saved. We should be driven to pray that for those who do not know Jesus, God will bring them to salvation. It should also compel us to preach and witness the Gospel as often as we can to as many as we can in the hope that the Holy Spirit may, at some point, regenerate their hearts.

THE FIRST FIVE BOWLS

Chapter sixteen begins the bowl judgments—judgments from which God's people will be protected, whether they are on earth or not. Keep in mind as we read and go through this section that God's ultimate goal is to establish a new creation—a new heaven on earth. So, what we see in these bowl judgments is God deconstructing creation before He recreates it. And if that does not make you see the absolute sovereignty of God, nothing will!

Revelation 16:1-11 says:

> *Then I heard a loud voice from the temple telling the seven angels, "Go and pour out on the earth the seven bowls of the wrath of God." So the first angel went and poured out his bowl on the earth, and harmful and painful sores came upon the people who bore the mark of the beast and worshiped its image. The second angel poured out his bowl*

> into the sea, and it became like the blood of a corpse, and every living thing died that was in the sea. The third angel poured out his bowl into the rivers and the springs of water, and they became blood. And I heard the angel in charge of the waters say, "Just are you, O Holy One, who is and who was, for you brought these judgments. For they have shed the blood of saints and prophets, and you have given them blood to drink. It is what they deserve!" And I heard the altar saying, "Yes, Lord God the Almighty, true and just are your judgments!" The fourth angel poured out his bowl on the sun, and it was allowed to scorch people with fire. They were scorched by the fierce heat, and they cursed the name of God who had power over these plagues. They did not repent and give him glory. The fifth angel poured out his bowl on the throne of the beast, and its kingdom was plunged into darkness. People gnawed their tongues in anguish and cursed the God of heaven for their pain and sores. They did not repent of their deeds.

There is a ton to unpack in these eleven verses. It may seem confusing that we read all those verses at one time, but we wanted to start with the full picture because there is definitely a full picture here. If you remember, the first six seal and trumpet judgments were poured out on a portion of the earth, or a portion of mankind. While the bowl judgments are the same judgments as the seal and trumpet judgments, one huge difference is that the bowls are poured out on the entire earth. They are complete judgments, not partial judgments.

Also, these first five bowl judgments are on the earth, not on people—although, as we will see, people are certainly impacted. But as we said, God is deconstructing the earth. He is reversing the Creation from **Genesis 1**. And just as He did in the Creation in Genesis, He is emphasizing His sovereignty over everything in creation. Throughout Scripture, we see that God is orderly and precise. He is not a God of chaos. He created the earth in **Genesis 1** in an orderly fashion, and He will de-create the earth in an orderly fashion. This flies in the face of evolutionists, who say the earth was created out of accidental pandemonium and will be destroyed in the same manner.

Through the progression and intensity of the first five bowls, God will dare the "scientists" to try and fix what will happen. But, of course, there will be nothing they can do.

The first bowl judgment will cause sores upon people. Here is an example of a judgment on the earth that will impact people. Credible scholars rightly see that what God will do in this judgment is pollute the earth's food supply. This polluted food supply will cause people to break out in sores. The judgments will be on the earth and progressing and intensifying with each bowl. This first judgment pollutes the food supply on land, like meat, vegetables, and fruit. When the food supply on land is no good, what is the next logical thing to do? Turn to the ocean for food, of course.

God will take care of this in the second bowl. As **Revelation 16:3** says, *"The second angel poured out his bowl into the sea, and it became like the blood of a corpse, and every living thing died that was in the sea."* God will pollute the ocean so that all of sea life dies. Now what? Well, perhaps the people will say to themselves, "At least we have fresh water to drink." Not for long! In the third bowl, God pollutes the rivers and springs of water. So now, those who will be on earth will have no food and no water.

Look at **Revelation 16:5-6** again. The angel in charge of the waters is cheering. It says, *"And I heard the angel in charge of the waters say, 'Just are you, O Holy One, who is and who was, for you brought these judgments. For they have shed the blood of saints and prophets, and you have given them blood to drink. It is what they deserve!'"*

If God's people will cheer when the wicked are ultimately judged, how much more will the angels, who have been with God and have seen all of the cosmic battles?!

Back to the bowls. The people will now have no food and no water. They may try to find solace in the fact that they still have the sun as an energy source and for warmth. When the fourth bowl is poured out on the earth, the heat of the sun is turned up, and it scorches people. Then, what will the people do? As unbelievable as it sounds, verse nine says, *"They cursed the name of God who had the power over these plagues. They did not repent and give him glory."* We may all be shaking our heads about now, but this is not the first time we have seen something like this in Scripture. Remember, Revelation is the ultimate fulfillment of Exodus—the final exodus. In the first exodus, God delivered His people out of Egypt and punished the nation who enslaved them. It is impossible to read chapter sixteen and not see the similarities between the bowl judgments and the plagues God imposed on Egypt. Even after suffering through ten plagues, including one where the firstborn of every family and livestock was killed, Pharaoh still did not repent.

This is exactly what we see in Revelation. After the first four bowl judgments, the people will be covered in sores and burns and be left without food or water. We can surmise that they will run to their government, political leaders, and scientists for help. You can almost imagine them desperately pleading, *"Fix this!"* just as Pharaoh's servants and magicians begged him to resolve the plagues. In the fifth bowl judgment, God will thwart any possibility of being able to fix things by plunging the Earth into darkness. So now those left on Earth will not only have no food and water and have sores and burns covering their bodies, but they will also lose the most crucial element to human existence—hope. This is the very antithesis of Isaiah's prophecy in **Isaiah 9:2**: *"The people who walked in darkness have seen a great light; those who dwelt in a land of deep darkness, on them has light shone."* Again, showing a stark contrast between those who are God's people and those who are not. The governments, the leaders, the beasts to whom they will have pledged their absolute devotion and loyalty will be able do nothing to help them. That is why they **Revelation 16:10** tells us, *"They gnawed their tongues in anguish."* And still, and *still*, they continue to curse God and refuse to repent.

We mentioned earlier that this passage should illicit a two-fold response from us—drop to our knees in gratitude before God and pray for and preach the Gospel to unbelievers. But there is a third response believers should have, especially when reading passages like we just did. God *is* sovereign over everything, but these verses in Revelation really hit home about just how sovereign. We are utterly and completely dependent on God for everything! Food, water, our health, our surroundings, warmth, light, and even the very breath in our lungs. As Christians, we should always be first and foremost thankful for the salvation we have received in Jesus, but our gratitude should by no means stop there! Did you eat today? Did you have a cup of coffee or glass of water? Were you able to see by the sun's light? Did you breathe today? These and so much more are things for which we should stop and take the time to thank our gracious God.

THE SIXTH BOWL—THE BATTLE OF ARMAGEDDON

Some may read through these bowl judgments and think God is just being mean; but right now, He is giving all the blessings He will one day take away—food, water, the sun, light—to the wicked as well as to His people. He is holding back His full wrath, giving people a chance to repent of their sin and evil. So, not only is He completely merciful, gracious, generous, and loving to His people always, but for now, He is also all those things to those who are not His people—those who revile His name, those who want Him out of their life and out of the world, those who get joy and pleasure out of perverting His Word and Truth, and even those who think it is funny to publicly denounce and curse God, daring Him to do something about it. And still, for now, He is holding His complete judgment back. That is the God we serve. That is Who He is.

And with that, we can move on to the sixth bowl judgment. **Revelation 16:12–16** tells of it:

> *The sixth angel poured out his bowl on the great river Euphrates, and its water was dried up, to prepare the way for the kings from the east. And I saw, coming out of the mouth of the dragon and out of the mouth of the beast and out of the mouth of the false prophet, three*

> *unclean spirits like frogs. For they are demonic spirits, performing signs, who go abroad to the kings of the whole world, to assemble them for battle on the great day of God the Almighty. ("Behold, I am coming like a thief! Blessed is the one who stays awake, keeping his garments on, that he may not go about naked and be seen exposed!") And they assembled them at the place that in Hebrew is called Armageddon.*

Here, again, we see that the partial judgments of the seals and trumpets will be complete judgments in the bowls. Both the seals and trumpets had judgments of war that would take place on parts of the Earth. Jesus warned us about this in **Matthew 24:6** when He said, *"And you will hear of wars and rumors of wars. See that you are not alarmed for this must take place, but the end is not yet."* Wars have been a part of the tribulation since Jesus' ascension and will continue to be a part of it until He comes back. But here in the sixth bowl, we see that in the future there will be a final war—the ultimate war—Armageddon.

With countless books, movies, and other media depicting it, Armageddon may be the most well-known occurrence in the entire book of Revelation, but it is oftentimes interpreted incorrectly. Dr. Voddie Baucham quotes an interesting statistic: "Only thirty-six percent of Americans believe the Bible is real; yet fifty-nine percent of Americans believe the events in the book of Revelation will come to pass. And at the top of that list of beliefs in events that will come to pass is the battle of Armageddon."[42]

What is this final, famous, sometime infamous, battle set off by the sixth bowl judgment? Remember we said that idealists believe that the book of Revelation depicts the cosmic struggle between Satan and the Church. The Battle of Armageddon is the final battle of that struggle. However, throughout history, many have tried to tie in specific events and people which they believed were the catalysts that would trigger the start of Armageddon. Some

---

[42] Voddie Baucham Sermons, "Voddie Baucham—Revelation 16:12-16—the Battle of Armageddon. YouTube video, 1:00:49, January 31, 2017,Retrieved March 22, 2021, https://www.youtube.com/watch?v=ncIZ0DX4r4c&list=PL_OPzWCIg29ERt3iop1b1taAa4Bh4WFQ9&index=17&t=1216s.

thought the battle was manifesting in events like World War I, World War II, and 9/11. Hitler, the Papal Dynasty, and Japan are just a few identities that people have attributed to the Antichrist or kings from the East, who assemble against God to fight in this battle.

We have already showed the problems with assigning specific people and/or occurrences to the events in Revelation. The problems are magnified when you try to do that with the battle of Armageddon. Neither John, his original audience, nor anyone up until the twentieth century would have had any idea who Hitler was or what 9/11 was. This passage also presents a problem to the futurists or dispensationalists who think the book of Revelation is a literal account of what is to come. Armageddon is the final battle—the final judgment. However, there is not actually a place on Earth called Armageddon, nor was there ever. Some will pass it off saying John meant to name a place called the Valley of Megiddo, located in Israel near the Palestine region. And they get this because *Armageddon* means "Har Megiddo" in Greek.[43] Megiddo is mentioned several times in Scripture. It was the location where several battles between God's people and their enemies were fought, including the battle between Gideon and the Midianites. In all these battles, God did the actual fighting for His people. So, we can see why some may think Armageddon, or "Har Mageddon" will take place at this site.

But there are two reasons we believe this is not the case. First, Scripture often uses a literal people group or place in a symbolic way (e.g. Babylon, Tyre, Jerusalem, the Temple). The literal is a symbol and pointer to the much bigger metaphoric. Knowing that, it makes perfect sense that the Lord would use the name of a literal battlefield where He fought for His people against their enemies for the ultimate battle when He will completely destroy His and His people's enemies. The second reason is that what is about to occur—the final judgment of all the evil of the world—could *never* happen on a literal

---

43 *The NAS New Testament Greek Lexicon*, s.v. "Armageddon," accessed March 23, 2021, from https://www.biblestudytools.com/lexicons/greek/nas/armageddon.html.

piece of land. Nowhere in the entire world is there land big enough for all the evildoers of the world to assemble.

Let us dig in by beginning with the drying up of the Euphrates River so kings from the East can walk upon it. Will God literally dry up the actual Euphrates River, or is this symbolic? Technically, it could be either, as God has certainly dried up bodies of water before; but since this battle does not take place on an actual piece of land, it is highly unlikely that it is literal. But literal or symbolic, there is one thing we can say for sure about drying up the Euphrates River. We may sound like a broken record, but since Revelation is the ultimate fulfillment of the book of Exodus, this is a definite reference to when God dried up the Red Sea to lead Israel out of Egypt and out of slavery.

There could be additional meanings as well. It could also be a reference back to Noah. Remember, the rainbow in the throne room was a symbol of the Noahic covenant. This drying up of the river could be a reference to when God dried up the water on the Earth after the flood so Noah and his family could prosper and repopulate the Earth. God also dried up the Jordon River so Joshua and the Israelites could cross it and take the Promised Land, their inheritance.

Finally, God has even literally dried up the Euphrates River before. He did it to expose Babylon to the Medo-Persian Empire, so they could conquer Babylon as punishment for overtaking the southern nation of Judah and holding them captive for seventy years. God's literal drying up of the Euphrates at that time was the fulfillment of prophecy in Isaiah and Jeremiah, where God said He would bring ultimate judgment on Babylon for their sin of conquering His people, although He was the One Who raised up Babylon to punish Israel for their sin. And through Babylon's punishment, God's people would be restored to the Promised Land and would rebuild their temple. In other words, God dried up the Euphrates to bring about the punishment of Babylon, who oftentimes represents evil in Scripture. So, while it is safe to say that God can certainly dry up any river anytime He wants, this drying up the Euphrates is almost surely a symbolic drying up harkening back to any or all of the preceding events, showing that God will ultimately punish evil and restore His people, bringing to completion the victory that Jesus won on the cross and at His resurrection.

We have a couple more notes on this passage about Armageddon. **Verse thirteen** says, *"And I saw, coming out of the mouth of the dragon and out of the mouth of the beast and out of the mouth of the false prophet, three unclean spirits like frogs."* Just as we have seen in earlier passages, the dragon (Satan), the beast, and the false prophet (the second beast) are the unholy trinity, or counterfeit trinity, who are the antithesis of the true Trinity—the Father, Son, and Holy Spirit. The unclean spirits coming out of their mouths are likened to frogs. Among other things, the frog has its origin in mud and lives in mud. They could be used here as a symbol of those who are born in sin and live in pollution. Frogs have also been used as symbols of harshness, empty babble, heretics, and insolence.[44] There is also a possibility that this is yet another reference to Exodus and the plague of the frogs.

Before we move on to the seventh bowl, **Revelation 16:15** contains the third beatitude that we see in Revelation: *"Blessed is the one who stays awake, keeping his garments on, that he may not go about naked and be seen exposed!"* This is a call for Kingdom people (believers) to remain vigilant and not be caught off-guard. Jesus' coming will happen at a time we will not know or expect. We must be sure we are not found vulnerable, meaning lacking in faith or wisdom. Compare this beatitude to Jesus' own words in **Matthew 24:37-44**:

> *For as were the days of Noah, so will be the coming of the Son of Man. For as in those days before the flood they were eating and drinking, marrying and giving in marriage, until the day when Noah entered the ark, and they were unaware until the flood came and swept them all away, so will be the coming of the Son of Man. Then two men will be in the field; one will be taken and one left. Two women will be grinding at the mill; one will be taken and one left. Therefore, stay awake, for*

---

44 Albert Barnes, "Revelation," StudyLight.org, accessed March 03, 2021, https://www.studylight.org/commentaries/eng/bnb/revelation.html.

you do not know on what day your Lord is coming. But know this, that if the master of the house had known in what part of the night the thief was coming, he would have stayed awake and would not have let his house be broken into. Therefore you also must be ready, for the Son of Man is coming at an hour you do not expect.

THE SEVENTH BOWL—IT IS DONE!

Hold onto your hat because the seventh bowl is about to be poured out! **Revelation 16:17-21** says:

The seventh angel poured out his bowl into the air, and a loud voice came out of the temple, from the throne, saying, "It is done!" And there were flashes of lightning, rumblings, peals of thunder, and a great earthquake such as there had never been since man was on the earth, so great was that earthquake. The great city was split into three parts, and the cities of the nations fell, and God remembered Babylon the great, to make her drain the cup of the wine of the fury of his wrath. And every island fled away, and no mountains were to be found. And great hailstones, about one hundred pounds each, fell from heaven on people; and they cursed God for the plague of the hail, because the plague was so severe.

These verses reinforce that Babylon is being used as the symbol for all evil and that Armageddon is not a literal place. The battle of God's final judgment is on all the evil of the earth. Seems pretty silly to even call it a battle. The announcement, *"It is done,"* occurs before there is even any fighting! Not at all like the sci-fi movies that depict this battle as the most devastating war the world has ever seen. This is a completely one-sided battle with God doing all the fighting. This may be a chilling passage, but it is also extremely comforting. God does not have to actually fight against evil. He is completely sovereign over it and can snuff it out whenever He chooses to with just a word. We will see the details of what occurs during Armageddon in upcoming chapters, but they will just reinforce that God does not even break a sweat to destroy all the evil in the world. When Armageddon, the final battle and final judgment on evil, happens, there will not be any struggle. God will assemble all the evildoers and simply say, *"It is done."* And that, my friends, will be the end of evil! The rest of this passage shows the power of God over nature, creation, and every living thing. With just His words, Jesus brings lightning, thunder, an earthquake that swallows up cities, mountains, and islands, and one-hundred-pound hailstones!

One last thing worth mentioning. When Jesus was crucified, right before He gave up His Spirit, He exclaimed, *"It is finished"* **(John 19:30)**. Immediately after Jesus' death, **Matthew 27:51-54** tells us:

> *And behold, the curtain of the temple was torn in two, from top to bottom. And the earth shook, and the rocks were split. The tombs also were opened. And many bodies of the saints who had fallen asleep were raised, and coming out of the tombs after his resurrection they went into the holy city and appeared to many. When the centurion and those who were with him, keeping watch over Jesus, saw the earthquake and what took place, they were filled with awe and said, "Truly this was the Son of God!"*

Before He died on the cross, Jesus was pronouncing that He had paid the penalty for the sins of His people and completed the work of taking the wrath of God and reconciling them to God. He was also proclaiming His victory of sin, Satan, and death—a victory He had decidedly won but would not bring to completion until His return. At Armageddon, we will see Jesus bring all that to completion! And what is more encouraging than that?!

CHAPTER 9
STUDY GUIDE

GETTING YOUR TOES WET

We quoted Dr. Voddie Baucham, who said, "Only thirty-six percent of Americans believe the Bible is real, yet fifty-nine percent of Americans believe the events in the book of Revelation will come to pass. And at the top of that list of beliefs in events that will come to pass is the battle of Armageddon."[45] Why do you think people, even in the secular world, are so obsessed with Armageddon?

What are some portrayals, sermons, or teachings you have seen or heard on Armageddon?

What are you most looking forward to in Heaven?

DIVING IN DEEP

The first fourteen chapters of Revelation show that God's purpose in patience is being played out. As **Romans 2:4** tells us, *"Do you presume on the riches of his kindness and forbearance and patience, not knowing that God's kindness is meant to lead you to repentance?"* How do these verses show that the purpose of God is to bring His people to repentance?

2 Chronicles 30:7-9

---

45   Voddie Baucham, ibid.

Luke 15:11-32

Acts 17:24-31

2 Peter 3:7-10

Revelation 15:2 says, *"And I saw what appeared to be a sea of glass mingled with fire—and also those who had conquered the beast and its image and the number of its name."* The "fire" is a reference to the Holy Spirit. The Holy Spirit has many functions in the life of a believer. This verse shows that the Holy Spirit enables God's people to stand against the beast because He has sealed all who belong to God. *What do you see the Holy Spirit doing for believers in the following verses?*

John 14:25-26

Romans 8:26-27

Ephesians 1:11-14

Galatians 5:19-26

Titus 3:4-7

Revelation shows us many already/not-yet events. *What is the already/not-yet events in the following verses?*

Matthew 24:6-14

Romans 8:28-30

Ephesians 2:4-6

THE FINAL EXODUS

BACK ON DRY LAND

When some read of God's judgment, they think God is just mean. Although it will not always be the case, right now, God is bestowing blessings and general revelation on unbelievers. This is called "common grace." *How do these verses show common grace?*

Jonah 3:1-10

Jeremiah 29:3-7

Matthew 5:43-46

Knowing that God will save all those He has chosen to save before the end comes, why is it still crucial that we witness the Gospel to both believers and unbelievers?

CHAPTER 10

THE MOTHER OF ALL PROSTITUTES AND OBSCENITIES

When Decius became emperor of Rome in 249, he decided to strengthen and unite the empire on the basis of religion, ordering all citizens to take part in a general sacrifice, pouring out a libation to the Roman gods and eating part of the sacrificial meat. The order was aimed particularly at Christian leaders in an effort to totally undermine Christianity and see it die out. Those who refused were imprisoned, tortured, and killed. Under the brutality of Decius, many within the Church caved to the pressure and sacrificed. Others obtained a certificate called a *libellus* stating they had sacrificed, as evidenced by papyrus examples of the certificates found at Oxyrhyncus. This libellus could be shown to the authorities as proof that they had obeyed Decius' order, whether they really had or not. Either way, by sacrificing to pagan gods or by obtaining proof that said they did, these churchgoers had become *apostate*—denying their faith and denying their Savior.

BEING COUNTERFEIT LEADS TO APOSTASY

Counterfeit Christianity is alive and well today, and not just in worship services packed with listeners giving rapt attention to someone telling them how great God thinks they are. Just about anyone might claim to be a Christian at any time, especially if they are running for political office! Progressive Christianity is creeping into churches and denominations that used to be solidly grounded in the truths of the Bible. They may support the truths found in Scripture and may even herald them, as long as these truths have no appearance of being viewed as unkind or unwelcoming. Progressives claim belief in the Bible but shy away from claiming it is authoritative, especially in passages they see as "stumbling blocks." In those cases, they claim there are no absolutes or that the faith is "still evolving."

Critical social justice creeping into the Church is another heretical movement. This "Woke Christianity" has been coming to the forefront as one of the biggest problems in evangelicalism as a gospel of social justice replaces the true Gospel message and liberation theology gains a new foothold. This is not the time for naïveté on the issue. This is not about fighting the injustices of prejudice; this is a raging battle that is anything but what it might seem on the surface. Critical Social Justice or Critical Race Theory is a *worldview*—one that is not based on the teachings of the Bible. In the words of Dr. Voddie Baucham, dean of theology at African Christian University in Lusaka, Zambia, "There are plenty of sincere, though perhaps naïve Christians who, if they knew the ideology behind it, would run away from the term 'social justice' like rats from a burning ship."[46]

Someday, each one of us may be called on to stand for what the Bible truly says, at the risk of losing everything. Persecution often weeds out the true believers from the counterfeits, who become apostate when things get tough. Should a Christian keep their mouth shut and obey government leaders at all cost? Should they bow to societal pressure just to keep the peace? Is it okay to "hide in the tall grass," hoping that no one will see us? Just how far is it okay to blend in with the culture, and when does that actually become stepping over the line and denying our faith?

BEASTLY WORLD GOVERNMENTS

Revelation 17 begins the final section of the book that is an *extended vision* of John's. So far, we have been introduced to the dragon, Satan, who uses deception

---

46   Voddie T. Baucham, *Fault Lines: The Social Justice Movement and Evangelicalism's Looming Catastrophe* (Washington, DC: Salem Books, 2021).

through the false prophet and violent state persecutions by the beast to wage war against Christ's Church. These "beastly" world governments empowered by Satan not only do evil against God's people, but they also assume rights that only God has, like giving others the right to unjustly take life at will by legalizing abortion or demanding that a couple limit their number of children.

In 2020, under the guise of "keeping citizens safe" from a virus that has a ninety-nine percent survival rate, governments hindered worship practices like gathering together and singing, while strip clubs were allowed to stay open. That same year, Thanksgiving, the United States' national day to give thanks to God, was strongly recommended to be canceled due to numbers of people "testing positive," despite questions about the accuracy of the testing. Gatherings larger than ten people not of the same residential address could have the police showing up at your door during Thanksgiving dinner because neighbors snitched on you for having more than a few cars in your driveway, which is exactly what they had been told to do.

This same year, privately-owned businesses were shut down worldwide, causing widespread unemployment, while bigger chain brand stores were allowed to remain open. The punishment for not obeying (unless you are serving a member of the ruling party, of course)—having your doors permanently closed, operating licenses revoked, or being given possible jail time. With businesses closed and people out of work, survival without the government's help becomes harder and harder. But in order to get help, compliance with their rules is mandatory; and throughout history, following the rules has often constituted sinning, like the churches of Pergamum and Thyatira that we saw in **Revelation 2**.

COUNTERFEIT GODS

The dragon, Satan, and the beast are *counterfeit* gods. They mimic God in some ways, but they fall woefully short! In **Revelation 17**, we meet their *counterfeit bride,* Babylon, which represents power, wealth, glamour, fame and all sorts of temptations. Babylon is not only something the wicked are drawn to; but she also seeks to entice the people of God away from their Savior. Babylon is a called a prostitute. This harlot and the beast work in tandem for a while. The beast uses force to try to get people to comply, while the harlot tries to entice them to comply to the world's standards through her temptations. Both will meet fitting ends.

COUNTERFEIT BRIDE

Here we get a zoomed-in look at this counterfeit bride and at her demise from **Revelation 16:19. Revelation 17** begins, *"Then one of the seven angels who had the seven bowls came and said to me, 'Come, I will show you the judgment of the great prostitute who is seated on many waters, with whom the kings of the earth have committed sexual immorality, and with the wine of whose sexual immorality the dwellers on earth have become drunk'"* **(Rev. 17:1-2)**.

The city of Babylon from the Old Testament times was a city full of worldly, sinful pleasures. Babylon is personified as a prostitute because she entices people to her worldly pleasures. She is not a pretty girl standing on a street corner minding her own business. She is a harlot, seductively wooing people to her by showing off her goods and motioning to come in and buy. It is the same picture as that of lady folly from the Proverbs.

The fact that Babylon is *"seated on many waters"* means that her pleasures are offered worldwide—something that is backed up by verse fifteen, which says these waters are *"peoples and multitudes and nations and languages."* We know they are worldwide because there are four things listed, symbolizing the whole earth. Babylon, the great seducer, and Rome, the beastly persecuting ruler of John's time, are the images John uses to describe temptation and violent persecution, but they are representative of worldly seducers and world powers all throughout history, until Jesus returns.

The angel takes John (conveyed by the Spirit in a vision) to a *wilderness* to get the full picture of this prostitute. Here, he sees a woman adorned in purple and scarlet, decked out with beautiful gold and jewels. That may sound good, except she was sitting on a red beast who was *"full of blasphemous* names, and . . . had seven heads and ten horns" **(Rev. 17:3)**. The description of Babylon's extravagance and luxury and the fact that she is holding a goblet of sin from her immorality, as well as the name on her forehead being *"Mother of Prostitutes and Earth's Abominations"* **(Rev. 17:5)**, shows John is getting the unedited picture of Babylon—a picture showing the filthy underbelly of the sin she is promoting that leads to spiritual death. And the cup she drinks from contains the blood of the martyred saints.

This picture is a contrast to another woman—the Bride of Christ, which is the Church. Here is the counterfeit bride in chapter seventeen. In **Revelation 21**, we will see Christ's radiant, spotless Church is the true Bride. Babylon is in a desert, while the Lamb's Bride freely drinks from *"the water of life"* **(Rev. 21:6b)**. Babylon is wearing purple and scarlet; the true Bride is radiant, *"clear as crystal"* **(Rev. 21:11)**. Babylon is *outwardly* adorned with gold and jewels; the true Bride is *inwardly* adorned having been refined through the fires of trial and tribulation, so now she *outwardly* reflects *"the glory of God"* **(Rev. 21:11a)**. Babylon is sitting on a red beast with seven heads and ten horns **(Rev. 17:3)**. This is the same symbolic beast from **Revelation 13** and also the beasts from **Daniel 7**. The beasts from **Daniel 7** symbolized real-world kingdoms, with rulers like Antiochus IV Epiphanes, who was horrific to God's people. This picture of the harlot sitting on the back of the beast represents all kinds of worldly temptations being supported by wicked rulers, who want to destroy the Church. The true Bride is supported on the firm foundation of the apostles and prophets, *"Christ Jesus himself being the cornerstone,"* as it says in **Ephesians 2:20**.

Seeing Babylon as the similar-but-counterfeit picture of Jesus' Bride is why some futurists believe Babylon is a false religion or a heretical church that will follow someone who is *the* Antichrist, at the very end times. Similarly, some Protestants think of Babylon as the Catholic Church following the Antichrist, who is the Pope, although that idea is not as prevalent as it once was. Some take this to be a literal new city of Babylon, but that really does not fit with any of the text.

John continues describing his vision, saying:

> When I saw her, I marveled greatly. But the angel said to me, "Why do you marvel? I will tell you the mystery of the woman, and of the beast with seven heads and ten horns that carries her. The beast that you saw was, and is not, and is about to rise from the bottomless pit and go to destruction. And the dwellers on earth whose names have not been written in the book of life from the foundation of the world will marvel to see the beast, because it was and is not and is to come **(Rev. 17:6b-8)**.

The text says that John *"marveled greatly"* at this woman and the beast. *Marvel* means to have "wonder, astonishment, amazement, or possibly even some level of admiration."[47] This is not here because the angel is rebuking John. It is a reminder to believers not to be enamored by worldly things. According to **Revelation 17:8**, it is those whose names have not been written in the Book of Life from the foundation of the world who chase after the things of the world.

THE MYSTERY OF THE BEAST

The angel is going to interpret the mystery of the beast, who upholds this counterfeit bride. Remember, when something is referred to as a *mystery* in the Bible, it is not something we track down the meaning of, like a detective; it is something which has not been revealed yet. The angel is going to reveal this mystery to John, but keep in mind that the different parts of John's vision are not necessarily chronological in order.

Revelation 17 gives us several descriptions of the beast, in addition to those of the harlot. The fact that this beast is *scarlet* **(Rev. 17:3)** refers back to the red dragon in chapter twelve who personifies Satan or evil and who was trying to kill the Church. The fact that he is also *"full of blasphemous names"* **(Rev. 17:3)** emphasizes that the beast clearly is out to do the work of Satan.

---

47 Greek Concordance, s.v. "ἐθαύμασα," accessed March 25, 2021, https://biblehub.com/greek/ethaumasa_2296.htm.

In **Revelation 13**, we saw this beast with a mortal wound that healed, which made the "whole earth" marvel at him. **Revelation 17:8** says the beast *"**was**, and **is not**, and **is about to rise from the bottomless pit** and **go to destruction**. And the dwellers on earth whose names have not been written in the book of life from the foundation of the world will marvel to see the beast, because **it was** and **is not** and **is to come**"* (emphasis added). To understand this, we should start by reminding ourselves of the four-fold pattern of Christ's life: He lived; He died; He rose from the dead; He ascended to Heaven. The angels praise Him in **Revelation 4:8**: *"Holy, holy, holy, is the Lord God Almighty, who was and is and is to come!"* What is said about the beast mimics these truths about Jesus. It *mimics* it, but it is different in showing that the beast, like the counterfeit bride, is also a counterfeit. Jesus ascended to the throne, but the beast is headed for destruction.

Moving on, the text says, *"This calls for a mind with wisdom: the seven heads are seven mountains on which the woman is seated; they are also seven kings, five of whom have fallen, one is, the other has not yet come, and when he does come he must remain only a little while"* **(Rev. 17:9-10)**.

Verse nine is one of those already/not-yet fulfillments. The seven heads of the beast are seven mountains, a reference to ancient Rome. The beast of John's days was the Roman Empire. Emperor Nero suffered a wound some thought looked mortal, but then he came back stronger. As we said in chapter five, the mortal wounds which have been healed means that evil keeps coming back.

Because the woman is seated on the beast, we know this is about more than Rome; it is going to have fulfillment worldwide. This beast in **Revelation 17** has seven heads that are also kings. The fact that they are kings represents their power. It is not a literal seven heads or seven rulers. Scholars have tried to pin these titles to different world leaders over and over again, without coming to a consensus. However, because there are seven of them—the number symbolizing perfect completion—this is symbolic of a perfectly complete number of rulers who bring God's perfect judgment. They all rule and reign here on earth according to their own sinful desires, but it is all part of the fulfillment of God's plan.

When Jesus triumphed over Satan with His sinless life, His death, and His resurrection, it bound Satan so that he could not deceive the nations for a period of time. There is a loss of some power there. He and his demons were not rendered totally ineffective, but they are limited for a certain period of time. At some point, though, Satan will be released from the bottomless pit, and things will get really bad. This was seen in chapter five when the locusts are released. This is what is meant by *"the other has not yet come"* **(Rev. 17:10)**. Satan and the demons will be released, and evil will seem to triumph for a short time throughout the whole earth. But just as we saw in **Revelation 14** when the two witnesses died, the wicked thought they had won, and their seeming victory only lasted for a short period of time. When it says, *"he must remain only a little while"* **(Rev. 17:10b)**, it is saying that when Jesus comes, Satan will be finished.

Jesus is talked about as the One *"who is and who was and who is to come"* **(Rev. 1:4)**. But in some of these chapters, He has been referred to as the one *"who is and who was"* **(Rev. 11:17, 16:5)** period. **Revelation 17:11a** is a play on words. The beast is described as *"the beast that was and is not"* again showing he is a counterfeit who is going to destruction when Jesus gets here. Those verses are talking about a time when Jesus has come again! **Revelation 17:11b** ends, *"It is an eighth but it belongs to the seven, and it goes to destruction."* This phrase represents an excess of evil unlike we have seen before. The eight symbolizing that it is so much evil, it is almost more than a perfectly complete amount, if that was possible! Because it is an eight that is really a seven, it also symbolizes the perfect *incompleteness* and perfect *counterfeitness* of the beast and Satan's kingdom.

Revelation 17:12-14 continues:

> And the ten horns that you saw are ten kings who have not yet received royal power, but they are to receive authority as kings for one hour, together with the beast. These are of one mind, and they hand over their power and authority to the beast. They will make war on the

Lamb, and the Lamb will conquer them, for he is Lord of lords and King of kings, and those with him are called and chosen and faithful.

In verse twelve, we are told that ten kings are given power for *"one hour."* That is not a literal ten kings, since the number ten is symbolic for completeness; it is showing us a *complete number* of kings or world leaders. And it is only one hour because Satan's future time of terrible assault on the Lamb and His Church will be short-lived. These leaders are *"of one mind, and they hand over their power and authority to the beast."* They will be so united in their purpose of destroying anything that has to do with Jesus and His Church that they will be willing to hand over their authority to the beast to make war on the Lamb and His Church.

THE LAMB AND HIS BRIDE

The *"chosen and faithful"* with the Lamb in verse fourteen are the believers. The Lamb is called *"the Word of God"* in chapter nineteen's battle description. That fits perfectly because the sword believers fight with, according to **Ephesians 6:17**, is the *"word of God."*

Like those ten evil kings are united in thought and purpose, believers are to be of one mind, too. We are to have unity, not only in the way we treat each other and in our love for each other, but also in our doctrine, at *minimum* on the essentials. Like we said in chapter two, that's what the apostle Paul was calling the Ephesian church to do in the familiar "speak the truth in love" passage. It's not about lovingly correcting your brother or sister in the faith about some sin they are committing. It is about correcting their theology and doctrine in a loving manner. We are to teach each other with correct theology and doctrine.

THEY USED TO LOVE HER, BUT THEY HAD TO KILL HER

The counterfeit beast and his counterfeit bride continue their disastrous work to *"peoples and multitudes and nations and languages"* **(Rev. 17:15)**—four things listed telling us it's throughout the whole world.

In the end, the beast and the ten kings *"will hate the prostitute"* **(Rev. 17:16)**. They will end up hating the luxurious, glamorous, lavishness that lures people to them; and in the end, they'll turn on Babylon. That sounds like something almost inconceivable, but Scripture says they *"will make her desolate and naked, and devour her flesh and burn her up with fire"* **(Rev. 17:16)**. Why do they do it? *"God has put it into their hearts to carry out his purpose by being of one mind and handing over their royal power to the beast, until the words of God are fulfilled"* **(Rev. 17:17)**. The counterfeit bridegroom kills his counterfeit bride.

We see this all over Scripture, where God's people think they will have to fight their enemies, who often far outnumber them. But when it is time for battle, they see their enemies have turned on themselves. King Saul found the Philistines attacking themselves in **1 Samuel 14**. Gideon's army found the Midianites doing the same. Seir, Moab, and Ammon—three of Judah's enemies—came against them in an allegiance with one another. What happened? The Ammonites and the Moabites turned on Seir, destroyed them, and then turned on each other.

And we see glimpses of that today. We see it in political parties that are divided by some wanting to keep the status quo and hold the normal party lines and even sometimes reach across the aisle, while others in their party want sweeping change of a whole government system. What they end up with is division, with no compromise, even when it comes to things like the heinous act of abortion. In 2020, Dianne Feinstein, a high-ranking Democrat, treated a pro-life Roman Catholic Supreme Court nominee very civilly during confirmation hearings and hugged Republican Lindsey Graham after the proceedings were finished. People from her party were outraged and called for her to step down from her position of top Democrat on the Senate Judiciary Committee because of it, which she agreed to do. Treating a United States Supreme Court nominee with respect and hugging a colleague wasn't looked at as common courtesy—it was looked at as treason against her party for not towing the party line hard enough. And that's just one example of how quickly and easily those in power will turn on each other.

No world kingdom lasts forever. Rome fell, partly because of its extravagance. Crumbling financially from within, its people under heavy taxation, reliance on slave labor, weakening of its military, overspending, government corruption, and political instability all played a part as outside forces threatened invasion. On top of the same problems that brought down Rome, citizens have opposing worldviews, causing countries to break apart and form smaller countries. Allies turn on each other and form other alliances. Jesus said, *"Every kingdom divided against itself is laid waste, and no city or house divided against itself will stand"* **(Matt. 12:25)**. The beast and the kings turn on Babylon the prostitute, and they utterly destroy her because it is their nature to destroy. They don't realize it, but they are fulfilling God's purposes in doing it.

Chapter eighteen begins by telling us that John saw another angel coming down from Heaven. This angel brings some very good news: Babylon the great has fallen, and now she's nothing but a place filled with demons and every other unclean and detestable thing imaginable.

THERE ARE NO RIGHTEOUS NATIONS—NO NATION ON EARTH IS "GOD'S COUNTRY"

God uses the beast to judge the prostitute because there are no righteous nations! The wicked are left to their sinful natures. Without the Holy Spirit regenerating a person's heart, that is the state they are in. And they will harden their hearts more against anything righteous. No country is immune to the temptations of power and wealth—wealth that is often made through luxurious living of the powerful on the backs of the middle class and the poor. While it is true that all people—rich and poor, ruler and those under them—are tempted by power and wealth, this is an indictment especially of those in power and the *"merchants of the earth"* who *"have grown rich from the power of her luxurious living"* **(Rev. 18:3)**.

COME OUT, CHURCH!

The Church is not to align themselves with Babylon because they belong to Jesus. Jesus says, *"'Come out of her, my people, lest you take part in her sins, lest you share in her plagues; for her sins are heaped high as heaven, and God has remembered her iniquities'"* **(Rev. 18:4-5)**. Do not be sucked in! Christians have to be in the world, but not of the world **(John 15:19)**. Jesus hung out with sinners, but He did not join them in their sin. We cannot avoid the world, and there are good things God gave us to enjoy in it. The counterfeits have distorted some of those good things and use them for sinful purposes—like alcohol, sex, food, and even gender differences, for instance. Babylon is seductive for a reason—to lure people in! As Christians, we need to stand firm against temptation to sin; and as churches, we need to stand firm against tolerance of the world's distorted views and not let them creep into our doctrine and theology. Christ's Church should look vastly different from the world.

WISE UP, CHURCH!

In addition to distortion, Babylon will be deceptive in trying to lure God's people away from truth. In 2021, a political group came to the forefront of the news in the United States. They used the truth that all lives matter because humans are made in the image of God, and many Christians fell for their lies simply because of their organization's name, Black Lives Matter. Because the name taken in and of itself is true, Christians promoted them, supported them, even marched with them, thinking they were doing a good thing. But in reality, if you looked at the underbelly of the organization's true mission, most everything they stand for goes directly against the Bible's teachings. That is exactly what is happening with critical social justice, with some denominations adding it as an integral part to the Gospel. But only Scripture can define what the Gospel message is. It is time for the Church to wise up and realize the world's definition of kindness and goodness often does not line up with how God defines holiness. Christians can not go blindly down paths they have not thoroughly investigated. It is also time to study Scripture.

We have to be trained by learning Scripture so that we can spot ungodly ideas in an instant.

God will repay Babylon for her wickedness and her assault on His Church. She lived in luxury, thinking she was *"a queen"* **(Rev. 18:7)**, but she was always a harlot, unloved by her counterfeit husband. God's judgment is always perfect—*"life for life, eye for eye, tooth for tooth"* **(Exod. 21:23-24)**. And while the Bible speaks of double blessings sometimes, Babylon will be repaid with *"double for her deeds"* **(Rev. 18:6)**. The wicked who assault Christ's Church will drink a double portion of the wrath of God. On the day of the Lord, *"her plagues will come"* and *"'in a single day, death and mourning and famine, and she will be burned up with fire; for mighty is the Lord God who has judged her'"* **(Rev. 18:8)**.

SHE'S GONE, GONE, GONE

Revelation 18:9-19 is a funeral dirge about Babylon's fall like the one from **Isaiah 21**. The *"kings of the earth, who committed sexual immorality and lived in luxury with her, will weep and wail over her when they see the smoke of her burning. They will stand far off, in fear of her torment, and say, 'Alas! Alas! You great city, you mighty city, Babylon! For in a single hour your judgment has come'"* **(Rev. 18:9)**. There is great mourning from all the people who participated in the sins of Babylon the prostitute because she is gone. **Revelation 18:11-14** says:

> And the merchants of the earth weep and mourn for her, since no one buys their cargo anymore, cargo of gold, silver, jewels, pearls, fine linen, purple cloth, silk, scarlet cloth, all kinds of scented wood, all kinds of articles of ivory, all kinds of articles of costly wood, bronze, iron and marble, cinnamon, spice, incense, myrrh, frankincense, wine, oil, fine flour, wheat, cattle and sheep, horses and chariots, and slaves, that is, human souls. "The fruit for which your soul longed has gone from you, and all your delicacies and your splendors are lost to you, never to be found again!"

Even those in the transportation industry will be lamenting Babylon's demise, crying out, *"'Alas, alas, for the great city that was clothed in fine linen, in purple and scarlet, adorned with gold, with jewels, and with pearls! For in a single hour all this wealth has been laid waste'"* **(Rev. 18:16-19)**. Every corrupt economic system of the world and those who profit from them will mourn the loss of the material goods that mean so much to them. It will all disappear quickly, *"in a single hour,"* when God finally says, "Enough!" And they will watch from a distance, but it will be too late to distance themselves from the counterfeit one they loved so much.

All corrupt economic systems are gone, done away quickly in God's mighty judgment. Those who lived in luxury and profited unjustly will wail and lament. But not everyone is singing this funeral dirge. Heaven is rejoicing because of God's judgment.

> *Then a mighty angel took up a stone like a great millstone and threw it into the sea, saying, "So will Babylon the great city be thrown down with violence, and will be found no more; and the sound of harpists and musicians, of flute players and trumpeters, will be heard in you no more, and a craftsman of any craft will be found in you no more, and the sound of the mill will be heard in you no more, and the light of a lamp will shine in you no more, and the voice of bridegroom and bride will be heard in you no more, for your merchants were the great ones of the earth, and all nations were deceived by your sorcery. And in her was found the blood of prophets and of saints, and of all who have been slain on earth"* **(Rev. 18:21-24)**.

At this point, all normal, pleasant things of everyday life are gone. Music, the sound of work, food, light—all gone. And so are the voices of the Bridegroom and the Bride. There is nothing pleasant on earth anymore.

THE FATE OF AN APOSTATE

Believers do not go through their Christian life totally sinless. Jesus died for all of the sins of His people for their whole lifetime. When Christians sin, they confess their sin and ask God for forgiveness, knowing that He will grant it because of Jesus. Persecuted believers often have a choice to make—will they stand their ground for Christ or apostatize and abandon the faith when persecution is imminent? **Hebrews 6:4-6** says:

For it is impossible, in the case of those who have once been enlightened, who have tasted the heavenly gift, and have shared in the Holy Spirit and have tasted the goodness of the word of God and the powers of the age to come, and then have fallen away, to restore them again to repentance, since they are crucifying once again the Son of God to their own harm and holding him up to contempt.

The early church, as well as others, had to deal with those in their congregation who did not bear up under persecution and denied Christ, later wanting to come back into the fold. Should they be allowed? Is the rest of the suffering Church supposed to forgive them? Does Jesus forgive them for denying Him? These are questions believers had to wrestle with in the past, and we may have to in the future.

Persecution is coming. If you are not experiencing it yet, be thankful to God. It isn't because the churches in your corner of the world have been wonderfully faithful and diligent; it's because God has been merciful. Christians who are suffering persecution in other countries are not suffering because they did not pray enough, or because they did not have enough faith, or because they didn't fight to keep prayer in school or to keep the social justice agenda out of it. Revelation shows us that someday persecution is going to be a worldwide problem, as God fulfills His purposes throughout the world. This is not a time for the Church to stay silent. We need to educate ourselves in the Scriptures daily. We need to know what it says. We need to proclaim the Gospel to a sin-sick, luxury-loving world. And we need to teach our brothers and sisters to stand as the Bride—the True Bride of Christ, their beloved Savior.

CHAPTER 10
STUDY GUIDE

GETTING YOUR TOES WET

No one is immune to the temptations of the world. Think about what things tempt you to sin and write them down or make a mental note of them.

Even things that aren't sinful can become idols if we love them too much. List some things in this world that enamor you.

DIVING IN DEEP

What do these verses say about temptation?

Psalm 119:11

Song of Solomon 2:15

Matthew 26:41

1 Corinthians 10:13

James 1:3

Not all messages or ideas that sound good, kind, or nice are actually biblical. The world will not only try to entice believers to sin; it will also produce lies and use distortion to distract God's people from what Scripture really says. What do these verses say about it?

Proverbs 5:1

Matthew 10:16

Romans 16:18-19

2 Timothy 3:14-17

2 Peter 3:17-18

BACK ON DRY LAND

How aware do you feel you are of worldly ideas that are creeping into the Church?

When you hear about organizations like Black Lives Matter, do you check them out before you share them on social media, send them money, etc.?

When you hear about something that might be occult or New Age creeping into the Church, do you check them out before you jump on the bandwagon?

CHAPTER 11
HOW IT'S ALL GONNA GO DOWN

We are in the home stretch! Revelation has been quite the roller coaster! In the last ten chapters of this book, we have covered eighteen chapters of the book of Revelation. We have looked at Jesus' letters to the seven churches, which represented actual churches as well as the universal Church for all time. We have seen how Christians have been, are currently, and will continue to be persecuted for their faith. We have seen how God's partial judgments on those who do not belong to Him have and will continue to unfold. We have seen how the counterfeit bride, Babylon, will be taken down handily. And we have seen that with very little effort, Jesus will bring His victory over Satan, sin, and death to culmination in the future. We would be remiss not to say that we have also seen some hard and disturbing images and events that have already occurred, that continue to occur, and that are still yet to occur. When you read the book of Revelation in its entirety, you cannot help but see the incredible kindness of our glorious God, Who has graciously woven in encouragement and hope for His people in between the sobering wrath that He will unleash on those who are not His. As we tackle the last four chapters of Revelation—two in this chapter and two in the next—we will see that more than ever.

Is there anyone who does not love a happy ending in a book? In fact, it seems to almost be a "must" for novels. No matter what the fictional heroes or heroines face throughout the book, their stories end on an "up" note. Sadly, though, art often does not imitate life. For many people, their very real, non-fiction stories do not end so happily. For any who die without coming to Christ—heartbreaking though it is—this will be the case for eternity. A sobering truth that should have us on our knees praying for the unbelieving world. However, the story is quite different for those who belong to Christ. If you have given your life to Christ, whatever your earthly story has been or is currently, it is *not* the end! The Lord God Almighty, the Creator, Sustainer, and Master of the entire universe and every molecule in it, has Himself written the end of your story; and it is about as happy as it gets! This incredible truth should have us on our knees in gratitude!

Let us start digging into **Revelation 19**. **Verses one and two** say, *"After this I heard what seemed to be the loud voice of a great multitude in heaven, crying out, 'Hallelujah! Salvation and glory and power belong to our God, for his judgments are true and just; for he has judged the great prostitute who corrupted the earth with her immorality, and has avenged on her the blood of his servants.'"*

Notice the first two words of this passage: *"After this."* What is this scene taking place after? Here is the umpteenth reminder that Revelation is not a chronological series of events. Chapter sixteen looked ahead to the battle of Armageddon—the final battle when Jesus will completely destroy all evil. Then, **Revelation 17-18** showed us how God will deal with Babylon. Obviously, if all evil is destroyed at Armageddon, that would include Babylon. As has been the pattern, first we got a big-picture view of the final battle in chapter sixteen. Then, beginning in chapter seventeen and continuing through chapter twenty, we get a zoomed-in look at the specificities of what will take place during that battle, including the destruction of Babylon.

Chapter eighteen ended with Babylon being thrown down in violence and destroyed. Moving into chapter nineteen, as we have often seen, there is rejoicing when God's judgment is passed on the wicked. In the first three verses of this passage, the multitude in Heaven who are crying out, *"Hallelujah,"* and praising God for His perfect justice are the people of God and may specifically be the martyrs. After all, they are the ones who have been crying out for God to avenge their blood. **Revelation 18:24** tells us about Babylon, *"And in her was found the blood of prophets and of saints, and of all who have been slain on earth."* And that is followed up in **Revelation 19:2** by the multitudes in Heaven shouting, *"[He] has avenged on her the blood of his servants."* Given all of that, these people rejoicing could very well be all who have paid the ultimate price for following Jesus. However, it may also be *all* the people of God. We know for certain that it is all the people of God who fall down and worship God when we get to **Revelation 19:4**, as they are represented by the twenty-four elders.

WILL THE TRUE BRIDE TAKE HER PLACE?

Chapter nineteen continues with another beautiful passage that continues giving us a glimpse into Heaven. **Revelation 19:7-9** says:

> *"Let us rejoice and exult and give him the glory, for the marriage of the Lamb has come, and his Bride has made herself ready; it was granted her to clothe herself with fine linen, bright and pure"—for the fine linen is the righteous deeds of the saints. And the angel said to me, "Write this: Blessed are those who are invited to the marriage supper of the Lamb." And he said to me, "These are the true words of God."*

Chapter eighteen was about the fall of the counterfeit bride, Babylon. You may remember, she was clothed in scarlet, adorned with jewels of the world, and drunk on the blood of the martyrs. She was the personification of "the world"—specifically, the evil that *can* come from power, lust, riches, fame, and the like. But now, here in chapter nineteen, we see the contrast of the counterfeit bride, Babylon, with the true Bride, the Church. We touched on this in the last chapter, but it is worth noting again the differences in the two. While the counterfeit bride was striding the waters of the Earth, the true Bride is falling down before God. While the fake Bride is drunk on the blood of the martyrs, meaning that she was heady with and reveling in *her* power and glorifying herself for destroying the people of God, the true Bride is rejoicing in the holiness and justness of God, worshipping *Him* and giving *Him* all the glory.

There is even a sharp contrast in how the two brides are dressed. Babylon is clothed in scarlet and purples, whereas the true Bride is in pure white. There is a scene from the movie *Gone with the Wind*, where Rhett Butler thought that his wife, Scarlet O'Hara, had cheated on him. They were heading to a party that night, and he made her wear a red, ornate gown because he said it made her look the part of a harlot.[48] Now, we are certainly *not* saying red is a bad color to wear, nor does wearing it make a statement about you. We love the color red. The point is that when red is compared to white, there is a stark difference. The color white is a symbol of purity and wholesomeness. It is the color brides and angels wear. The contrast is evident. But perhaps the biggest contrast between the counterfeit bride and the true Bride of Christ is that while Babylon will be thrown down with violence and destroyed, the true Bride will be at her marriage banquet!

In verse nine, we see another of the seven beatitudes contained in the book of Revelation: *"'Blessed are those who are invited to the marriage supper of the Lamb.'"* The beatitudes throughout the Bible are all pictures of the Kingdom of God. For example, the ones found in **Matthew 5**, the Sermon on the Mount, are all pictures of what Kingdom life should look like. And here we are in **Revelation 19**, seeing Kingdom life being lived out! For those who are citizens of the Kingdom of God, there will be a celebration of that citizenship. This is what the true Bride being given to the Bridegroom Jesus and attending the wedding feast is all about!

We have all probably been to some pretty spectacular weddings. We see some where no expense is spared on food, decorations, centerpieces, the cake, favors, and even ice sculptures! Nonetheless, none of the weddings any of us have ever attended, no matter how grandiose, will compare to the wedding of Jesus and his Bride, the Church! It is not even possible to image how amazing

---

48   *Gone with the Wind*, Directed by Victor Fleming, United States: Selznick International Pictures and Metro-Goldwyn-Mayer, 1939, DVD.

it will be because it will be like nothing ever seen on earth! And for those of us who were brides once, we get to wear a white gown again! Well, maybe it is more like a robe, but you get the point.

THE RIDER ON A WHITE HORSE

> *Then I saw heaven opened, and behold, a white horse! The one sitting on it is called Faithful and True, and in righteousness he judges and makes war. His eyes are like a flame of fire, and on his head are many diadems, and he has a name written that no one knows but himself. He is clothed in a robe dipped in blood, and the name by which he is called is The Word of God. And the armies of heaven, arrayed in fine linen, white and pure, were following him on white horses. From his mouth comes a sharp sword with which to strike down the nations, and he will rule them with a rod of iron. He will tread the winepress of the fury of the wrath of God the Almighty* **(Rev. 19:11-15)**.

Don't you just love this picture? During this amazing wedding feast, Jesus will claim His Bride, the Church. Of course, Jesus is the perfect Bridegroom, and as such, He does what you would expect a perfect husband to do—He protects His Bride. These verses are a picture of Jesus as He sets out to judge and avenge the mistreatment of His Bride by the wicked. One difference, though, is that unlike humans, Jesus sets out to make war *"in righteousness,"* meaning those He judges and releases His wrath on justly deserve it. We have said this before, but it is certainly worth repeating to remind ourselves that we, too, deserve that wrath and judgment, but Jesus has already endured it for us. Yet one more thing to bring us to our knees in gratitude.

In this passage, Jesus is called by the names, "Faithful," "True," and "the Word of God." These are all names we have seen used for Him before. **Hebrews 10:23** tells us, *"Let us hold fast the confession of our hope without wavering, for he who promised is faithful."* Jesus describes Himself by the names, *"Faithful and True."* In **Revelation 3:14**, we read, *"And to the angel of the church in Laodicea write: 'The words of the Amen, the faithful and true witness, the beginning of God's creation.'"*

Finally, there is the well-known passage in John's gospel where John states outright that Jesus is the manifestation of the Word of God: *"In the beginning was the Word, and the Word was with God, and the Word was God"* **(John 1:1)**.

If you recall, way back in chapter three, we looked at why there are not a lot of physical descriptions of Jesus in the Bible, even though He had met thousands of people in the thirty-three years He walked the Earth. Well, here we are in chapter nineteen, and here is that symbolic description: *"His eyes are like a flame of fire, and on his head are many diadems, and he has a name written that no one knows but himself. He is clothed in a robe dipped in blood"* **(Rev. 19:12-13)**.

Some of this symbolism should be easy to decipher since we have seen some very similar earlier in chapter five of Revelation. As in chapter five when we read that Jesus had seven horns and seven eyes, this verse in chapter nineteen does not mean that Jesus is literally wearing a bunch of crowns on His head. This image most likely has a dual meaning. First, Jesus is the King of kings and Lord of lords, as verse sixteen says is written on His thigh. The many crowns symbolize that He is the true King, Who has complete authority over every other leader who has ever lived or will ever live. Also, the multiple crowns denote that Jesus is the perfect Fulfiller of the three major offices of God's people that are listed in the Bible—prophet, priest, and king.

Throughout Scripture, God appointed men to these three offices over His people. Some examples, among many, are Isaiah being anointed as a prophet, Aaron being anointed as high priest, and David being anointed as king. Sections, from the Heidelberg Catechism and Westminster Confession of Faith show that the imperfect men who were appointed to these offices were always meant to point us to the only One who could execute the offices perfectly. Jesus is not just our Savior; He is also our Prophet, Priest, and King. The Heidelberg Catechism tells us that God the Father ordained Jesus for these roles with the anointing of the Holy Spirit.[49] The Westminster Confession of

---

[49] "Heidelberg Catechism (1563)," The Heidelblog, January 31, 2021, https://heidelblog.net/catechism.

Faith gives details about exactly how Jesus executes each of these offices. The point of both church catechisms is to emphasize that it's because Jesus is fully God that He has the power to execute these offices to perfection; and because He is fully Man, He is qualified to fill them.[50]

It is clear that it would have been impossible for a mere man to fulfill any of these offices to God's expectation. But that was never God's intention. Everything in the Old Testament and everything in Scripture is meant to point us to Jesus. So, when we read verses like **Deuteronomy 18:15**, **Leviticus 4:20b**, or **1 Chronicles 17:11**, know that while God is speaking into the circumstances surrounding the verses, He is ultimately pointing His people to the One Who would perfect and forever reign as His people's Prophet, Priest, and King. **Hebrews 1-3** tell us that Jesus has done exactly that.

Just like the "many diadems" on Christ's head is not meant to be taken literally, Jesus' eyes are not actually on fire. We have seen this imagery before in **Revelation 1:14** and **2:18**, although we did not define it then. The symbolism is the same in those passages as it is in **Revelation 5:6**, when John said Jesus had seven eyes. It signifies Jesus' holiness, authority, omnipotence, and omniscience.

The last image we are given of Jesus is that He is clothed in a robe dipped in blood. This again takes us back to **Revelation 5:6**, where John described Jesus as looking like a Lamb Who had been slain. If you recall, that pointed to Jesus' being wounded at His crucifixion when He took upon Himself God's wrath for the sin of His people. While it temporarily "appeared" that Jesus had been mortally wounded and lost, He crushed Satan, sin, and death at His resurrection.

THE LORD'S ARMY

Revelation 19:14 says, *"The armies of heaven, arrayed in fine linen, white and pure, were following him on white horses."* Can you imagine what a magnificent picture

---

50 Westminster Divines, "The Westminster Shorter Catechism, (1647) by Westminster Divines," Ligonier Ministries, December 21, 2009, https://www.ligonier.org/learn/articles/westminster-shorter-catechism.

this will be?! Can you also imagine an army going off to war in pure white linen? That would be ludicrous! That is, unless you are completely confident about the win. Jesus has every reason to be confident about the outcome of the war He is about to fight. Not only has it already been won and is just waiting for Him to bring it to completion, but this image is also a picture of Jesus going to the battle of Armageddon that we saw in chapter sixteen. And that battle, as we saw, ended just by Jesus saying, "It is done." We can be fairly certain that those white robes and white horses were still sparkling even after Armageddon.

There is some irony to note in this image. The way Jesus makes His entrance in **Revelation 19** is the way the Jewish people had expected Him to come the first time. They wanted a great military leader who would avenge them and set them free from their earthly oppressors, the Roman Empire. Obviously, Jesus didn't come anything like that the first time. Instead, He humbly rode in on a donkey with no army and no fanfare. Jesus is forever turning the worldview of things upside down!

The last image to deal with in this passage is Jesus' weapon, His sword. As **Revelation 19:15** tells us, *"From his mouth comes a sharp sword with which to strike down the nations, and he will rule them with a rod of iron."* We probably do not even need to state that Jesus does not literally have a sword coming out of His mouth. We probably also do not need to mention that Jesus hardly needs a sword or any other weapon to fight against anyone. So, what is with this sword? The book of Hebrews is a great place to get the answer. **Hebrews 4:12** says, *"For the word of God is living and active, sharper than any two-edged sword, piercing to the division of soul and of spirit, of joints and of marrow, and discerning the thoughts and intentions of the heart."* Time to put all that homework to good use and connect the dots. Why will Jesus be able to completely defeat all of evil just by saying, *"It is done"*? Since Jesus is God and the Manifestation of the Word of God, every word out of His mouth is the Word of God. As the Hebrews verse tells us, the Word of God (a.k.a. every word Jesus speaks) is sharper than any sword and pierces a person to their very depths. As God,

Jesus knows all, sees all, and judges all. This is how He pierces us. Despite the facade with which we may be fooling the world, He is not fooled, and He and His Word can and will expose all. For those of us found to be sincere in our love of God, we are imputed the righteousness of Christ and will be at those glorious, heavenly worship services. For those who are not, though—including Satan, the beasts, Babylon, and everyone else who does not have Jesus as their King and Savior—with just a word, Jesus will condemn them for all eternity.

THE FLESHY FEAST

Revelation 19:17-21 says:

> *Then I saw an angel standing in the sun, and with a loud voice he called to all the birds that fly directly overhead, "Come, gather for the great supper of God, to eat the flesh of kings, the flesh of captains, the flesh of mighty men, the flesh of horses and their riders, and the flesh of all men, both free and slave, both small and great." And I saw the beast and the kings of the earth with their armies gathered to make war against him who was sitting on the horse and against his army. And the beast was captured, and with it the false prophet who in its presence had done the signs by which he deceived those who had received the mark of the beast and those who worshiped its image. These two were thrown alive into the lake of fire that burns with sulfur. And the rest were slain by the sword that came from the mouth of him who was sitting on the horse, and all the birds were gorged with their flesh.*

Here again is proof that Armageddon will not be much of a battle. We also see another huge contrast between the people of God, the true Bride, and the wicked, the counterfeit bride. While the true Bride will be at the most spectacular wedding reception ever, feasting on the finest of foods, the evil will be at the *"great supper of God."* Instead of feasting, they are getting feasted *on* by birds! And these will not be sparrows or robins; the birds mentioned here will more likely be turkey vultures, crows, and vultures—the kind of fowl we see eating dead animals on the side of the road.

We saw that Jesus will destroy the beast, the false prophet, and all the wicked merely by saying, *"It is done."* We may have been picturing that those on the other side would just drop dead at His words; but now that we are getting the particulars of the event, we see that is not the case at all. Without any resistance at all, the beast and false prophet are captured and *"thrown [alive] into the lake of fire that burns with sulfur."* Jesus will then speak an earthquake into occurrence, have one-hundred-pound hailstones fall on people, and tell the birds to feast on the flesh of His enemies.

We cannot help but be sobered by what will happen to those who do not belong to God, but we should also take a moment to be awed that Jesus is able to destroy everything evil in the world and will not even break a sweat! That is the incredible power and sovereignty of the God we serve!

THE MILLENNIUM—PRE, POST, OR A?

As we begin chapter twenty, we want to give a word of caution. We have been careful to do our due diligence throughout this whole book, but never is that more crucial than when interpreting **Revelation 20**. Otherwise, this chapter will trip us up, as it has many others. Let us start by taking just the first three verses. **Revelation 20:1-3** says:

> *Then I saw an angel coming down from heaven, holding in his hand the key to the bottomless pit and a great chain. And he seized the dragon, that ancient serpent, who is the devil and Satan, and bound him for a thousand years, and threw him into the pit, and shut it and sealed it over him, so that he might not deceive the nations any longer, until the thousand years were ended. After that he must be released for a little while.*

These verses on the "thousand years," or millennium, are the most debated and thought to be the most difficult passages in the entire book of Revelation. Scholars are split as to whether this is a still-yet-to-come event, if it will happen right before Jesus' Second Coming, or if it is happening right now. In fact, there are three schools of thought that are named for how these thousand years are viewed.

The first one is post-millennialism. Post-millennialists hold to the notion that Jesus will not come back until after the thousand years of Satan being bound occurs. While most in this camp do not think the one thousand years is a literal thousand years, they believe that at some point in the future, Jesus will bind Satan for a set number of years (represented by one thousand), during which time Christians are to establish God's kingdom on earth (i.e., Christianizing the world). After this, Jesus will return and let Satan out, and the final battle will occur. An easy way to remember this is that post-millennialists think Jesus comes post (after) the thousand year (literal or symbolic) binding of Satan.

Next, there is pre-millennialism. If you know your linguistics, you have probably guessed that pre-millennialists believe that Jesus comes back *before* the thousand-year binding of Satan. Pre-millennialists believe that after all we have read so far in Revelation happens, Jesus will come back and physically reign on earth for one thousand years. Most all in this camp believe that the one thousand years is a literal thousand years during which Jesus will sit on His throne as King on earth with His people. They believe that during Christ's reign, the earth will be a great place. It will not be Heaven on earth yet, but it will be pretty great because it will be "Christianized" with Jesus as King. There are problems with this view. There is no scriptural evidence of the earth ever being "Christianized." Pre-millenialists cannot even agree on or account for exactly what the world being "Christianized" means. For example, there is no definitive view on sin during this period. With Jesus physically reigning as King, will Christians reigning with Him sin? Some think they will, and some think they will not. If they do continue sinning, how will this time be any different than it is now? If they no longer sin, that will mean they will be perfected, and, according to Scripture, that only happens when we go to Heaven or when Jesus establishes Heaven on earth.

The third view on the millennium is where we fall, and that is the amillennial view. Amillennialists believe the one thousand years of Christ's reign is symbolic, like most of the other numbers in Revelation. Since the number "one thousand" is used as symbolic throughout the book as a number of completeness, Amils see the one thousand years as the complete time period between Jesus' first and second coming. Dr. Voddie Baucham takes it even further, saying one thousand is ten to the third power. Ten is a number of completeness, and three is a number of completeness with a reference to the Trinity; so one thousand, or ten to the third power, is a complete godly reign.[51]

But as we always say, Scripture must interpret Scripture, so we do not want you to take our word or even Dr. Baucham's word on this. Let us look at scriptural proof that Jesus' reign is happening now. The Kingdom of God is mentioned 126 times in the Gospels and a total of 160 times throughout the New Testament. Most of these references come directly from Jesus. The Hebrew word for kingdom is *malkut*, and the Greek word is *basileia*. Both terms primarily mean **"rule"** or **"reign,"** and both terms refer to the **exercise of God's power**, dominion, or sovereignty. **Psalm 103:19** illustrates this: *"The Lord has established his throne in the heavens, and his kingdom rules over all."* And as Jesus tells us in **Luke 17:21**, *"'The kingdom of God is in the midst of you.'"* Jesus is telling us He is the Kingdom, or reign, of God. So Jesus' first coming was the ushering in of the Kingdom of God on earth. Jesus is both the Manifestation of the reign of God and the King of that reign! Certainly sounds like He is currently reigning!

The above passage says Satan will be bound for a thousand years. While there is no doubt that Satan is being restrained by God right now, he is not as bad as he could be or will be sometime in the future. But this binding of Satan here in **Revelation 20** is a very specific restraint. This binding of Satan has to do with his not being able to deceive the nations. Satan is at work making

---

51 Voddie Baucham Sermons, "Voddie Baucham—Revelation 20:1-3—When Is the Millennium?," YouTube video, 1:03:25, February 3, 2017, https://www.youtube.com/watch?v=OyEq07uMOHc&list=PL_OPzWCIg29ERt3iop1b1taAa4Bh4WFQ9&index=21.

war on believers, and it does not say he is being bound from doing that. What the text *does* say is that he is being bound from deceiving the nations. If you remember, "nations" was part of the believers on earth—*"peoples and multitudes and nations and languages"* **(Rev. 17:15)**. What this passage is saying is that Jesus is limiting Satan's power so he is unable to veil the Gospel from believers. Paul must have known this, for he says in **2 Corinthians 4:3-4**, *"And even if our gospel is veiled, it is veiled to those who are perishing. In their case the god of this world has blinded the minds of the unbelievers, to keep them from seeing the light of the gospel of the glory of Christ who is the image of God."*

The Gospel is spreading and flourishing, bringing people to Christ because God is not allowing Satan to blind the minds of those He has chosen to save. Satan is unable to keep believers from the Gospel because the Holy Spirit regenerates their hearts and testifies to the truth of it. So as a result, the Gospel has been increasing and thriving in all nations since the coming of the Holy Spirit at Pentecost, even in the midst of history's most horrific persecutions.

Jesus keeps Satan's power to deceive God's people from the truth of the Gospel at bay, which is shown symbolically here by keeping him chained in a pit. But then the text says Jesus will release him for a short time.

Once again, this book is not in chronological order. These verses in **Revelation 20:1-3** actually happen at the beginning of the one-thousand-year period, or at Jesus' ascension. It is at the end of the thousand years, right before Jesus' Second Coming, that Satan and his demons will be released for a short time. Remember what **Revelation 9:1-11** said. Here is a quick excerpt: *"[An angel] was given the key to the shaft of the bottomless pit. He opened the shaft of the bottomless pit, and from the shaft rose smoke . . . Then from the smoke came locusts on the earth . . . They were allowed to torment them for five months."* We just read in **Revelation 20:1** that an angel was given the key to lock Satan in the pit. That is a direct correlation to **Revelation 9:1**, where the angel has the key to open the pit and let Satan out. It is also a reference to **Revelation 1:18**, where Jesus said He holds *"the keys of Death and Hades."* Right now, Satan is being restrained from blinding believers to the Gospel, but Jesus is also holding him back from doing his worst on unbelievers. Think back to the locusts coming out of the pit in **Revelation 9** after the fifth trumpet. They symbolized Satan and his demons. And at that point, when the pit is opened, God will give unbelievers over to Satan and his demons. But it will only be for a time—until God says, "Enough is enough," as we saw when we exposited **Revelation 9**.

REIGNING WITH CHRIST AND BEING RESURRECTED

Revelation 20:4-6 says:

> Then I saw thrones, and seated on them were those to whom the authority to judge was committed. Also I saw the souls of those who had been beheaded for the testimony of Jesus and for the word of God, and those who had not worshiped the beast or its image and had not received its mark on their foreheads or their hands. They came to life and reigned with Christ for a thousand years. The rest of the dead did not come to life until the thousand years were ended. This is the first resurrection. Blessed and holy is the one who shares in the first resurrection! Over such the second death has no power, but they will be priests of God and of Christ, and they will reign with him for a thousand years.

This is a picture, a recapitulation, of the vision we saw in both **Revelation 6** and **Revelation 12**. In **Revelation 6**, the martyrs are gathered around the throne room, saying, "'O Sovereign Lord, holy and true, how long before you will judge and avenge our blood on those who dwell on the earth?'" **(Rev. 6:10)**. Then we saw another perspective in chapter twelve that showed why there are martyrs. It is because according to **Revelation 12:17**, "Then the dragon became furious with the woman and went off to make war on the rest of her offspring on those who keep the commandments of God and hold to the testimony of Jesus." Now, here in chapter twenty, we get yet another perspective. This is a picture of what is happening with the martyrs now, as well as all other believers. None of these have forsaken their love for God or taken the mark of the beast because they had already been marked (or sealed) by the Holy Spirit and have been spiritually protected. As Jesus said in **John 6:39**, *"And this is the will of him who sent me, that I should lose nothing of all that he has given me, but raise it up on the last day."*

All who have been given to Jesus have been made heirs to the kingdom—joint-heirs with Christ—as we see in **Romans 8:17**, which says, *"And if children, then heirs—heirs of God and fellow heirs with Christ, provided we suffer with him in order that we may also be glorified with him."* So, right now, those who belong to Jesus who have died are co-heirs and are reigning with Christ from Heaven. This is not a future event. It is happening now. The thousand-year reign is happening now!

Knowing this makes the next verses a little easier to interpret. All believers who have died are reigning with Christ in John's vision, but those who will still be alive at the time of Jesus' Second Coming are the ones who are still to be raised. The first and second resurrection coincide with the first and second births mentioned in Scripture. If you recall, our first birth is our physical birth, and our second birth is our spiritual birth.

Everyone is physically born of their mother—that is the first birth and is a commonality shared by every human being. Another commonality is that since Adam and Eve, all, except Jesus, are born spiritually dead because of their inborn sin nature. However, that is where the similarities end. Those who God has chosen will, at some point in their life, be made spiritually alive. In other words, they will be brought back to life or resurrected. Jesus referred to this as being "born again," meaning it is our second birth. Since our second birth only occurs by our being resurrected by the Holy Spirit, we can also call it a believer's "first resurrection." To try and put this simply, a believer being born again is the same as a believer's first resurrection. This makes perfect sense as to why the first resurrection has no impact on unbelievers. Unbelievers do not realize they are spiritually dead. They go through life not caring that we, as believers, have been spiritually resurrected and reborn. They are blinded to the truth of the Gospel and their need for Christ.

This also shows us why believers need not fear the second death, as the verses in this passage tell us. The second death occurs when we physically die. For believers, we have no need to fear this since that is when we join Christ and reign with Him in Heaven. Rather than fear it, we should be longing for it!

This is directly tied to the second resurrection. When Jesus comes back, all will be resurrected. For believers, this means our already-glorified souls will be given new, wonderful physical bodies. For unbelievers, though, this resurrection means that their physical bodies will join their souls condemned to Hell forever.

THE DEFEAT OF SATAN

Revelation 20:7-10 says:

> And when the thousand years are ended, Satan will be released from his prison and will come out to deceive the nations that are at the four corners of the earth, Gog and Magog, to gather them for battle; their number is like the sand of the sea. And they marched up over the broad plain of the earth and surrounded the camp of the saints and the beloved city, but fire came down from heaven and consumed them, and the devil who had deceived them was thrown into the lake of fire and sulfur where the beast and the false prophet were, and they will be tormented day and night forever and ever.

In these verses, we see a zoomed-in picture of what will happen at Armageddon. We have already seen that Satan will be released to have his way with unbelievers for a short time and that he and his evil minions will line up to fight Jesus and His followers. We have also seen that it will not be much of a battle.

Futurists like to hone in on Gog and Magog, but this is not the first time we see them. They are mentioned in **Ezekiel 38-39**. **Ezekiel 38:1-6** says:

> The word of the LORD came to me: "Son of man, set your face toward Gog, of the land of Magog, the chief prince of Meshech and Tubal, and prophesy against him and say, Thus says the Lord GOD: Behold, I am against you, O Gog, chief prince of Meshech and Tubal. And I will turn

> *you about and put hooks into your jaws, and I will bring you out, and all your army, horses and horsemen, all of them clothed in full armor, a great host, all of them with buckler and shield, wielding swords. Persia, Cush, and Put are with them, all of them with shield and helmet; Gomer and all his hordes; Beth-togarmah from the uttermost parts of the north with all his hordes—many peoples are with you.*

Gog and Magog represent the evil kingdoms, who join forces with Satan to persecute and torment the people of God. We have already seen in Revelation what the fate of these kingdoms is, but Ezekiel was shown it back in **Ezekiel 38:18-23**:

> *But on that day, the day that Gog shall come against the land of Israel, declares the LORD GOD, my wrath will be roused in my anger. For in my jealousy and in my blazing wrath I declare, On that day there shall be a great earthquake in the land of Israel. The fish of the sea and the birds of the heavens and the beasts of the field and all creeping things that creep on the ground, and all the people who are on the face of the earth, shall quake at my presence. And the mountains shall be thrown down, and the cliffs shall fall, and every wall shall tumble to the ground. I will summon a sword against Gog on all my mountains, declares the LORD GOD. Every man's sword will be against his brother. With pestilence and bloodshed I will enter into judgment with him, and I will rain upon him and his hordes and the many peoples who are with him torrential rains and hailstones, fire and sulfur. So I will show my greatness and my holiness and make myself known in the eyes of many nations. Then they will know that I am the LORD.*

THE RESURRECTION OF THE DEAD

Revelation 20:12-14 says:

> *And I saw the dead, great and small, standing before the throne, and books were opened. Then another book was opened, which is the book of life. And the dead were judged by what was written in the books, according to what they had done. And the sea gave up the dead who*

> were in it, Death and Hades gave up the dead who were in them, and they were judged, each one of them, according to what they had done. Then Death and Hades were thrown into the lake of fire. This is the second death, the lake of fire. And if anyone's name was not found written in the book of life, he was thrown into the lake of fire.

This is a picture that simultaneously shows the judgment of God that every unbeliever will have to face when they physically die, as well as the final judgment at the very end before Jesus establishes a new heaven and new earth. Everyone—absolutely everyone—will face God when they physically die (the second death). If your name is in the Book of Life—meaning you have been chosen by the Father, saved by the Son, and sealed by the Holy Spirit—you have nothing to fear because it is not the sin-tainted record of what you have done that God the Father will see, but Jesus' spotless, perfect record. Upon our death, our souls are immediately taken up to Heaven, where our new, glorified bodies will join us when Jesus returns and resurrects everybody who has ever lived.

For those whose names are not in the Book of Life, upon their death, they will have to face God the Father on their own merit. And as *"all have sinned and fall short of the glory of God"* **(Rom. 3:23)**, their souls are condemned to Hell for eternity. At the second resurrection, which this passage depicts, they will be thrown into the lake of fire for eternity.

The end of this passage shows that once Satan and all evil are destroyed, death is also destroyed because everyone will be immortal. Hell is sealed up (the destruction of Hades). Everyone left at this point will be alive forever with Jesus in the new heavens and new earth.

CHAPTER 11
STUDY GUIDE

GETTING YOUR TOES WET

Do you find it more assuring that God has included details about how His final judgment is all gonna go down, or would you rather not know? Why or why not?

When you read the book of Revelation in its entirety, you cannot help but see the incredible kindness of our glorious God, Who has graciously woven in encouragement and hope for His people in between the sobering wrath that He will unleash on those who are not His. *How have these interludes with glimpses into Heaven given you encouragement and hope?*

Besides being a book to encourage persecuted Christians, the book of Revelation is also a book meant to show the sharp contrast between those who belong to God and those who do not. *What are some of the sharp contrasts that have stuck out to you so far?*

DIVING IN DEEP

We did not mention it within the text of this chapter, but **Revelation 20** contains another of the beatitudes. **Revelation 20:6** says, *"Blessed and holy is the one who shares in the first resurrection! Over such the second death has no power, but they will be priests of God and of Christ, and they will reign with* *him for a thousand years."* Knowing what we do about the beatitudes—that they are a picture of kingdom life for believers that is not yet perfected but will be in Heaven or when Jesus returns—*how would you explain this beatitude to someone?*

Revelation 19 shows the sharp contrast between the counterfeit bride, Babylon, and the true Bride, the Church. There is even a distinct difference in how the two brides are dressed. Babylon is clothed in scarlet and purples, whereas the true Bride is in pure white. This is not a commentary saying wearing red is evil, but red and white are used symbolically in Scripture. *What do these verses say about these colors?*

Isaiah 1:16-20

Daniel 11:31-35

Matthew 17:1-2

Matthew 27:27-29

Jesus sets out to make war *"in righteousness,"* meaning those He judges and releases His wrath on justly deserve it. We, too, deserve that wrath and judgment, but Jesus has already endured it for us. *What do these verses say about God's righteous judgment and wrath and how we are protected from it?*

Nahum 1:2-8

Matthew 10:26-33

Romans 1:18-23

2 Peter 2:4-9

BACK ON DRY LAND

There will be cheering and rejoicing by believers when God passes final judgment on evil and unbelievers. This is a future picture for us. For the present, our hearts should break for unbelievers, knowing what they will face one day if they do not come to saving faith in Christ. *How can we both be encouraged that God will one day execute His perfect justice and have compassion on those who will be under that judgment?*

When Jesus rides on His white horse, Scripture says that He will have many diadems on His head. The multiple crowns denote that Jesus is the perfect Fulfiller of the three major offices of God's people that are listed in the Bible—prophet, priest, and king. *How does it help and encourage us to live our life on this side of Heaven knowing Jesus is our:*

Prophet—

Priest—

King—

CHAPTER 12

WHAT WILL ETERNITY BE LIKE?

Take a moment and think about your easiest relationship. This is not necessarily the person you love the most. It might not be your spouse, or your parents, or your siblings, although it could be. This is the person, or sometimes a small group of people, who think like you, act like you, can even finish your sentences for you. They are your family, regardless of the vast genetic differences you might have.

Now, imagine that kind of relationship with everyone you meet, everyone who is around you, every day, for eternity. The apostle Peter wrote that God has promised us *"new heavens and a new earth in which righteousness dwells"* (**2 Peter 3:13**). That means that every believer will be free from sin, a me-centered pride, prejudice, hate, and injustice.[52]

Coming to the very end of the book of Revelation, we have seen that Jesus and His Church's enemies have been destroyed and cast into the lake of fire for eternal, unending punishment, and the heavens and earth as we now know them have been deconstructed. Now, John gets a vision of what is next for Christians after our final exodus—a new heaven and new earth—starting with **Revelation 21:1-2**: *"Then I saw a new heaven and a new earth, for the first heaven and the first earth had passed away, and the sea was no more. And I saw*

---

[52] Paul W. Swets "What Is the Meaning of the 'New Heavens and New Earth'?," in *The Coming Glory: Hope Now for Life after Death* (Rapid City: CrossLink Publishing, 2019).

the holy city, new Jerusalem, coming down out of heaven from God, prepared as a bride adorned for her husband."

The first question that most people have when they hear about the new heavens and earth is, "Is it *totally* new, or is it the earth we have now but *restored to perfection* in some manner?" That is a difficult question, and commentators disagree on the answer. To begin taking a look at that question, it is helpful to begin with what the Bible says about our *bodies* from the old earth—they are resurrected and made new.

When a believer dies, their soul is immediately in Heaven at the side of Jesus. We know this because Paul tells us he is torn between a desire to continue his fruitful labors spreading the Gospel and his desire *"to depart and be with Christ, for that is far better"* in Philippians 1:23. He says the same in his second letter to the Corinthian church **(2 Cor. 5:8)**. Although it is often talked about in terms of "forever," Heaven is not our eternal home but instead is an intermediate place of rest for a believer's weary soul until Jesus comes again and our soul is clothed in its resurrected body. When Christ comes, the elect who have already fallen asleep—or, in other words, have died—God will bring with Jesus from Heaven at His Second Coming **(1 Thess. 4:14)**. All believers will get their resurrected bodies at the same time!

In **Philippians 3:20-21**, the apostle Paul says, *"But our citizenship is in heaven, and from it we await a Savior, the Lord Jesus Christ, who will transform our lowly body to be like his glorious body, by the power that enables him even to subject all things to himself."* According to this verse, our bodies will be transformed from what they were to something new. One important point to be made here is that if our bodies are transformed to be like our Savior's, then we are not turned into angels! Angels are another type of created being, different than humans. So, if you have been reading books from people who said they have died and gone to Heaven and saw their dead relatives with wings, you know what they are saying is either made up or the person has an active imagination and has never read parts of the Bible.

In **1 Corinthians 15**, Paul makes the argument that if Jesus rose from the dead, then believers will, too. He starts out reminding the Corinthians that they know Jesus was resurrected from the dead because afterward, He appeared to Peter and the twelve apostles, then to more than five hundred believers at one time, most of whom were still alive at that time **(1 Cor. 15:6)**. Paul argues that death came through Adam, but Christ came to give resurrected life to His people. In fact, the last enemy he came to conquer was death, according to **1 Corinthians 15:25-26**, which says, *"For he must reign until he has put all his enemies under his feet. The last enemy to be destroyed is death."* Christ overcame death and was raised on the third day. Jesus is the "firstfruits" of the harvest of resurrected bodies, and the rest will be raised at His return.

What will our new bodies be like? They will be imperishable **(1 Cor. 15:42)**. No longer will there be leprosy or cancer or Alzheimer's. Our new bodies will be immortal—they will never die **(1 Cor. 15:53)**. And if Jesus is the Firstfruits of the harvest, we can look to what we know about His resurrected body and glean some insight from that. From chapter twenty-four of Luke's gospel, we know that Jesus walked and talked with men on the road to Emmaus. And when he appeared to His disciples a while later, Luke records:

> *And he said to them, "Why are you troubled, and why do doubts arise in your hearts? See my hands and my feet, that it is I myself. Touch me, and see. For a spirit does not have flesh and bones as you see that I have." And when he had said this, he showed them his hands and his feet. And while they still disbelieved for joy and were marveling, he said to them, "Have you anything here to eat?" They gave him a piece of broiled fish, and he took it and ate before them"* **(Luke 24:38-43)**.

If our bodies are *resurrected* and made glorious—not annihilated and made over again—what about the Earth and heavens as we know them? The wording in **Revelation 21:1** seems to say that the old is gone, and everything will be made new. And yet again, there does seem to be some continuity between our old bodies and our new glorious ones. So, is it the same with the new heavens and earth? **Second Peter 3:10** says, *"But the day of the Lord will come like a thief, and then the heavens will pass away with a roar, and the heavenly bodies will be burned up and dissolved, and the earth and the works that are done on it will be exposed."* The stars, the sun, and moon are burned up—there is major destruction to the heavenly bodies with fire—but it does not speak of *total annihilation* of the Earth. **Romans 8:22** says that all of *"creation has been groaning"* because of the effects of sin and hopes to be set free from its bondage to corruption. For living creatures, that includes freedom from death. "Waiting to be set free" sounds more like renewal than annihilation of everything. It actually makes sense that the Earth would be purified, much like it was by the Flood in Noah's day. The flood washed the slate clean. This time, it will be cleansed by fire. The Earth will be a place for us to live clean, with no sin, nothing marred by sin's effects—a totally moral world in every way. This leads us to talk about *"the sea was no more"* **(Rev. 21:1)**.

Does this mean no more beach? Many people have asked this question and lamented that it sounds like a depressing idea! To our fellow beach lovers, we can say, "Take heart!" **Jude 1:13** uses the word "sea" for wicked mankind, likening them to raging waves. Likewise, **Isaiah 57:20** says, *"The wicked are like the tossing sea,"* and there are lots of other examples of the sea being a place of unrest, turbulence, and so on. This verse in Revelation about there being no more sea is not talking about there being no ocean or beach or not having any bay! It is talking about no more *wickedness*. That is reiterated in verse four, where Jesus wipes away our tears because there is no more crying and no more pain, emotional or physical. No longer will we watch our loved ones dying, feel the pain of losing a beloved pet. We will not suffer with guilt or shame or any of the other effects of sin because there will be no more sin.

This is a new home—a holy place, where God will reside. It is the heavenly home of Christ and His Bride. This brings us to *"the holy city"*—the *"new Jerusalem"* **(Rev. 21:2)**. This is not a literal city coming down out of Heaven from God. This is the Church. This is the same imagery from **Revelation**

11—the temple of God, the place where God resides. To reiterate, that is a picture of God's people. God resides with His people, alluding to **Ezekiel 40-48 and 1 Corinthians 3:16**, like we talked about in that chapter. **Revelation 21:2** says this is the *"bride adorned for her husband,"* Jesus. This is reiterated in **Revelation 21:9-10**, which says, *"Then came one of the seven angels who had the seven bowls full of the seven last plagues and spoke to me, saying, 'Come, I will show you the Bride, the wife of the Lamb.' And he carried me away in the Spirit to a great, high mountain, and showed me the holy city Jerusalem coming down out of heaven from God."*

The heavenly city is in the shape of a cube. The only place in the Bible the shape of a cube was the Holy of Holies, where God resided. The people were separated from that part of the temple, and only the high priest could enter in once a year. But when Jesus died, the curtain dividing us from being before God's throne was torn in two, and the way was made for men to enter the Holy of Holies without a priest as intermediary. Christ is the perfect and forever High Priest, Who opened the way for us, if we are believers. This perfect city is *"the dwelling place of God ... with man. He will dwell with them, and they will be his people, and God himself will be with them as their God. He will wipe away every tear from their eyes, and death shall be no more, neither shall there be mourning, nor crying, nor pain anymore, for the former things have passed away"* **(Rev. 21:3-4)**. Just like in Genesis before the fall of man, God will dwell in the midst of His people. We will be His people, and He will be our God. From the beginning, the pattern for the Kingdom of God is God's people in God's perfect kingdom under God's rule with God's blessing in a perpetual, ongoing sabbath rest of enjoyment in His presence!

The destruction of God's enemies and the consummation of the salvation of His people is *"done!"* The *"Alpha and the Omega, the beginning and the end"* has come to His people, to satisfy their thirsty longing for redemption from sin and all its effects and to let them freely drink *"from the spring of the water of life"* **(Rev. 21:6)**. Believers who stand firm *"will have this heritage ... But as* *for the cowardly, the faithless, the detestable, as for murderers, the sexually immoral, sorcerers, idolaters, and all liars, their portion will be in the lake that burns with fire and sulfur, which is the second death"* **(Rev. 21:7-8)**.

The wicked will remain in an unregenerate state forever. This is a warning to people who renounce their faith or who compromise their beliefs because of pressure from the beast or the seduction of the harlot. They suffer the "second death" of the burning lake. Their first death was their bodily death. The wicked having a second death in the lake of fire means their resurrected bodies will stand before the Judgment Throne and then be tormented in Hell forever. Those verses and many other parts of Scripture throw the idea of universalism (everybody gets saved in the end) right out the window.

When the angels had finished carrying their bowls of wrath, one of the seven came to John and carried him away to a mountaintop. From there, he could see the holy city, Jerusalem. **Revelation 21:11-26** describes it as:

> *Having the glory of God, its radiance like a most rare jewel, like a jasper, clear as crystal. It had a great, high wall, with twelve gates, and at the gates twelve angels, and on the gates the names of the twelve tribes of the sons of Israel were inscribed—on the east three gates, on the north three gates, on the south three gates, and on the west three gates. And the wall of the city had twelve foundations, and on them were the twelve names of the twelve apostles of the Lamb. And the one who spoke with me had a measuring rod of gold to measure the city and its gates and walls. The city lies foursquare, its length the same as its width. And he measured the city with his rod, 12,000 stadia. Its length and width and height are equal. He also measured its wall, 144 cubits by human measurement, which is also an angel's measurement. The wall was built of jasper, while the city was pure gold, like clear glass. The foundations of the wall of the city were adorned with every kind of jewel. The first was jasper, the second sapphire, the third agate, the fourth emerald, the fifth onyx, the sixth carnelian, the seventh chrysolite, the eighth beryl, the ninth topaz, the tenth chrysoprase, the eleventh jacinth, the twelfth amethyst. And the twelve gates were twelve pearls, each of the gates made of a single pearl, and the street*

of the city was pure gold, like transparent glass. And I saw no temple in the city, for its temple is the Lord God the Almighty and the Lamb. And the city has no need of sun or moon to shine on it, for the glory of God gives it light, and its lamp is the Lamb. By its light will the nations walk, and the kings of the earth will bring their glory into it, and its gates will never be shut by day—and there will be no night there. They will bring into it the glory and the honor of the nations. But nothing unclean will ever enter it, nor anyone who does what is detestable or false, but only those who are written in the Lamb's book of life.

This is the description of the Bride of Christ, the Church. If you will remember our discussion about Babylon, the counterfeit bride, from chapter ten, you will see the contrast is striking. Some take this to be a literal city of Jerusalem coming down out of Heaven, where Christ will reign for a literal thousand years on an Earth that still has sinners in it, doing something special with ethnic Israel. But there are some problems with that view. In order for that to be true, it would mean that God has two sets of people—the Church and ethnic Israel, who some believe will be then be "weeded out" by persecution after the Church is raptured out of here. But the Bible talks about God having just *one* people group—the Church—which already includes any Jews who are saved by faith, as well as the Gentiles who are. Paul talks about unity of the Jewish believers and Gentiles in Ephesians and other places in the Bible.

Revelation 21 creates another problem for those who hold to that view because they believe that someday a *third* Jewish temple will be built, and the Old Testament sacrifices will resume. But **Revelation 21:22** says there is *"no temple in the city."* To think that Jesus is going to reign on earth for a thousand years while Old Testament sacrifices are reinstituted goes against Scriptures like **Hebrews 9:12**, which says, *"He entered once for all into the holy places, not by means of the blood of goats and calves but by means of his own blood, thus securing an eternal redemption."* **First Timothy 2:5** says, *"For there is one God, and there is one mediator between God and men, the man Christ Jesus."*

Another take on this description of the Bride coming down out of Heaven is for it to be a *literal* view of what *Heaven* will be. This is where the ideas of "pearly gates" and "streets of gold" you hear talked about in Gospel songs and some hymns comes from. Some talk of this as a literal city, maybe even Heaven's capital city, where God dwells, as if it's the Washington D.C. of the our eternal home, with other cities in this new world, too, and we will be able to go in and out of the open gates to explore, visit family, and do other things. But if we go back and read verse nine of this chapter again, we see, *"Then came one of the seven angels who had the seven bowls full of the seven last plagues and spoke to me saying, 'Come, I will show you the Bride, the wife of the Lamb.'"* That is how this description of the New Jerusalem begins. So, this is a symbolic description of the Church, not a literal city of any kind.

It is the Church that has been made perfect and radiant and whose lives have been secure with Christ in Heaven this whole time. Believers' lives have been "hidden,"—or, in other words, "kept safe" in Heaven. Paul says this in **Colossians 3:1-4**, which says: *"If then you have been raised with Christ, seek the things that are above, where Christ is, seated at the right hand of God. Set your minds on things that are above, not on things that are on earth. For you have died, and your life is hidden with Christ in God. When Christ who is your life appears, then you also will appear with him in glory."*

The Church is described in this very symbolic picture as *"having the glory of God"* **(Rev. 21:11)**. It is exactly what we were created to do—be God's *tselem*—His image representing Him to the world. Here, we reflect Him and His glory perfectly, clear as crystal. God's people will have no imperfections distorting what God is like any longer!

The book of Revelation starts with the seven churches—some of which are full of sinful imperfections. Revelation ends with the glorious, perfected Church, who have been made holy. God's people are being transformed by the work of the Holy Spirit living in us, washing us and perfecting us with the Word (like the picture of the husband and wife in **Eph. 5:26**), so that some day, this Bride is what we are!

The New Jerusalem has high walls and angels at its gates. This signifies that believers are safe. There will not even be the possibility of attack from our enemy Satan and his minions or our own sin because we do not have a sin nature anymore. In **Revelation 11**, God's people (the temple) were safe as far as their salvation went but were vulnerable to attack from the enemy. Here, God's people are safe for eternity and have absolutely no vulnerability physically or emotionally. And there will not be another fall of man that starts this whole process over again, like in Genesis, because all traces of sin are in Hell for all eternity.

The gates bear the names of the twelve tribes of Israel, and the wall of the city is laid on foundations of Christ and His twelve apostles. This signifies the complete Church comprised of all the Old Testament believers and the New Testament believers. Again, this shows *one* people of God, not two separate groups of people.

This city is measured, and its shape is a cube—twelve thousand stadia. Many take that measurement and translate it into 1,380 miles or 2,221 kilometers and talk about how big this city is. But remember, this is the Church, so it is *people* being measured, not a city, just like we saw in **Revelation 11**. And it is a cube fashioned after the Holy of Holies, where God resided above the ark of the covenant. There is only one other place in the Bible that is a cube—the inner sanctuary in Solomon's temple, where the ark of the covenant was. This is another symbolic picture that signifies that God is with His people.

The angel also measured the wall, which we said signifies protection, at 144 cubits. These numbers are multiples of twelve, symbolically representing the people of God. This is the complete number of the people of God, completely and totally protected, with God dwelling among them.

Twelve stones are also mentioned here. They correspond (although some names might have gotten changed in translation) to the twelve stones in the high priest's breastplate that had the names of each of the tribes on them. The high priest wore that into the Holy of Holies; He did that once a year to make atonement for sin. It is yet another picture of God residing with all of His people!

Verse twenty-two tells us this city has no temple in it. There is a lot to say about this—more than we can possibly cover here. The tabernacle, or "tent of meeting," was where God would be in the midst of His people. **John 1:14** tells us, *"The Word became flesh and dwelt among us."* Jesus came and "tabernacled" with us. There is no need for a temple in **Revelation 21** because God the Father and God the Son are the Temple, and they are there. And the *"new Jerusalem"* (God's people) is the temple of God the Holy Spirit, as we already said.

All of this sums up perfectly the picture from **Ephesians 2:11-22**, which says:

> *Therefore remember that at one time you Gentiles in the flesh, called "the uncircumcision" by what is called the circumcision, which is made in the flesh by hands—remember that you were at that time separated from Christ, alienated from the commonwealth of Israel and strangers to the covenants of promise, having no hope and without God in the world. But now in Christ Jesus you who once were far off have been brought near by the blood of Christ. For he himself is our peace, who has made us both one and has broken down in his flesh the dividing wall of hostility by abolishing the law of commandments expressed in ordinances, that he might create in himself one new man in place of the two, so making peace, and might reconcile us both to God in one body through the cross, thereby killing the hostility. And he came and preached peace to you who were far off and peace to those who were near. For through him we both have access in one Spirit to the Father. So then you are no longer strangers and aliens, but you are fellow citizens with the saints and members of the household of God, built on the foundation of the apostles and prophets, Christ Jesus himself being the cornerstone, in whom the whole structure, being joined together, grows into a holy temple in the Lord. In him you also are being built together into a dwelling place for God by the Spirit.*

God has one group of people comprised of believing Jews and Gentiles, who were once alienated but were brought together in Christ, who will abide with God one day.

In our eternal home, we will not need the sun or the moon anymore. Does that mean that there will not be any sun or moon or stars to enjoy in the new heavens and earth? Who knows? The important thing to remember is the sun and the moon are to govern the days and nights. They govern time for us. But we will be in God's presence for eternity. Time has no bearing in eternity. The glory of God is the Source of the light, and Jesus shines that light on His Bride, who radiates it through her purity. Will there really be *"no night"* there? Maybe or maybe not. The main point is God's people will be safe because *"nothing unclean will ever enter it, nor anyone who does what is detestable or false, but only those who are written in the Lamb's book of life"* **(Rev. 21:27)**.

Revelation 21 is the ultimate fulfillment of **Isaiah 60:1-63:6**. But there is one more chapter in Revelation to discuss. People have all kinds of ideas about what they will do when they get to Heaven or when we are living on the new earth. Some say they will ask God questions about things that happened in this present life or for answers to all sorts of things they want to know. It is obvious that some believe we will float around on clouds. Some people think they will be bored. Stop right there. The only response to being in front of our perfectly glorious, perfectly holy God is to fall on your face in humble worship, like Moses and Aaron in **Numbers 20:6**.

Some have ideas of what the place will be like. We cannot rely on any of the "I have been to Heaven" books. They are fake. We know that because no one has seen God, except the One Who has come down from Heaven—Jesus—according to **John 1:18**. Most of the writers of those books are so preoccupied with stories about angels and dead relatives that we know for certain they are fake. No one who even has a vision of God does anything but fall down with their face to the ground in worship or in fear and shame! A person's gaze certainly would be fixated on the glory of God, not other things! In addition to that, no one who was brought back from the dead in Scripture talks about what happened while they were dead—not Lazarus; nor the widow's son, whom Elijah raised in **1 Kings 17:17-24**; nor Eutychus, whom Paul brought back to life in **Acts 20:9-12**. We need to let go of any ideas we have garnered from the "tours of Heaven" books and stick solely to Scripture!

This final description of our forever home contains elements from the Garden of Eden before the fall of man, particularly from **Genesis 2:8-10**, where it says:

> *And the LORD God planted a garden in Eden, in the east, and there he put the man whom he had formed. And out of the ground the LORD God made to spring up every tree that is pleasant to the sight and good for food. The tree of life was in the midst of the garden, and the tree of the knowledge of good and evil. A river flowed out of Eden to water the garden, and there it divided and became four rivers.*

In **Revelation 22:1-5**, John describes a bright, flowing river that's clear as a crystal running through the middle of the city. Its Source is God. On the side of the river stands the tree of life yielding twelve kinds of fruit and bringing healing to His people from every tribe, tongue, and nation. We will worship God, and we'll see His face. We can because His mark—the seal of the Holy Spirit—is on us. But those without His seal won't be there.

The curse and stain from Adam's sin is gone. This is the Kingdom of God—God's people in God's perfect kingdom under God's rule with God's blessing in a perpetual, ongoing sabbath rest of enjoyment in His presence!

Revelation ends with an epilogue, much like the prologue, reaffirming that these are Jesus' words and are *"'trustworthy and true. And the Lord, the God of the spirits of the prophets, has sent his angel to show his servants what must soon take place'"* **(Rev. 22:6)**. Jesus is coming soon. *"Blessed is the one who keeps the words of the prophecy of this book'"* **(Rev. 22:7)**. This is the sixth beatitude in the book of Revelation.

What does John do at this point? He gets another rebuke from an angel because he falls down to worship at his feet. Jesus appointed an angel to show

John these things, but angels are never to be worshipped. They are fellow servants of God, along with the prophets and all believers. It is God alone Who is to be worshipped.

The words of the book of Revelation weren't given to John for him to seal up. They were to be heard and learned and studied! The time is near, and the Church needs to hear them. The prophet Daniel was told, *"Many shall purify themselves and make themselves white and be refined, but the wicked shall act wickedly. And none of the wicked shall understand, but those who are wise shall understand"* (**Dan. 12:10**). John is told the same here in **Revelation 22**. Jesus' sheep will cooperate with the Holy Spirit to become more and more holy like their Savior. The wicked goats will still act like goats. Goats never turn into sheep. They can't. The last beatitude in the book of Revelation is *"blessed are those who wash their robes, so that they may have the right to the tree of life and that they may enter the city by the gates"* (**Rev. 22:14**). Beatitudes are about believers and kingdom life. This one tells of the life that's to come for those who have washed their robes in the blood of Jesus. It is contrasted in the next verse about those who are not believers: *"Outside are the dogs and sorcerers and the sexually immoral and murderers and idolaters, and everyone who loves and practices falsehood"* (**Rev. 22:15**).

Jesus sent an angel to give John a message for the Church. It was for the seven churches of John's day, and it is for all of God's people until Jesus comes again. There is a warning from Jesus about adding to Scripture or taking from it, which is also warned about in **Deuteronomy 4:2** and **12:32** and **Proverbs 30:6**. This should be a red flag for those who want to cherrypick Scripture they like while ignoring the rest. It should make the hairs of the necks stand up on those who re-word and re-write Scripture and then call it a *translation* like the Passion Translation or the Mirror Word both do. And it should make believers consider carefully what they're studying. The book ends with a testimony from Jesus: *"'Surely I am coming soon.' Amen."* It is followed by a response from His bride: *"Come, Lord Jesus! The grace of the Lord Jesus be with all. Amen"* (**Rev. 22:20-21**).

CHAPTER 12
STUDY GUIDE

GETTING YOUR TOES WET

Close your eyes and imagine what a world without sin would be like. What things will you be glad to never see again?

What sounds will you be glad to never hear again?

What are the things you will be most glad to see changed in others? In yourself?

DIVING IN DEEP

The greatest blessing of being in the new heavens and earth will be unhindered fellowship with God—"God with us." *What do the following verses have to say about God being amongst us?*

Exodus 25:8

Exodus 29:45-46

Leviticus 26:11

1 Kings 6:13

Ezekiel 37:26

How do the following Scriptures show God working out this covenant promise?
Isaiah 7:14

Matthew 1:23

If you are a believer, consider the great lengths God has gone to in order for you to have unhindered fellowship with Him. Do you believe that will help you stand firm in the face of trial and temptation—even persecution?

BACK ON DRY LAND

Scripture does not tell us what Heaven is like. Read **Luke 23:43**, **John 14:2**, **1 Corinthians 2:9**, **2 Peter 3:13**, **Philippians 3:20-21**, and **1 Peter 1:4**.

Which of these makes you desire Heaven most?

Why?

CONCLUSION

Our hope in writing this, as well as when we did the podcast series by the same name, was that the book of Revelation would no longer be something to be ignored on the basis that it was too hard to understand, nor that it would be looked at as having imagery too scary to study closely, nor that it would any longer be seen as some sort of code to crack. We hope that we have accomplished this and that the book has actually taken the place it is supposed to as an encouragement to believers to persevere under any circumstances.

Revelation is God's final revealed word to those who are His. By studying and understanding this book, you will be led to a greater understanding of all that comes before it. As you know by now, it is not a roadmap of history to plot the day and time of Jesus' Second Coming, nor is it a book of strange symbols and images for us to try to decipher. Instead, it shows us the struggle between God's people, the Church, against our enemy Satan and his minions throughout the time between Jesus' first and second comings. This battle is shown in recapitulated visions and viewed from different vantage points, as if they were different camera angles showing the same thing.

The main point is this—Jesus has already won the battle, and some day, He will destroy Satan and the demons and throw them in the fiery pits of Hell for all eternity. In fact, everything sinful and everyone who is an enemy of God will share that fate. Sin will be banished from the life of God's people, and we will live for eternity in the blessed presence of God forever and ever. Amen.

BIBLIOGRAPHY

Anaday, Joe. "The Beast Rising From The Earth: Revelation 13:11-18." Sermon. Emmaus Reformed Baptist Church, Hemet, California, September 24, 2017. http://emmausrbc.org/2017/09/24/sermon-beast-rising-earth-revelation-1311-18.

Barnes, Albert. " Revelation." In "Albert Barnes' Notes on the Whole Bible." StudyLight.org. Accessed March 3, 2021. https://www.studylight.org/commentaries/eng/bnb/revelation.html.

Barrett, D. B. and T.M.Johnson. "World Christian Trends—AD 30-AD 2200. 2001. https://archive.gordonconwell.edu/ockenga/research/documents/WCT_Martyrs_Extract.pdf.

Baucham, Voddie T. *Fault Lines: The Social Justice Movement and Evangelicalism's Looming Catastrophe.* Washington, DC: Salem Books, 2021.

Beeke, Joel R. *Revelation.* Grand Rapids: Reformation Heritage Books, 2016.

Benson Commentary. s.v. "Proverbs 9." Accessed March 11, 2021. https://biblehub.com/commentaries/benson/proverbs/9.htm.

Blue Letter Bible. s.v. "–Elegchō." Accessed March 13, 2021. https://www.blueletterbible.org/lang/lexicon/lexicon.cfm?Strongs=G1651&t=ESV.

Clash of the Titans. Directed by Louis Leterrier. Warner Brothers. 2010. 1:46:00. Video file.

Dictionary.com, s.v. "Abyss." Accessed March 20, 2021. https://www.dictionary.com/browse/abyss?s=t.

Duguid, Iain M. "Daniel/Chapter 13/Prepared for Battle." In *Daniel*. Phillipsburg: P & R Publishing, 2008.

Easton's Bible Dictionary, s.v. "Abaddon." Accessed March 20, 2021. https://www.biblestudytools.com/dictionary/abaddon.

Foxe, John. "Chapter II: The Ten Primitive Persecutions." In *Foxe's Book of Martyrs*. Christian Classics Ethereal Library. Accessed March 19, 2021. https://www.ccel.org/f/foxe/martyrs/fox102.htm.

Gone with the Wind. Directed by Victor Fleming. United States: Selznick International Pictures and Metro-Goldwyn-Mayer. 1939. DVD.

Greek Concordance. s.v. "ἐθαύμασα." Accessed March 25, 2021. https://biblehub.com/greek/ethaumasa_2296.htm.

Guzik, David. "Revelation 1 – Introduction; A Vision of Jesus." Enduring Word.com. Accessed November 1, 2021. https://enduringword.com/bible-commentary/revelation-1.

Halley, Henry H. "Essay." In *Halley's Bible Handbook*, 25th ed. Grand Rapids: Zondervan, 2000.

"Heidelberg Catechism (1563)." The Heidelblog. January 31, 2021. Accessed March 25, 2021. https://heidelblog.net/catechism.

Josephus, Flavius, and William Whiston. "Essay." In *The Antiquities of the Jews*. McLea: IndyPublish.com, 2001.

Lightfoot, J.B., Trans. "The Martyrdom of Polycarp." Early Christian Writings.com. 1990. http://www.earlychristianwritings.com/text/martyrdompolycarp-lightfoot.html.

Lowry, Linda. "The 10 most dangerous places for Christians." Open Doors USA. org. January 15, 2020. https://www.opendoorsusa.org/christian-persecution/stories/the-10-most-dangerous-places-for-christians.

McDonough, Dr. Sean. "New Testament Survey II—The End of All Things." Lecture. Gordon Conwell Theological Seminary's Dimension of Faith Program. May 2017.

Merriam-Webster, s.v. "Apocalyptic." Accessed March 30, 2019. https://www.merriam-webster.com/dictionary/apocalyptic.

"Myanmar." Open Doors USA. January 12, 2021. https://www.opendoorsusa.org/christian-persecution/world-watch-list/myanmar.

NAS New Testament Greek Lexicon, s.v. "Armageddon." Accessed March 23, 2021.

Osman, James C. "The Posture of a Soldier." In *Truth or Territory: A Biblical Approach to Spiritual Warfare*. Kootenai, ID: James C. Osman II and Kootenai Community Church Publishing, 2015.

Paxson, Christine and Rose Spiller. "An Unobtainable Directive Part 1," *No Trash, Just Truth* Podcast, July 27, 2020, 20:26. https://www.buzzsprout.com/615385/4319417.

Paxson, Christine and Rose Spiller. *No Half-Truths Allowed—Understanding the Complete Gospel Message*. Greenville: Ambassador International, 2020.

Ramsay, W.M. and E.M. Blaiklock. "Philadelphia." BiblicalTraining. org. Accessed April 1, 2021. https://www.biblicaltraining.org/library/philadelphia.

"Salmon Color Guide: Why Salmon are Pink, Orange or Red," Wild Alaskan Company, April 16, 2018, https://wildalaskancompany.com/blog/heres-why-salmon-are-pink-orange-or-red.

Saver, Christof and Thomas Schrirrmacher. "Father forgive them." *Christian History Magazine* online. Issue 109. 2014. https://christianhistoryinstitute.org/magazine/issue/109-persecuted-church.

"Sermons on the Book of Revelation." Transcript of sermon delivered at Christ Reformed Church. 2002. http://kimriddlebarger.squarespace.com/downloadable-sermons-on-the-bo.

Strong's Concordance. s.v. "Apóleia." Bible Hub.com. Accessed March 24, 2021. https://biblehub.com/greek/684.htm.

Strong's Concordance. s.v. "Ptócheia." Accessed March 31, 2021. https://biblehub.com/greek/4432.htm.

Strong's Exhaustive Concordance. s.v. "biblaridion." Accessed April 1, 2021. https://biblehub.com/strongs/greek/974.htm.

Study Notes for Revelation 2:6—Nicolaitans. *ESV Study Bible: English Standard Version.* Wheaton: Crossway Bibles, 2016.

Swets, Paul W. "What Is the Meaning of the 'New Heavens and New Earth'?" In *The Coming Glory: Hope Now for Life after Death.* Rapid City: CrossLink Publishing, 2019.

Tacitus. "The Annals." Alfred John Church and William Jackson Brodribb, trans. Classics.mit, 109 A.C.E. http://classics.mit.edu/Tacitus/annals.10.xiv.html.

Theopedia. s.v. "Cyrus I. Scofield." Accessed February 21, 2021. https://www.theopedia.com/cyrus-i-scofield.

Urban Dictionary, s.v. "Kracken," accessed March 21, 2021, https://www.urbandictionary.com/define.php?term=Release%20the%20kraken.

Vine, W. E. "Essay." In *Vine's Complete Expository Dictionary of Old and New Testament Words: with Topical Index.* Nashville: Thomas Nelson, 2000.

Voddie Baucham Sermons. "Voddie Baucham—Revelation 16:12-16—the Battle of Armageddon." YouTube video. 1:00:49. January 31, 2017. Accessed March 22, 2021. https://www.youtube.com/watch?v=ncIZoDX4r4c&list=PL_OPzWCIg29ERt3iop1b1taAa4Bh4WFQ9&index=17&t=1216s.

Voddie Baucham Sermons. "Voddie Baucham—Revelation 20:1-3—When Is the Millennium?" YouTube video. 1:03:25. February 3, 2017. https://www.youtube.com/watch?v=OyEqo7uMOHc&list=PL_OPzWCIg29ERt3iop1b1taAa4Bh4WFQ9&index=21.

Westminster Divines, "The Westminster Shorter Catechism," Ligonier Ministries. December 21, 2009, https://www.ligonier.org/learn/articles/westminster-shorter-catechism.

Westminster Divines. "The Westminster Larger Catechism (1648)." Ligonier.org. May 12, 2021. https://www.ligonier.org/learn/articles/westminster-larger-catechism.

"What was the leviathan the Bible talks about?" Got Questions Ministries. Accessed March 21, 2021. https://www.compellingtruth.org/leviathan.html.

DISCOGRAPHY

Luther, Martin. "A Mighty Fortress is Our God." Public Domain.

For more information about
Christine Paxson and Rose Spiller
and
The Final Exodus
please connect at:

www.proverbs910ministries.com

Ambassador International's mission is to magnify the Lord Jesus Christ and promote His gospel through the written word.

We believe through the publication of Christian literature, Jesus Christ and His Word will be exalted, believers will be strengthened in their walk with Him, and the lost will be directed to Jesus Christ as the only way of salvation.

For more information about
AMBASSADOR INTERNATIONAL
please connect at:

www.ambassador-international.com

If you enjoyed this book, please consider leaving us a review on Amazon, Goodreads, or our website.

Also check out Chris and Rose's Podcast: No Trash, Just Truth! *Streaming now on all platforms.*

MORE FROM AMBASSADOR INTERNATIONAL

To some people, saying David had a godly heart is almost offensive. How do you apply that description to a man whose legacy includes neglecting responsibilities, lust, adultery, murder, deception, hypocrisy, and callous indifference? *David: The Godly Heart of a Sinful Man* examines David's heart, identifying specific character qualities that influenced his response when confronted with his sin.

Job, the book and the man, is well-known even in the public arena. However, the main character of the book is the Triune God. Moreover, some have suggested that the book of Job focuses on the larger problem of evil in a good God's world. By definition that would include the concept of victimhood. However, Dr. Jim Halla thinks that approach misses major issues. *The Book of Job: God's Faithfulness in Troubled Times* presents an in depth look into Job and how it applies to the New Testament, Jesus, and us.

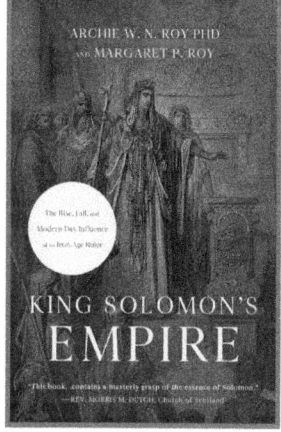

King Solomon is known as the wisest and richest man to have ever lived, but who was this man really? Even though we read his words in the Bible, this man who was the son of "the man after God's own heart" remains a mystery to this day. Even his death is veiled in conspiracy theories. How could a man who was granted his greatest wish by God Himself be so enamored with the pleasures of this world—hungry for sex, power, and more wealth? In *King Solomon's Empire*, Archie and Margaret Roy take an in-depth look into the life of the wise king and the kingdom he led.

www.ingramcontent.com/pod-product-compliance
Lightning Source LLC
Chambersburg PA
CBHW062156080426
42734CB00010B/1704